MOGULS

ALSO BY

MICHAEL PYE

The Movie Brats

(WITH LYNDA MYLES)

MOGULS

INSIDE THE
BUSINESS
OF SHOW
BUSINESS

MICHAEL PYE

Holt, Rinehart and Winston
New York

Library of Congress Cataloging in Publication Data
Pye, Michael, 1946-
Moguls.
Bibliography: p.
Includes index.
1.   Theatrical producers and directors—Biography.
2.   Performing arts—History.   I.   Title.
PN1583.P9   790.2'092'2 [B]   79-22533
ISBN: 0-03-052426-1

First Edition

Designer: Amy Hill
Printed in the United States of America
1 3 5 7 9 10 8 6 4 2

For East Preston Street,
with love

CONTENTS

Twelve pages of photographs follow page 148.

ACKNOWLEDGMENTS

I AM VERY GRATEFUL to the dozens of people who shared memories, knowledge, and papers with me while I was preparing this book. Among others, I thank: Eric Barnouw, David Brierley, Rosemary Chiaverini, Judi Dench, Margaret Gardner, Frederick Gerschon, David Golding, Peter Guber, Seth Herbert, Ruth Kaplan, Gail Kellogg, Stephen Komlosy, David Land, Norman Lear, Ronnie Lippen, Andrew Lloyd Webber, Joshua Logan, Kevin McCormick, Frank Mewshaw, Chester Migden, Donald Murrey, Trevor Nunn, William S. Paley, Stanley Penn, Alan Sapper, Suzanne Schwartz, David Shaw, Ginny Smyth, Jules Stein, Robert Stigwood, Beryl Vertue, William Wilkinson. For help in research I depended on Angela Francis, and on Michael Jackson, Maureen O'Toole, and Therese Stanton. I owe special thanks to the staff of the New York Public Library at Lincoln Center, the librarians of the *Sunday Times* (London), and the staff of the U.S. Justice Department in Washington. I also thank the librarians of the American Film Institute, the British Film Institute, the California Labor Commission at San Francisco, the U.S. Federal Archive at Laguna Niguel, the Motion Picture Academy of Arts and Sciences, the Securities and Exchange Commission, the University of California at Los Angeles, and *The Wall Street Journal*. While I was working, friends were immensely supportive; I particularly thank Regina Cornwell for all her help, and Celia Haddon,

ACKNOWLEDGMENTS

Michael Klein, Lynda Myles and the East Preston Street collective for their constant support. In the beginning, Peter Wilsher, while editor of the London *Sunday Times Business News,* set me thinking about the business of show business. Anthea Morton Saner and Mike Shaw at Curtis Brown were much more than agents. Jennifer Josephy at Holt, Rinehart and Winston and Maurice Temple Smith had faith, hope, and finally charity. And while it might have been possible to write this book without John Holm, it would not have been worth it.

Nassau, Bahamas
April 1979

1
MOGULDOM

YOU WILL NEED AN INVITATION. Between sidewalk and party stand the black-tie guards, ready to check your papers. To pass them, your face must be known or your card of invitation be in order. It may only be a party, a celebration, but it is held in an exotic land.

Past the guards there are ladies, crisp in black and white, who bob through the crowds with good champagne. Sleek people, pretty like putti, dress the stairs and look directly at solid, jowly men. Half-famous faces hold poses to the room, asking for recognition. Distant music underscores chatter and little laughs in the corner. There is a cabal of journalists, eyes alert; a simper of bankers; men with Pentax cameras slung around their necks; and glittering, visible, omnipresent stars. Across a library of stuffed books, under cold crystal chandeliers, the house is full of waiting people, ranked and ready for an entrance.

The light is too careful and the guest list too precise. Everyone is famous; every room is dazzling. On the invitations was the name of a mogul, a man who has power in show business. This is his production. A public relations firm chose the guests. The caterers found the house and made it almost alive with a neat, bought taste. This party is a device that asks for our attention and our affection. It says the mogul is a powerful man, and that he is of substance. It speaks of money and authority. It also asks that we like the man for the silk and kindness of it all, the taste and the excitement, and, most important, that we play our proper part when, finally, he appears.

Stars could dazzle down stairways, taking the eye. A mogul darts through a side door, ruddy faced and sandy haired, hotly aware of all the eyes around him. He is absurdly ordinary, a man of a certain age, a certain standing, without disguise. Flashbulbs chorus a welcome. The mogul walks to the stairs and there around him are a flock of stars, strong, bright faces and affectionate smiles. There are gestures, laughter, and greetings. Together, mogul and stars form a line, and the men with Pentaxes record it for posterity. However, the friendly laughter around the mogul's eyes cannot quite disguise his care and alertness. Tonight he is visible and individual, but tomorrow he will assume again his public, corporate identity. He will melt into a line on a movie poster ("Robert Stigwood presents . . .") or the logo on a record sleeve ("RSO" . . .) or an occasional figure in the trade papers ("Robert Stigwood in multi-million deal . . ."). We have a rare privilege tonight, which is: to see the man himself in the middle of his calculated glamour.

He is the model of a modern impresario, architect of an empire of movies that made more than $100 million, records that routinely sell in millions, stage shows that run like *Jesus Christ Superstar*. He found and glorified stars like Cream and the Bee Gees. In short, he guides and influences and manipulates our popular culture—the songs and stars and dances that we consume, and also the pervasive attitudes they contain. We are brushed by his flights of taste. He is famous for his fantasticated premieres, with Hollywood searchlights raking the sky and troops of celebrities being marshaled in some witty place, like a New York subway station groaning with midnight lobster. He knows how to play promoter, publicist, and fairground barker, all at once. He is also known to be cold, shrewd, strong. He is a bright and icy operator, with both image and substance. He is an individual who has acquired the means to shape our dreams.

Movies and music and television are powerful, insidious forces that shape and reinforce our attitudes and prejudices and aspirations.

Behind their influence are the minds and money of moguls. They are the powerbrokers of show business, more than mere producers. They have a personal influence of great range. Once, in a time when there could be a dragon circus of entrepreneurs, those moguls could make empires of their taste—huge structures of financial intrigue and showman's flair that ossified into corporations. Now, newer moguls make their treaties with the empires their predecessors built. The meaning of mogul remains, in show business, the man or woman of exceptional power who can at least appear to operate for himself and even, on the surface, by himself. It is the nature of the moguls' power that has changed. Jules Stein was able to take control of 60 percent of show business from a simple start in a Chicago doctor's office. William Paley was able to build a network, CBS, which became one third of American broadcasting and long the richest third. In a corporate society, full of giant corporations, their creations have become the powers with which a Robert Stigwood has to deal. And yet, his individual taste still emerges and it is vastly consumed.

Moguls themselves perform for us a glittering dance. They have marvelous parties, yachts, and fur-lined Rolls-Royces, flash as well as power. In show business the ostentation and the balance sheet remain as entwined as they ever were in the grand days when Rockefellers, Astors, and Carnegies were in business. There are obvious, melodramatic risks; each movie, each record takes a chance on our taste. There are machines that survive precisely because they know the art of minimizing those risks, but the gambles remain. There are grandiose, superlative rewards; seven-figure salaries are more common in show business, in Twentieth Century-Fox and Warner Communications and the rest, than in the family of Ford. All is extreme—business as well as show.

Robert Stigwood is like that. In twenty years he has soared and crashed, gone from a small-time London agent backed by a schoolboy's inheritance to an ephemeral power in music; then, when his little empire crashed, he came back to a deal that gave him a half share in the Beatles; when that foundered, he nursed the Bee Gees, made his company public five years after it was created, launched massive shows on bravado and nerve, and went private once more because of hidden debt and grand ambition. Even then, his roller-coaster progress had barely begun. He came back, again, and again he was dealing in millions—of records, dollars, theater tickets. He took public glory and a fine facade, a promontory in Bermuda, a house with a screening room in Beverly Hills, an acre of burlap and Chinoiserie in New York. He seems a perfect and old-fashioned mogul; yet he is not. For more than a decade, Stigwood's progress has been supported, bankrolled, sponsored by the European electronics giant Philips/Siemens. Ultimately, his brave, brash dealings all depend on corporation managers in dark suits who visit his companies to talk of group management philosophy. While he is a wild success, the managers are happy to stay distant. Nobody is cruel enough to remind him that he, too, is dependent on the studios and networks and corporations and conglomerates, the ones who have the risk capital and scale to minimize their risks, and who therefore hold a position of dominance in how a movie or show or record can be sold to the public. Robert Stigwood is allowed to appear as mogul and risk-taker, to give a public performance of an entrepreneur, star of the corporation's finest production.

This book is about the men and the machines who have wide and subtle influence over all the entertainment that we have—the powers that set our standards, change our minds, by the half-examined TV series that we never question or rock movies or double albums. They are less often called to justify themselves than the fashionable newsmen who disseminate information, and they do not willingly articulate the scale of their power. But they are more important to more people in more ways than a newspaper owner or a political figure. The moguls are the old men who built corporations that limit, define, and control our popular culture; they are the handful of younger men who have real power to manipulate those machines and show us what they want. They have changed with the structure of the economy of the West, from entrepreneurs to managers, from competition to the monstrous sell, and have profited. Their appetites, their ambitions, have shaped our culture. They fit the type and genus of moguls.

THE FIRST OF THEM made steel, or chemicals, or banks. They were Astors, Rockefellers, Morgans, or Du Ponts. They were a species of operator, of founding figure. Their other names are "tycoons" or, less politely, "robber barons."

The moguls outside show business set the definition for the breed. They have a fine-honed sense of self-interest. Their power was personal, not derived from standing in some corporation. They could run their money as they wanted, even speculate against their firstborn corporation if it seemed a good prospect. They acted more as financiers than as manufacturers, and their money built the oppressive, bustling industrial expansion of the late nineteenth century. They were manifestly different from the businessmen who had come before; business was abstract to them, a matter of paper and stocks and not of plant and products. They were the natural men to build the faceless corporations that succeeded them.

But they were neither private nor discreet about wealth itself. Their cash had a gaudy face. They flaunted wide estates, grand yachts, grandiose parties, and extravagant gifts. Boasting was a business expense, a means to establish credit, command attention, show status. Even philanthropy was useful: it tended to bring love and affection. Ostentation was an important factor in the old moguls' power.

It took time for the first movie dealers, hiding from complicated lawsuits in sunny Hollywood, to metamorphose into moguls. They began wisely. Movies, like television and the talent agency business later, were among the few distinctively twentieth-century businesses that generated sufficient cash flow and attracted enough stock exchange glamour to permit a mogul to play with money as he wanted. Their shares were glittering, highly valued against their real earnings. The movie men had landed in cinema by accident, but they came with the monstrous qualities of moguls. They ran their studios with arbitrary power. They kept flocks of writers tethered at their will, and snapped autocratic orders at contract producers, directors, and stars. They had the power to make and break careers. They loved ostentation, the grand parties that disguised risk and trouble. They could achieve outrage, like Harry Cohn of Columbia who electrified a boardroom chair to embarrass lunchtime guests; and Carl Laemmle of Universal who had his life written down in 1930 in a bid for the Nobel Peace Prize; or William Fox whose final ruin came when he was convicted of bribing a federal judge. The moguls had megalomania, or else, more kindly, they were larger-than-life caricatures of the entrepreneurial spirit. With the coming of talking pictures, and the brief Wall Street love affair with movie shares, they became kings of merger, financiers and manipulators of companies.

They were at their height when a young eye doctor crept into their business in Chicago. Jules Stein was quiet, analytic, brilliant, cold. He deserted medicine and took to booking bands; he gave names to orchestras, promoted their leaders, and invented the one-night stand for touring bands. He turned the music business upside down. He even bought radio time to keep his clients in work. His power came to be resented by some of his own clients, respected by his rivals, and feared by the dance halls and theaters he could boost or ruin. He bought his way into Hollywood and took control of more than 60 percent of the starriest performers in American show business. With the help of a client, Ronald Reagan, he engineered a startling deal that allowed him to head the only talent agency, MCA, that was allowed by the guilds of screen actors and writers to make as many TV programs in its own right as it wanted, with no restrictions. Stein flourished. His new business accounted for one third of American prime-time television. He virtually programmed NBC, from outside. His power was anonymous and quiet, never written down, and never publicly discussed by his men in dark suits; their savage discussions were kept private. It was a power that profoundly influenced the tone and ideology of all American television, and since it most affected film for television, it fed the series and fantasies to the world. It also shifted the balance of power between stars and studio in Hollywood, reinvented the band business, and in the 1970s tried to make itself a fourth network in American television. Yet its sole, central purpose was the enrichment of Jules Stein and his family.

This is a true mogul, a financier and not at first a manufacturer, operating with high intelligence and technical brilliance with no concern for any public responsibility. Jules Stein changed show business, fashioned a monstrous machine that now owns Universal Pictures and the onetime Decca Records as compensation for the talent agency that was abandoned amid fierce legal pressure in 1962. The most he wanted was to make a fortune.

The help to Judy Garland, the nighttime deference to Bette Davis's moods, the brief career as backing band and dance instructor to Mae West were only one career. He dealt in cars and real estate, liquor, antiques, nightclub favors, stocks and shares. He built other businesses all on the meager capital and huge cash flow that an agent needs and makes. He learned business, he says, from a three-year correspondence course, and the result was a power almost beyond control. It became a corporate state with managers, a show-business megacompany. Jules Stein was an architect of the change in the meaning of moguls' power—except that he lived on long enough to seem an exotic creature, the founder of a corporation grown bloated, faceless, and huge. He survived to see the change.

SELLING, RATHER THAN MAKING, was the megacompany's obsession, and the reasons were a tragedy. Only show business used to spend as much on selling as on making, but industry soon caught up. A cold cure like Contac appeared with $13 million worth of advertising in the hope of capturing $16 million worth of sales in its first year. Selling was one desperate device to absorb some of the unusable surplus that was flooding America, the money nobody knew how to use or invest to make jobs for the chronically unemployed. It was also the foundation of fortunes—indirectly for Jules Stein, since it allowed for the growth of commercial radio and television, and directly for William S. Paley.

In 1890, when Paley's grandfather had just arrived in prosperous style in Chicago, Americans spent $360 million on advertising. In 1929, when Paley's little adventure in radio had turned into a network, the bill was $3.4 billion. In 1957, when television was in its prime, all advertising media in the United States absorbed a staggering $10.3 trillion. Selling replaced price-cutting as a way to persuade people to spend. Competition in the classical sense gave way to huge corporations with the powers and privileges of strict monopoly in the nineteenth century. They controlled their own economic environment to a staggering degree. It was the spending of those corporations that made a new fortune for William Paley.

He had a million dollars from his family's business and he used it to buy a hobby—a ramshackle radio company whose competition was the monstrous Radio Corporation of America cartel. He took the company and invented the network. His innovations persuaded local stations to cede the power to program to a distant force on Madison Avenue. Networks, with no legal existence to subject them to controls, came to dominate American broadcasting; Paley's style, ambitions, and concessions made them. He defended his creation against Washington with shrill and adroit campaigns. He demanded deadening self-restraint to make sure the networks were not controlled by others. Scandal forced him into political and religious balance of a sort, but all his employees always sensed the awful dangers in comment, opinion, analysis, and challenge. He poached talent; he made concessions to sponsors; he aimed low. For all his private style and grace, he helped fashion the gross narrowness of American television. He made CBS into a vast machine and then pleaded that its vastness prevented anything much more than the crassly commercial. It was a profitable trap. It made some people believe that networks were the only way to run broadcasting—until the technology changed.

The story of the achievements of CBS, in news and current affairs, in informing America, quite pales alongside the story of how a rich boy came to steal away the public airwaves and turn them into a private corporation. Taste and appetite and ambition in William Paley conflicted and jostled, and the products were the network and the conglomerate that was based upon it.

INSIDE THE CORPORATIONS, moguls gave way to managers. The
new men seemed poor imitations. They were anxious about their
jobs, nervous, cautious, and without glamour. They suffered like
those of the second generation in steel or automobiles or chemicals
from Victorian Britain to Detroit after Ford: they were thought ef-
fete alongside the tiger enterprise of their fathers.

Yet in show business the mogul survived, flaunting his wealth,
power, and outrage. David Merrick played the role on Broadway
and salvaged the New York stage in the process. To him, the part
of a mogul was a mask; it allowed him to cut away his poor-boy
past and arrange to be born as a tycoon. It attracted backers at first
and audiences later. Merrick as monster was a salable, promotable
commodity; the mogul pose had become something to be exploited,
theatrically. Behind it, Merrick was the sharp, efficient businessman, meticulously checking his productions, allowing no leakage of
money from his private network of businesses. He had the advantages of scale, of spreading risk and advertising budgets, of watching costs. But he chose not to appear as the businessman. He saw
the dollar value of a mogul's pose, battling critics, snarling at actors, staging outrageous stunts. He did what the public expects a
mogul to do. He played the legend.

Others had to rewrite the rules. Bright new recruits to show-business companies were no longer eager artists desperate for a break.
They were fresh from business school, shiny with theory. Peter
Guber was like that. He went, by accident, to Columbia Pictures in
the late 1960s when Hollywood was starting to quake and fall.
There had been absurd overspending, blindness, and optimism.
Guber saw its consequences. He survived in a corporation of bitter
infights. He spent ten years among the knives, soaring in the hierarchy as others quit, finally coming to run worldwide production for
the studio. He observed the corporate reality of show business in the
1970s and preserved some private dreams. He helped the company
back from near bankruptcy and saw it into profit. He quit, then, to
be his own man, to make his own movies. He knew he would have
to deal with the monster powers and the studios and the machine he
had so recently left, and he determined to play the corporate game

11

from outside. He fought and he schemed and he became a power—half-owner of a massively successful film and record company. He knows he depends on the machines, but, mogul-like, he has found a way to live between them and depend on them without pain.

Guber found his strategy; thousands of others are still searching. For there is always this difference between show business and other industries, however close they grow otherwise and however they share the same economic pressures and process. Few men and women want a Bessemer converter of their own or an assembly line, yet that is what they would need to enter the steel business or the truck trade. Many people want to make a particular movie, cut a particular record, make a star's career, or act as agent to a star. They want to enter show business and they think they have only brief need of the studio machinery. They need skills in making deals, and making those deals mean something. They are in great need of conduits—people who can link ideas and the machine of show business, who can make an enterprise out of encouraging the enterprise of others. They need, in short, moguls.

The corporate powers are not the only necessary conditions of making movies, television, theater. Governments, also, intervene. The great subsidized theatrical companies are among the largest theatrical operations in the world. They demand political sense and diplomatic skill; they also require an impresario, a man who knows how to make the money that alone will guarantee survival. Trevor Nunn, head of the British Royal Shakespeare Company, is such a mogul—fulfilling a national obligation to maintain a national institution and, at the same time, acting as director, scholar, tout, and fixer. Survival depends on his skill. Failure would never be forgiven. His unfriendly burden puts him among the moguls.

AT A MOGUL'S PARTY, the machine of show business is remote. It is stashed away behind the glamour. It seems as irrelevant as thoughts of power and politics as you laugh at a farce or scream at a horror movie or empathize with soap opera characters in some extremis. But the machine is vital. It makes the hidden ideas of programs as well as the quality and appeal of them. It is insidious.

For the story of any business only stops at the outer reaches of its social influence. Cars and Henry Ford are the necessary condition of certain sorts of city, certain sorts of mass transport, even of gross individualism and the history of Los Angeles and the growth of post-war suburbia. Henry Ford intended only to make the car available, massively. In doing so, he did not intend the form of cities, the growth of fringe areas at the expense of inner cities, or any of the other consequences. His intentions are irrelevant. His business made possible massive social change.

In the same way, the bland ideas, the conformist statements about woman's role and man's proper behavior that fill the airwaves and find echoes in our lives, may all be reinforced by what show business produces even if the moguls would strenuously deny any such intention. It is not that William Paley set out to brainwash America. It is that he created the machinery that could do nothing but make possible the brainwashing of America. It is not a matter of pursuing his intentions. We have to look at the careers of individuals to see how the machine came about, and how it is now run, before we can hope to assess or understand the particular potency of popular culture. We already make assumptions in general talk that it is, indeed, potent. Exposure to frequent scenes of violence seems to cut sensitivity to real brutality, and we acknowledge that. We see phenomena that have close links with the show-business products—postwar suburbia with its concern for hearth and home and private pastimes like television; and teenage identity, expressed in rock that gave a banner to the generation of superkids barreling their way out of the suburbs with too much pocket money, a second-hand car, and an appetite for a social identity of their own. Social phenomena and our entertainment, our diversions, are closely linked.

Popular culture itself is both limited and produced by the machine of show business. We must examine the story of that machine—and of the treachery and glamour, cunning and capital and power that are at work. Here, there are moguls, performing powers—Jules

Stein, William S. Paley, David Merrick, Peter Guber, Trevor Nunn, and Robert Stigwood. They are exotic creatures in a strange land. They are, some of them, legends. But through their very public postures, their fantastications as well as their deals, we can see something extraordinary emerge. We can watch the change in our own popular culture over five decades—and the changes in the machine that makes it.

2

JULES STEIN:
10 PERCENT

I HAVE HAD FOUR CAREERS," Jules Stein insists. "Four careers." He is an old man now, little and dry and sharp, sitting in a dark wood office flanked by sporting prints and antique furniture. He works on the thirteenth floor of a building on Madison Avenue, with the offices of the New York Jets and Rodgers and Hammerstein on the floors below. It was once an eccentric speculation, this building; Stein owns it. It was an island in the emptying middle of Manhattan, surrounded by blankness. Stein held on, and he was right. His office now overlooks the site for IBM's monstrous new corporate headquarters. His investment was acute. Stein looks from the desk across to the window, and through the window to the prospects below. "It was a good buy," he says, "whatever they thought."

He has done business in real estate, in antiques, on the stock exchanges, and in show business: he has been a doctor, ophthalmologist, agent, and corporate head. In 1960, he was the ultimate power in more than half of American show business, agent to the stars in theater, cinema, television, radio, and music. He had created filmed drama for television and kept it bland. He became the power that dominated the schedules of NBC. He created the one-night stand for dance bands and a profession for himself at the same time. He ran the music business so toughly that no dance hall would stand out

17

against him. He expanded to Hollywood with patience and cunning and a ready checkbook, overturning the balance of power between studios and stars. He presided over the discovery that stars could sell their shows like corporations and save tax, or take a share of profits as shareholders. Almost a third of prime-time television in the 1950s came from the corporate machine he fashioned. When finally the Justice Department put his business in a courtroom and challenged its scale and powers, he had already decided to abandon his agency. He had made an empire out of his 10 percent commissions, and now the empire would be enough for him. He bought a record company, Decca, and a film company, Universal, and a studio, a bank, a hotel, a gift company, an electronics business, and he bid for the right to bottle Coca-Cola in Los Angeles. He even owned a sizable share of a national park—Yosemite. All these were packed inside a corporation run, according to its own underwriters, for the personal tax convenience of Stein and his family. Like a mogul in the age of railroads or early banks or steel or oil, he never wanted power in show business one half as much as he wanted the privilege of managing his money as he wished, of building and holding a fortune that could run by its own independent rules. He had made himself a mogul.

For years he was quiet and retiring, seen sometimes in a corner talking business at an A-list party in Hollywood. His face was hardly known. In his last years, set down from his post at the head of MCA, he blossomed in public. Like some Astor, he suddenly had great parties, where proper people come with their Vuitton bags and celebrate each other. Like a Rockefeller, he gave huge donations to medical research, a new philanthropist in town. He did the cruel business of amassing his fortune in private; later, he published the fortune to the world.

For he wanted to be remembered. His lives were set out like goods in a market for buyers to inspect. There was Stein the real estate man who owned all the offices in which his own corporation did business. There was Stein the dealer in antiques who filled his corporation's offices with good pieces that were collected in the chaos of Europe after World War II. With great care, each piece was kept labeled with a metal tag. "It's helpful to be a dealer," he said, "because it gives me a sense of what things are really worth." His enthusiasm for antiques was shared and prompted by his formidable, graceful wife, Doris, who bought him a desk and a breakfront soon after their marriage; he proceeded to translate his passion into 50 percent of Stair and Company in New York, a store on Fifty-seventh Street called the Incurable Collector, and 10 percent of Malletts, the London dealers.

He would like to be remembered also as a man with a seat on the New York Stock Exchange and a shrewd market sense that allowed him to invest for his friends and guarantee their stake. He wants his medical career remembered, brief as it was; there was a paper on distill and telescopic lenses as applied to nearsightedness that Zeiss valued highly enough to distribute fifty years ago. He wants immortality from his name on an eye clinic at UCLA, a hundred kindnesses and checks that went to work against blindness. All this, for he is old, Dr. Stein, old and weak, and he fears he will be forgotten. Business is not enough to make a man immortal. Show business is even less.

He changed show business in America. He built the corporation and the attitudes that now shape movies, television, and music. He was a brilliant dealer and a substantial philanthropist. But the achievement to be remembered is the twisting and forming of popular culture. That is Jules Stein's memorial.

THE STORE WAS SMALL AND CLUTTERED, a general store in South Bend, Indiana. Jules Caesar Stein grew up there, a boy who played violin for money and showed great academic promise. By the age of twelve he was in prep school, and by the age of fourteen he had a dance orchestra of his own. "The favorite tune," he remembers, "was 'Alexander's Ragtime Band.'" Little legends still cling to him. There is Stein telling his schoolmates he wants to be an aviator, sitting grim-faced as they spin him on a piano stool to prove his sense of balance. There is Stein at college, making his fraternity house profitable; and Stein at eighteen, back in South Bend drinking

19

wine from the slipper of a pretty girl. At eighteen, also, he graduated from the University of West Virginia. If he was ever a child, the time was hurried by a brilliant academic career and the music that helped pay for it.

He was already a small-time booking agent at eighteen. Sometimes his band had more offers than they could honor. Stein found other outfits and booked them, for a cut of the fee. His own music was society-sweet, insubstantial, and untouched by jazz; "schmaltz," he says. With his music money he spent a year in postgraduate biological research at the University of Chicago, retreated for two years to build his bankroll, and went to Vienna to study postgraduate medicine. While at Chicago he met William Goodheart, the wizened and sour-tempered little man who became his partner. Together, they took and sold what musical jobs they could find. Stein played backup band for Mae West in vaudeville. "I used to take her down to the black joints," he remembers, "and she learned to shimmy there. She was the first white woman to do the shimmy. She was an attractive woman, voluptuous even, but she was much older than she likes to admit." He had money in his pocket. Even after Vienna he returned with $300 in the bank. It was a start.

As Kenneworth Music, he and Goodheart booked bands into the South Side cabarets and speakeasies of Chicago. At the same time, Stein was a working doctor, an internist at Cook County and then a specialist out on his own. He remembered toying with dermatology and with ophthalmology, the two branches of medicine with the fastest turnover of patients; he chose eyes. His academic work had been respectable. His practice, in a $1-an-hour address on Jackson Boulevard, made him $50 a week. He had no sentimental feeling for hard times and he had fierce ambitions. As he examined eyes, he booked bands. He had no thought of going back to the bandstand himself; he admits he was not that good. Instead, he organized bands and sold them to bookers, pocketing whatever the cabaret or hotel was prepared to offer and paying out only what the band demanded. That, along with his 10 percents, was the basis of a business. "I had a young assistant," he remembers, "and he'd ring up about bookings while I had a patient in the chair. I'd be saying:

'Can you read this, can you read this?' and all the while I'd be speaking down the phone. We had Hushaphones in those days, a box around the speaker so nobody could hear what you were saying, and I couldn't have done business without that.''

His show-business apprenticeship had been erratic but long. In 1924, he gave it form. With $1,000 in capital and himself as president, Stein founded Music Corporation of America. He began to apply the principles he had learned, some from a three-year correspondence course in business studies, some from experience. Individually, they were only common sense or ambition. Together, the ideas of MCA changed the music business.

THE LINE CAME FILING ONTO STAGE, suits dark and respectable, horns ready. Bands in any ballroom, any theater sounded much the same. Arrangements were on sale across the nation. A band leader's name meant little, since his music was much like any other man's. There was no special following for the ordinary dance bands. They did a keen, professional job, stayed in a single town for years, and belonged to a solid union. It was regular work.

In the 1920s, the spreading influence of jazz and the migrant black bands strutting from the South combined to break that static picture. Even the stuffiest ballroom musicians began to experiment with style. It might be some direct jazz influence, or it might even be a symphonic approach like Paul Whiteman's band, which later played Gershwin's *Rhapsody in Blue* at Carnegie Hall under the plushy management of Sol Hurok. Stein saw a way to capitalize on the change. He began to move bands from place to place, offering them regular work, more money, and a name in place of the careful anonymity of ballroom work. Band leaders liked the idea; it was their names and their faces that the public came to know. Dance halls and hotels liked it because audiences did expand and business did improve when name bands arrived with their individual and often mobile following. When Stein went into business, the one-night stand and even the week-long engagement were unknown in the band trade; by the mid-1930s, every musician had learned to live with grueling night rides and the ubiquitous bus. MCA called a booking for more than a week "permanent."

The one-night stand created a business for Jules Stein. Band leaders had enough to do without worrying about the next month's itinerary or the credit rating of some hotel three states away. Stein and Goodheart took care of all that. Within months of opening, MCA had a virtual monopoly of booking bands around Chicago. A local radio station realized that every band it played on every peak-time show, between 8:30 P.M. and midnight, was supplied by MCA. The partners had to import bands from the East and West to meet the demand. At the same time, hotels and dance halls needed help organizing their weekly schedules. Instead of regular men who went on stage month after month for a fixed fee, needing little attention from a harassed management, there would be some strange band that had to be found, checked, evaluated, and paid. It was easier to trust those matters to MCA, and the agents were only too happy to help—on certain conditions.

From the start, MCA wanted "exclusives." If they booked a band, they wanted to be its sole agent. If they helped a hall, the hall must repay them by booking from MCA mainly, if not exclusively. It wasted time and energy, Stein thought, to be forever matching some small band with some small hall. Individual attention was downright inefficient. Instead, he persuaded bookers that MCA could offer a constant flow of talent, often better than they could usually afford, if they agreed to deal only with that one agency. That gave Stein a steady market for his wares. He could now offer work every week of the year to band leaders. He could also offer the services of his other companies—a deal on insurance, perhaps, or a new house in the suburbs, or a spanking-new Rolls-Royce. To the club owners, he could offer anything they needed from cigarettes to bandstands, favors to stars. During Prohibition, Stein even bought certificates for bonded warehouse stocks so that he was ready for the day drink could again cross the American border legitimately.

He packaged everything. For a flat fee, a hotel received its entertainment for a year, its hatcheck girl, its star attractions. With

Stein's other business interests, he already had a small empire. He left medicine aside, and dropped the title "Dr."; "I didn't want anyone in the business calling me 'Doc.' " He was fashionable, sharp, and public; he took to the boulevards of Chicago in a fine raccoon coat and a grand Rolls-Royce, escorting lovely ladies to his newly bought estate overlooking Lake Michigan. On Sundays at the Palace he would join the crowds who came to hear Jack Benny or Sophie Tucker and watch with respect the file that followed Al Capone as he walked to his usual seat. Stein was vulnerable and he learned that suddenly. Like anyone booking bands he had done business with mobsters; they controlled the cabarets. Now the trouble started. Unions, angry with Stein's blows at local orchestras, began to fight back. The mobs offered protection for which Stein would not pay. Firebombs broke nine times in clubs that Stein controlled. Waiters went on sudden, unexplained strike. The mobster Roger Tuohy, who had already snatched James C. Petrillo, head of the musicians' union, and ransomed him for $50,000, now threatened Stein. He was an easy target, a boulevardier, a ladies' man. He refused gun and bodyguard. He decided to face Tuohy out. His only defense was a hurried insurance policy against kidnapping arranged with Lloyds of London; the premium was $5,000, the amount insured was $75,000. "They tried to muscle in on me and I never let them," Stein says. "I had the guts of a fool."

He was less vulnerable than he seemed simply because he never quite fitted the business he chose, or the company he kept. "In those days," he says, "agents were loathsome, they were dishonest. Our company has given dignity to a good profession." Gangster against doctor was an unfair match, like setting knives against marble. Stein's incongruity saved him.

GUY LOMBARDO CAME SOUTH from Canada to play at a Cleveland restaurant called The Music Box when he was twenty-three. His music was sweet and restrained, the sort that made decorum fashionable again after years of semijazz. It appealed to Stein and Goodheart whose tastes were basically conservative. They never en-

couraged progressive musicians who usually found a home with
GAC or some other rival agency; instead, MCA held on to the
money-spinning middle-of-the-road types like Xavier Cugat, Sammy
Kaye ("swing and sway . . ."), and Wayne King. Stein liked what
he heard of Lombardo, and he planned.

Goodheart made the first approach, a direct offer in Cleveland
which was rebuffed. "Nix," said Lombardo. "I'm doing fine without an agent." Stein was prepared to wait. His lead attraction was
the Coon-Saunders' Kansas City Nighthawks, and they were on the
wane; stars like Isham Jones and Abe Lyman had refused to sign
up; and although MCA had prospered in the heartlands, it was
largely because the fancy East Coast agencies were too preoccupied
with filling New York halls and hotels. Stein needed one unquestioned star name with which he could lever his way into the New
York market. With just one name he might hope for exclusive contracts; he had a list of adequate bands to fill the other weeks. Without it, he would be a Chicago agent all his life.

He gambled. In 1928, with not a superstar to their names, Stein
and Goodheart opened a New York office. Carefully, Stein investi-
gated the Manhattan hotels. With his information assembled, he was
ready to try Lombardo once again. By this time, the band leader
had begun to dream of Manhattan dates. His only doubt was
whether MCA could deliver them. He watched with fascination as
Stein assessed each possible hotel. The St. Regis was rejected; the
room was too large for soft music and the clientele too stuffy. The
New Yorker crowd nursed their cocktails with stolid indifference to
the musicians' skills; they were not likely to respond to Lombardo's
style. That left the Roosevelt Hotel among the bidders for Lombardo's services. It was a happy coincidence. The Roosevelt was
not yet established, and it needed the services of an agent like MCA
almost as much as Stein needed a Manhattan showcase. Lombardo
played and took the town by storm, surviving even the Depression
years with a steady following and an accelerating fee.

Stein was established in New York. The big names now began to
gravitate to MCA. Sometimes they came by friendly contact; Lom-

bardo himself was helpful. Eddy Duchin was a friend of his, a pianist who had the devoted public, if not the outrageous showmanship, of a Liberace. "When we'd leave the Roosevelt Grill for the spring," Lombardo said, "we'd make sure they gave jobs to our friends. We believed in taking care of people we liked. That's why we got Eddy Duchin away from Leo Reisman's band and put him with MCA."

Sometimes bands arrived through Stein's close attention to his own intelligence network and his other duties as an agent. He went prowling New York night spots with a dance team called Veloz and Yolande, his clients in search of an orchestra that could go on tour with them. He found Shep Fields and helped him construct a touring band that became famous. Information, the foundation of MCA's later success in Hollywood, brought him the band of Ben Bernie. The crash of 1929 left Bernie stranded in California with no cash and no work. The nightclub he was playing failed to come up with a paycheck at the end of the week. Times were hard. He had to borrow the $1,000 he needed simply to ship the band back to its base in New York. Stein heard about the story and made a strategic phone call. He understood the problems, he said, and would like to help. There was a break of journey in Milwaukee that might interest Bernie, and a possible two weeks at the College Inn in Chicago, if he would be interested. "Good pay," Stein said, "and the place has a wire to a good radio station." The radio link was a success. Stein had acquired another client.

Out from New York and Chicago, the agency spread its business. Stein began to book ice shows; he went to Hanover to inspect a midget circus which he found, he says, "too disgusting" for America; he sold to fairs and parks and country places as well as big-city palaces and smart New York hotels. In the 1930s, MCA advertising sheets ranked more than a hundred tiny monochrome pictures of band leaders, all neat and available. "Other Parks and Fairs Have Struck Real Pay Dirt When They Prospected with MCA Attractions," said the copy, indulging a strain of metaphor that the company later quelled. "If you have been getting 'fool's gold' in return for your efforts, 'pick' your date and *stake your claim* on MCA's gold mine of orchestras and entertainment—and then get set for the biggest boom since the California Gold Rush.''

Stein's business was clever and growing, close to the point where its very size would become a competitive advantage which few rivals could match. Size meant bands always available to halls, and work always available to bands. It was an attraction in itself. It made some band leaders feel trapped and bitter, some dance halls feel under siege, and most rivals in the agency business feel edgy and insecure. The complaints and the battles were about to start.

"I WON'T SEE YOU for many a day" sang the band leader Jack Teagarden at a 1940 recording session, "because I'm on the road for MCA." It was a rueful little protest at the power of MCA. It found echoes among the agency's clients and customers—and victims. As Stein expanded his business, it became more and more clear that he ran by ungenerous rules. He was not interested in new and unproven talent; he was prepared to poach bands, once they were established names, from other agencies; his machine was so efficient that the band leaders caught within it sometimes felt their lives were being dominated by the interests of MCA. Instead of representing them, they felt the agency was running them. They found it profitable, but uncomfortable.

Inside the agency there were occasional dissidents. Willard Alexander was one. His musical taste was at odds with the smooth society music Stein preferred. His enthusiasms made him appear eccentric within MCA's meticulous operation. It was Alexander who managed Count Basie, and defended him when other MCA executives wanted to drop the band. Basie had been a disappointment in the barrackslike space of the Roseland ballroom in New York, and his earning potential was marked down by the MCA moneymen. Alexander disagreed. Basie had stars like Billie Holiday working with him. The music was more than impressive; it was extraordinary. Alexander resorted to all the tricks he knew to hold Basie as a client and keep him in work. There was a small club called The Famous Door which he hoped might book a band as intimate as Basie's; the trouble was that the club itself was small, and it preferred a small and cheap combo to a major band. Alexander went to work on the owners. He talked of the virtues of air conditioning, and how much more comfortable the club could be. The management were interested. He offered to lend the club $2,500 to install air conditioning. They accepted gratefully. They also accepted Count Basie.

Alexander clashed again with his bosses over Benny Goodman. Stein and Goodheart were unimpressed with the band; Alexander was the advocate. When, in 1939, Alexander left MCA for the more congenial taste of the rival William Morris Agency, Goodman was left stranded with Stein, the unwilling client of an unenthusiastic agency. He refused to set foot in any MCA office, despite his contract, and he would not talk to any man from MCA. He let it be known that he considered the bookings MCA arranged for him to be deliberately humiliating. He felt he was being punished for being a bad client.

The Goodman row was one of the legends that began to tarnish MCA's reputation among musicians. The dark-suited men with their neat white shirts and their precise calculations were undoubtedly good for many of their clients, superlatively good. They also had a streak of opportunism. Their rival agents were resentful of Stein's success and understandably worried about keeping their own most successful clients. For MCA would use whatever means came to hand, always within the law and its own ethical standards; often the means was the power of the checkbook. The band leader David Rose, for example, was a private in the U.S. Army in the war years, but his military duties left him the time and taste for the highlife at night spots like the Mocambo in Hollywood. They did not, however, leave him the money for his pleasures. MCA spotted that, and offered Rose a $20,000 advance on his services if he would leave his agent and join their list. The money would, of course, cover any possible embarrassment when the bills from the Mocambo rolled in. Rose considered and asked his own agent, Jimmy Saphier, if he could match the offer. Saphier, a small but efficient operator, simply did not have the cash. MCA had a new client. Even among their established clients, MCA

would attempt occasional adjustments of loyalties. They were discovered trying to lure the singer Kitty Kallen to strike out on her own
and leave the band of Harry James, another of the agency's clients.
It was, perhaps, solid and good advice to a burgeoning career, but
it happened to coincide with a period of agency displeasure with
James, who was opting for home life with Betty Grable and an offer
of steady work as a music director in a movie studio rather than the
constant tours that made 10 percent for MCA.

On the road, the band leaders caught the rumors of disaster among
halls and hotels that would not play MCA's game. Stories became
fables, warnings to the rest. Once, in an Ohio town, there was a large
dance hall that refused to sign an exclusive deal with MCA, and a
small dance hall that agreed. The two were cat-claw competitors, at
each other constantly. The smaller hall took all the good things that
MCA had to offer, like the Benny Goodman Orchestra in a hall barely
able to support some polite teatime band, while the larger hall went
deeply into debt. After a time, the man from MCA returned to Ohio
and proposed some new negotiations. This time, the larger hall
signed an exclusive contract, the MCA bands poured onto the bandstand, and the small establishment went bankrupt within two
months.

The same sort of pressures applied if MCA had the bulk of a
hall's business, but lacked the magic exclusive. Frank Dailey ran a
New Jersey night spot called Meadowland for some fifteen years,
booking amicably from MCA's list among others; between fall 1943
and fall 1945, he took 72 out of 104 of his bands from Jules Stein's
agency. The one thing he would not concede was an exclusive deal.
In fall 1945, a larger hall opened for business in direct competition
with him and accepted MCA's terms. Suddenly, Dailey could do no
more business with MCA. The agency froze. Only a handful of personal friends, like Tommy Dorsey, defied the agency and played for
Dailey.

The anger MCA stirred was too general to be kept a secret. The
agency's exact methods, however, stayed hidden. To register the
extent of disquiet over Stein's operations it was only necessary to
open *Variety*. There was Tommy Dorsey telling the world: "They

make me so mad I could cut their throats, but I've got to play ball with them." When his MCA contract finally expired, he took a full-page advertisement: "Whew . . . ," it read, "I am finally out of the clutches of you-know-who." But dozens of other clients were wholly content with Jules Stein. They were richer and busier than they had ever been before. Stein's ideas of exclusive contracts, his habit of buying radio airtime and providing packages of entertainment from announcers to star bands to fill it, all provided constant, lucrative work. If Stein was operating against the law in any sense, the facts were hidden; if he was not, then his record suggests a sharpness quite enough to generate his power. Nobody knew for certain.

Then the city government changed in San Diego, California. For the first time MCA's business was out in the public view.

MISSION BEACH IN SAN DIEGO had all the paraphernalia of an overpriced seaside amusement park. There was a ferris wheel, a glass house, a merry-go-round, a roller coaster among the scooter cars and the shooting galleries. Beside the gaudy mechanical attractions stood a ballroom. It did not have much of a commercial record, but it did have possibilities.

Big-name bands played Mission Beach with little success; the house speciality became western music, played by Bob Wills and his band. The whole operation earned only $74,000 in 1944, and the ballroom contributed barely a quarter of that. It would not have been big business for many men, but for its owner, Wayne Daillard, it made sense. He also controlled Mission Beach's closest rival, a single-story ballroom seven miles across town called Pacific Square. Between the two, Daillard was the music business in San Diego. When the city government changed, his position changed with it; the lease on Mission Beach was put up for tender by the new administration. Normally it would have been a soundless contest, easy and private. But Daillard's opponent was a brash man from out of state named Larry Finley, and he was determined to win.

Finley knew the music business from the wings. Once he had been a band leader, calling himself Larry Fields and acting as pianist,

29

leader, drummer, saxophonist, and booker. He had been advertising manager to a bedding firm, sending out a singing team who performed at the storefront to reward any shop that sold enough mattresses. He had been involved, variously, in cafés in Syracuse, the Dorsey Brothers' Casino Garden in Santa Monica, a skating rink, a jeweler's called Gary's, and an upstairs ballroom in San Diego called the Trianon. Mission Beach fitted neatly into his own ambitions for San Diego. He wrote a bright prospectus for an "Amusement Center for the Whole Family." He promised to slash prices, to ban alcohol so that "parents will be happy to permit their sons and daughters to spend an afternoon or evening of fun at the ballroom without fears or qualms." He also promised the city more rent than Daillard had paid—$20,000 plus 2 percent of his gross takings.

He let it be known that he would put big bands and main attractions into Mission Beach, despite its dubious track record. Before the end of October 1944, he made the necessary pilgrimage to the white colonial mansion in Beverly Hills that served as MCA's headquarters in the area. There he met Larry Barnett, orchestra coordinator for the agency. "I told Barnett that I had to have MCA bands if I got the Beach," he said, and "that I wanted to buy the majority of the attractions from MCA. He advised me at the time that they had a ten-year deal with Daillard, but if I got Mission Beach, it would change the picture considerably in San Diego and he would work something out for me to enable me to obtain MCA bands." Barnett made it clear he did not like the idea of change in San Diego. The promise of bookings was vague. More, as Barnett later admitted, "I also told him he might not be wise to open up."

Barnett's warning made some commercial sense. "I didn't think the town was big enough to have two ballrooms battling against each other and both splitting the business and neither of them would make any money." But he had a prior contracted loyalty in the battle. Wayne Daillard knew what made his business work; at Pacific Square he had a huge sign that promised dancing on Tuesday, Thursday, Friday, Saturday, and Sunday with the help of "MCA," acknowledged in letters as large as the Pacific Square name, with the slogan

"World's Greatest Bands." The agency was to be embarrassed by Daillard's enthusiasm, and, even worse, by the deal they had signed with him on May 3, 1944. In a letter from Beverly Hills, MCA promised him first refusal on all orchestra bookings offered by the agency for engagements at ballrooms, open-air pavilions, or street dances in the county of San Diego. Only theaters, concerts, and radio broadcasts were left out. If MCA and Daillard could not agree on a band within forty-eight hours, the act could be offered elsewhere, but not for less than Daillard had been asked. In return, MCA demanded and got its traditional exclusive. Daillard had to book at least thirty-five of the agency's bands each year, or accept a minimum of 75 percent of MCA's offers. If he had a weekly house band, some second-string outfit to keep the customers dancing between star names, he must book that band from MCA for at least forty-eight weeks out of every fifty-two. In effect, MCA said it would give Daillard its active blessing if he would give the agency all his business.

Nothing suggests the deal was rare. It was the essence of Stein's business philosophy: control as absolutely as possible without being involved in ownership, minimize your risks to the greatest degree possible. It was cozy and clever. It also infuriated Larry Finley. He went to law. A handful of indiscretions among members of the MCA staff gave Finley the handle he needed to sue Jules Stein and his associates for conspiracy in restraint of trade under the Sherman Act, a private man's civil antitrust suit.

MCA made mistakes, uncharacteristic of an agency that always disapproved of unnecessary records, paperwork, or memos. Its employees went on record. Daillard indiscreetly promised the San Diego council his links with MCA as a guarantee of quality at Mission Beach, and claimed the agency represented 95 percent of the big-name bands in the country. In Beverly Hills, meanwhile, an MCA salesman named Harold Bishop—always known as H. E. Bishop—began his own personal campaign to help Daillard. Lawrence Barnett, his boss, was later unable to remember if he had encouraged Bishop and Daillard or not. Bishop, certainly, pulled out all the stops. He even called other talent agencies, asking them to withdraw letters they had sent in support of Finley's bid. It would, he wrote, be "bad business" for them and the band business in San Diego and for the bands that they represented to antagonize Daillard, who had been a profitable source of business in employing their bands at Pacific Square and at Mission Beach over the years. The other agencies paid attention; they had been in the habit of splitting their commissions with MCA should they be lucky enough to sell a band to Pacific Square. Even MCA's rivals, it appeared, were made to respect an MCA exclusive deal.

Bishop's campaign and MCA's warnings came to nothing. The new San Diego administration took the Mission Beach lease away from Daillard and gave it to Finley. He started operations in January 1945. His troubles had barely started.

On February 27, MCA offered the services of Ted Fontana, Bob Chester, Jack Teagarden, and their bands; for Teagarden, Finley would have to pay $2,250 a week as an advance against 50 percent of the gross takings. Finley refused the deal for a simple reason: he knew that Teagarden and Chester were already booked to appear in a spectacular battle of music at Daillard's Pacific Square just three days before they would come to Mission Beach. Daillard was paying the same price as Finley, but for the first San Diego showing of the bands. Finley was annoyed, but at least he had signed no contract. Next he booked the singing King Sisters for the Beach, offering $1,500 a night for them to appear on February 10 and 11. He sent a letter of acceptance, but it was not acknowledged. He knew why from the San Diego papers within a few days. The King Sisters were promised in huge advertisements for Pacific Square—on February 2, 3, and 4. Finley's sense of persecution grew. MCA would refuse him information, bands, and deals. Each name band that he tried to book appeared, it seemed, in the rival dance hall at Pacific Square. Because MCA dominated the market for "name bands," the star attractions whose names alone would pull a crowd, Finley's business suffered; he was losing money on the second-rank bands he could book. His anger took him to the law.

IT WAS THE FIRST TIME Jules Stein had given a deposition in a lawsuit. For twenty years, MCA had been a very private power. Now Stein found himself sitting in a lawyer's office, room 806 of the Union Bank Building in Los Angeles. He was waiting to tell the story of MCA.

His direct involvement with the Finley case was small. He faintly remembered a business meeting with Wayne Daillard, and he had meet Larry Finley "once, in the Beverly Hills Hotel lobby, for about half a minute." But his role in MCA, and the agency's business, were material issues in the lawsuit, and at ten in the morning on August 8, 1945, the lawyers tried to unveil the truth. They got something less than the full story, but Stein's statement remains the fullest account of Music Corporation of America ever given under oath and in his own name by an officer of the company.

Stein was modest. He was, he said, "a theatrical executive" and of his duties with MCA he claimed that "I am only the president." The lawyers wanted to know his exact duties. They came forth like a catechism answer. "Coordination of all the companies, the affiliated companies, the corporate problems, the establishment of new employment opportunities in various fields of the amusement business, the handling of union relations, and the usual problems that are attendant upon an institutional head." He claimed some distance from the agency's day-to-day operations. He did not, for example, know whether MCA bands did more business than those of all other agencies combined. At first, he could not tell the lawyers if MCA did more business than its largest rival, but he changed the record to show a more direct answer: "In my opinion, it does." On counsel's advice, he quietly refused questions on the corporate relationship between Music Corporation of America and its affiliates. His sole sign of quickness and distaste came when he was asked about his medical background, and whether he had once been an optician. "An optician fits glasses," he said. "An oculist is a physician and an M.D."

In the questioning of Jules Stein, there were certain vital points. MCA was sued under the Sherman Act, the federal legislation against restraint of trade. The act applies only to trade between states. Finley's lawyers had to show that MCA was engaged in shipping something—bands, publicity, contracts—across state borders. If MCA booked the vans that carried the instruments, or organized a bus for each band, then it might come within the Sherman Act; if it merely booked bands between Los Angeles and San Diego, the point might be impossible to establish. The lawyers also had to prove that the "name bands" really were as important to the survival of dance halls as Finley suggested, and that Stein controlled enough of those bands to make his lack of cooperation damaging to Mission Beach. Last, they had to prove that MCA did in some real sense control the bands. If bands were free to make their own bookings—both sides admitted that it did happen on occasion—then Stein might seem to have the power only to inconvenience Larry Finley. There would be no offense and no question of damage. But if MCA did control the bands, then the jury would have to find that the agency had life and death powers over ballrooms throughout the country, and Mission Beach in particular.

Stein laid out the structure of the MCA empire, but with patches of discretion. Its corporate parts were the Music Corporation of America, the band-booker; MCA Artists Ltd., which handled legitimate theater and ice shows; Management Corporation of America, a more recent unit that booked clients on radio and found them personal-appearance spots; and California Movie Company, an agency (despite its name) with functions similar to Management Corporation. The New York office handled the East Coast, Chicago the heartlands, and Los Angeles, aided by San Francisco, handled the Pacific States. "Cleveland handles Ohio and perhaps part of Michigan," Stein reported, "and they interlock with some in Chicago and New York. I think they go as far as Pittsburgh in the East. Dallas handles Texas and goes as far up as Kansas City. There is no sharp demarcation." As for numbers of staff, Stein thought there were some twenty-five workers in Los Angeles for Music Corporation of America, of whom perhaps six worked with bands and orchestras; in New York there were the same number, "or somewhat more"; other offices were far smaller, with only Chicago even in the same league as New York and Los Angeles. The Atlanta office, indeed, had been "discontinued" in the 1940s.

Stein's evidence suggests a careful central core to the agency— proper records, careful accounts, and a liaison system designed to prevent double bookings or overlaps. Each office held a booking chart on each client, but there was no master file of contracts except in the accounts department. Each office found bookings in its own area—by mail or telegram or telephone and "also on permanent engagements by personal contact of the executive." MCA's private definition of permanency was more than one week. Responsibility for all this lay with individual heads of offices. "There was no such thing as one-night stands before we got into the business in 1924," Stein claimed, "and as you develop one office and that territory, you spread on to another territory and then you correlate." He admitted the peculiar importance of his innovation. Of the bands, he said: "I would say that most of them would like a fine permanent engagement where they could make as much money as they could make by traveling about, but the income on traveling around is sometimes substantially more."

Minor details emerged of MCA's way of doing business. There was a neat device to improve cash flows: deposits from halls or hotels. On single engagements, for example, "as a rule deposits are required, particularly from newer employers. The balance of the monies are paid to the leader upon completion of the engagement and we refund to the leader the balance of the monies collected as a deposit, if deposits are required, and less the commission to which we are entitled." Instead of waiting until a band leader was paid and could write a check for their commission, MCA took the use of the money up front. Their commission, Stein reported, ran at "an average up to twenty percent on one-night stands" and up to 10 percent on permanent engagements. The whole machine worked, he added in an aside, without benefit of a teletype machine.

He insisted on the limits to MCA's role. "We cooperate with the attractions," he said. "We don't build these bands." He conceded that MCA would help—by "putting [bands] in territory wider than their local environment . . . going into hotels or cafés or other places where they may have broadcasting facilities . . . important hotels.'' But that was all part of an agent's duties as laid down in the standard contract, ''to represent, counsel, advise and book.'' Their client was the band leader, and it was his business who played in his band. Stein admitted that the band leaders were tied to MCA by exclusive contracts, worldwide, for up to seven years, and that although they kept the right to make their own bookings, that was ''not a general practice.'' He reported that MCA would take its cut in any case—weekly or monthly, by check from the band leader. He did insist, however, that the agency only advised and booked. It did not control bands, and its services were strictly limited. ''We don't have a publicity department,'' he said. ''We have had it on several occasions, but it is limited now to preparation of window cards and newspaper matter and securing photographs to be sent out in advance of the attraction.'' The band leader arranged his own transport, sometimes with MCA's advice, but no more; and although MCA supplied the itinerary for each tour, ''our service is completed with the sending of the itinerary.''

Stein's claim was too bland for Finley's lawyers to stomach. Surely, they asked with great courtesy, MCA was at least concerned with whether or not the band arrived to play its date? ''We know they are performing the engagement,'' said Stein, drily, ''because if they weren't on the engagement, you would know within a few minutes of the time they were to get there . . . somebody would call frantically wanting to know where the band was.''

HOW THE MCA MACHINE WORKED was only part of the examination. Just as important to Finley's case was the scale and the power of that machine. Wayne Daillard had claimed MCA represented 95 percent of the name bands in America; he had hoped that claim would win him Mission Beach. Now Stein was challenged to say exactly how powerful his agency had become, to say if MCA really did rule the music business.

He began with an evasive technique that was used again when the Justice Department went after MCA. He listed the bands that MCA did not represent. In 1946, they did not book Jimmy Dorsey or Woody Herman or Benny Goodman, although the rows with Goodman had been legendary while he was a client. They had nothing to do with Duke Ellington, Paul Whiteman, Spike Jones, Charley Spivak, or Count Basie, who had parted from MCA as soon as possible after Willard Alexander quit and left him without a protector there. The list seemed to come more fluently than the account of MCA's own clients. Under some gentle pressure he conceded that MCA was the largest agency in the band business, although he did not agree that it was larger than all its rivals put together. Stein was inclined to believe there were some thousand "organized orchestras" in America; MCA represented only 200. What he did admit was a hefty number—the $1.5 million that clients paid MCA each year in agency commissions, implying that those bands could earn at least $15 million a year.

The lawyers wanted to know who the clients were. They started with definitions. It was important to establish that "name bands" mattered, and that MCA controlled many of them. Stein proposed that a "name band" was "any band with a name which can be publicized, promoted, or become of popular and public interest." It was none too helpful a definition. The definition, he said, posed a problem which "even the American Federation of Musicians, the social security divisions of the Government, and the Treasury Department have been unable to solve." He found it hard to account for popularity. "[It] might be the personality of the orchestra leader, might be his arrangements, might be the fact he has extremely fine musicians. However, some of the finest musical orchestras in the country have not developed any popularity at all." But surely all the clients of MCA had a national name? "We represent some attractions," Stein said, "that are of local interest in small communities."

His stalling produced no clear answer. That was left to Lawrence Barnett, the MCA band coordinator in Los Angeles. Stein said the majority of bands represented by the agency earned less than $1,000 a week. It was not clear whether he meant that their average income every week of the year was less than $1,000, or whether they always earned less than $1,000 while working. Either way, MCA's own figures, confirmed by Stein, showed that MCA bands as a whole earned an average of roughly $1,440 a week. If most were indeed under $1,000, there had to be a galaxy of stars hidden in the apparent drabness of the low earners. There was. Barnett told the lawyers in his deposition that 50 of MCA's 200 bands earned more than $3,500 a week, and 75—among them Harry James, Artie Shaw, Guy Lombardo, Xavier Cugat, Gene Krupa, and Sammy Kaye—earned more than $2,500. They were the substantial gloss and glitter in the $15 million machine.

The jury found against MCA. The court records show that the jury asked for additional guidance on the complex legal questions, and even warned at one point that further deliberation would be useless. With time, they reached a decision. On April 10, 1946, judgment was entered for Larry Finley in the amount of $55,000 plus $7,500 to cover his attorneys' fees. MCA lost a later appeal. For the first time, the courts said MCA was taking and winning its power outside the law.

HOLLYWOOD REBUILT ITSELF after the financial earthquakes of the 1930s. It ran almost like a real business again. Paramount had gone into near bankruptcy; United Artists had almost tumbled; the old guard had, some of them, been turned out of office for a while as others tried to salvage an economic disaster. Yet there was still visible money in the movie industry. Loud flesh peddlers, unlovely figures with brash attitudes and sharp practices, handled the talent. MCA could do that better. Its cold, detached, calculating men could run the flesh merchants out of business. Its decorum could improve the agent's image. Billy Stein, brother to Jules, went to California in 1932 to inspect the business. Jules Stein rented a house there in 1936, convinced it was worth his time and energy to acquire 10 percent of Tinseltown. In 1938, he bought out the management contract on his first movie stars and sent out a young, eager man, tall, gaunt, and serious, to help in the business. His name was Lew Wasserman. Within a decade, Wasserman was the most powerful man in show business.

Jules Stein's first buy was less than inspired. For some tens of thousands—reports said $40,000—he bought the management contract on the Ritz Brothers, a fading batch of brother comedians who had briefly glittered in some early 1930s musicals. Their real strength lay in the nightclubs, but their contract with Twentieth Century-Fox called for two more movies for the studio and one outside. Nobody seemed very interested in making those movies. After a while, Stein allowed his first movie stars to go back to Lou Irwin, their original agent. The brothers returned to nightclub work, making $12,000 a week in 1946, with their last guest appearance on the screen in 1976. The brief liaison with MCA seems neither to have hurt nor helped either side.

Stein was determined. For him, the band business had become tedious and complex, hedged with union regulations that were hurting his brilliant package deals. Radio was blossoming, but he needed another arena. If he was to make it in the movies, he needed—as he had needed Guy Lombardo—the names that would give him leverage. To get them he would wheedle, connive, poach, scheme, or simply buy. As in the music business, Stein was quite honest and quite ruthless. He had the unique advantage of thinking methodically in a disorganized business, understanding that 10 percent of most people's profits is a better living than a constant series of gambles on making profits of your own. He stood outside the business because he was not unduly concerned whether a particular movie was made, or even what money it took in at the box office. His concern was with the careers of the talent, the indispensable talent. He wanted names that would surely continue earning for MCA, properties that arrived with a guarantee of a generous yield. Stars, like stocks and shares, required him to take a view on future earnings and then decide if the price was right.

His first superstar was Bette Davis. She had survived a dramatic dash to London and a British lawsuit over breaking a contract, and now she was back at Warners. Her career was shining bright. She had won her first Oscar for *Dangerous* in 1935; she was on her way to her second for *Jezebel,* and a nomination for a third in *Dark Victory*. She would make an excellent start to Stein's Hollywood list. To win her, he set out to indulge a Hollywood character called Eddie "The Killer" Linsk. He was without work at the time, but he had friends; notable among them was Harmon Nelson, then husband to Bette Davis. Stein found Linsk and gave him a job at $150 a week. Linsk delivered Ms. Davis. In the same way, a few years later, Stein acquired Eddie Bracken, a comedian with a sizable following after *The Miracle at Morgan's Creek*. In that case, Stein traced Bracken's best man, Monte Juro, and hired him. Soon after, Bracken was on the MCA client list.

Where contracts were not for sale, Stein bought agents or agencies. He bought out Johnny Beck, Jr., from Associated Artists and made him head of MCA's motion picture division. Through Beck Stein came to meet the hierarchy of Hollywood, the ancient moguls still asserting their power. The meetings were sour. Stein was quiet, cold, and discreet, which was not like an agent; he was an interloper, and yet he had swiftly acquired stars like Errol Flynn, John Garfield, John Forsythe, and Paul Henreid. Rumors of his background as doctor and scientist were disconcerting to men like Louis B. Mayer, the onetime junk dealer, who felt some rare inadequacies in his presence. Beck engineered a meeting between the two at Mayer's office. Stein brimmed with fulsome politeness. "Thank you very much," he said, "for this meeting." Mayer was brusque. "I didn't do it for you," he said, staring at Beck. "I did it for him." There was an awkward pause before he added, incongruously, "But you must be a very nice man to have men like this working for you."

When it helped, Stein could remember and use his music background. He admits to using it on occasion with MGM. On the West Coast, they were the operating arm of Loews, Inc., which on the East Coast had theaters that were in constant need of the sort of name bands represented by Stein. If MGM would not come up to scratch on a contract, it was simple for MCA to suggest potential trouble in arranging bookings for Loews. Stein preferred diplomacy to threats, but the force of his diplomacy was hard to miss. His own diversification matched the diverse interests of the entertainment companies, and made them vulnerable. It was an extra card to put alongside his established principles of buying big names for leverage and never taking on talent until it was established and earning.

As well as names, he acquired some social momentum. In the band business there were no indispensable parties, no places where an agent must be seen. In Hollywood, to be visible was to be real. According to Bette Davis, Stein chose another way. He was, she has said, "seldom ever seen. Few people even knew what he looked like. He preferred to live this way." Beck and the rising Wasserman made many of MCA's necessary public appearances. But Stein had a circuit of his own. He liked to play gin rummy, his only recorded game, at five cents a game and no more; for that he would visit perhaps the Samuel Goldwyn household and play with Harpo Marx or Danny Kaye. He liked the gloss of social life, the Roman titles, and the grand style that was to be found about the movie colony. He frequented Elsie Mendl, a rich French interior decorator and a fearful snob who had acquired a penniless English knight and taken him to Hollywood. The couple maintained a sense of status so exact that they even divided their dinner parties into those who were significant and therefore invited to eat, and those who were less significant and might call for drinks when the others had finished dinner. Stein was not happy, ever, to be relegated to the minor league. He once arrived after dinner in business clothes—a decent suit, a white shirt, a dark tie. The director Otto Preminger, concerned by his appearance, took him aside and asked where he had left his dinner jacket. "No dinner," said Stein, firmly, "no dinner jacket."

If he went to "A-list" parties with the elite of the industry, he would often talk business in a corner. His own entertaining had a deliberate splendor, but it was as much for pleasure as for business. His agency was expected to be cold. "Some of the other agents," he says with distaste, "were nothing more than baby-sitters." He sometimes came close to his clients. He would sit by Bette Davis in her darker moods, reassuring and consoling, and he is said to have been the man who taught Gene Kelly to save money. But he had no ambition to be a father figure. He was not a polo player like, say, Darryl Zanuck; he saw no need to go out to sports or parties or events simply to be seen and make contacts. "I do not live on the golf course," he says. "I learned long ago how to study. I don't read much fiction. I would rather deal with corporation tax problems and intricacies of corporate structure. I relax that way." His style was visible in the MCA offices with their antiques and proper, unflamboyant corporate taste. It showed in his mansion in Beverly Hills on Angelo Drive, with the collection of antiques. The man was stylish, but he did not seem to need ostentation. He did his social duty and graced some grand tables, but he was not obviously clawing his way into the social apparatus of Hollywood. He seemed remote from how such moguls are supposed to live. That was deliberate. He was pulling back from the day-to-day business of the agency. He knew now how to run that. At weekly meetings, he took the head of the table and watched his agents do gladiatorial battle, each talking up his own achievements and denigrating those of the others. That fierce competition ran throughout the agency. It contrasted oddly with the somber exterior that MCA presented, the dark suits and dignity that made the place seem to some inmates like a mortuary. However, with such a degree of ferocity going into the daily running of the business for which Stein had set the principles, he now needed to be nothing more than a strategist for his financial interests, except when a special client had some special trouble. Stein had built a power that was almost abstract. It ran for itself. It answered to no one. Its innovations were about to change Hollywood and shape television when it appeared. To Stein, the manipulator of money, the old-style mogul, the revolutions that he caused were not significant. MCA used its power only in the interests of MCA. From this point on the story of Jules Stein is the story of the machine he had created.

THE BEST OF THE LISTS belonged to Leland Hayward. In the early 1940s, Stein had bought out the agency interests of CBS; William Paley detected an unhealthy attention on the part of the Justice Department to his company's dual role as agent and employer, and put the CBS agency up for sale to keep things looking quite proper. While the transaction made MCA huge, it was the deal with Leland Hayward that gave it unquestioned influence and authority in Hollywood.

Hayward was a Hollywood outsider, much like Stein. He was an easterner, with white flannels, linen underwear, and the accent of a man who had been to Princeton. Among the richer ethnic mix of the movie business he seemed a gentleman agent, almost quaint. He had started with sharp improvisation. While drinking late at the Trocadero in New York, he listened attentively as the management complained that business was bad, and what the place really needed was an attraction like Fred and Adele Astaire. Hayward, who was without work or money at the time, recognized his chance and pelted down the street to the theater where the Astaires were gracing *Lady Be Good*. He offered the $4,000 the Trocadero had offered every week and persuaded the Astaires to accept. He pocketed $400 in commission and reckoned it was the easiest money he ever made.

By the 1940s, Hayward's list was formidable. His list of writers alone would have made him a power. He represented Walter de la Mare, Julian Huxley, Theodore Geisel of the Doctor Seuss books, Ben Hecht, and Dashiell Hammett. He even acted for A. E. Housman, who earned $24.15 for MCA in 1949, after the Hayward list had been bought. His list of stars was incomparable. He spoke for Boris Karloff, Greta Garbo, Fred Astaire, Henry Fonda, James Stewart, Gene Kelly, Fredric March; he both represented and loved Katharine Hepburn, and he represented, loved, and married Margaret Sullavan; he was the business voice of directors like Joshua Logan, Billy Wilder, and William Wyler. The Hollywood aristocracy, directors and dancers, writers and actors took his advice. But all that was not enough for Hayward. His wife, Margaret Sullavan, was implacably hostile toward his business. She hated the telephone; Hayward was addicted to it. She thought it was a rival to her family. Stein remembers Hayward marooned in the countryside, utterly forlorn, trudging to the nearest drugstore for the sheer and necessary pleasure of calling the office to see how things were going.

Family pressures were reinforced by Hayward's own ambitions. Stein was perfectly happy to be the top agent in town but Hayward wanted to be a creator and a producer. He refused to stick to any one thing even though he was a success. Late in 1944, Hayward opened his first Broadway production, *A Bell for Adano;* Margaret Sullavan's attitudes had been honed to a cutting edge, and even Hayward was beginning to admit that the agency business tied him down too much. It was time for a deal.

On March 31, 1945, Hayward and Stein signed. Hayward handed over his business to MCA, with the promise that he would nurse his clients for at least three years and be available to the agency after that if he was needed. He abandoned nothing; he moved his desk from 9200 Wilshire Boulevard to the imposing MCA headquarters on Santa Monica Boulevard that was so often mistaken for the city hall in Beverly Hills. He made a point of persuading his clients that MCA would be even better agents than he had been on his own; he went out to woo such new clients as Jerome Robbins, the director and choreographer, and to win back some brief defectors like Astaire and Rogers. Few resisted the deal. Clifton Webb, the waspish and aging character actor, claimed he had not been told what was happening and took legal steps to escape his contract with MCA; he told the court he would never have signed again with Hayward had he known "the actual facts." Mostly, though, clients were impressed with the sense of balance-sheet wisdom that MCA exuded, and Hayward was still there to comfort and advise them. He came to think of himself as the agency's elder statesman. If some senior client like James Stewart had to decide which movie to make or which contract to sign, Hayward was there. His presence, week by week, gave Stein and Wasserman valuable help. He was able to reassure old clients and gave the agency advice on the theater world, which was new to them, and the movie world in which they were still learning their business. The only disruption came with the writers. Because MCA saw no real difference between representing an actor and representing a writer, the top literary agent of Hayward's operation was quickly disillusioned with the new arrangement. He went out on his own when MCA refused him the top job in their writing department. That was how MCA lost the services of Irving Paul "Swifty" Lazar, the man who later organized coups like the selling of President Nixon's memoirs.

By 1945, and the deal with Leland Hayward, MCA was attracting some public attention. The phrase that appeared was always the same: "the star-spangled octopus." The cliché stayed with Stein's empire until the law broke up the business. MCA was generally regarded as a private state, invulnerable to government action, adhering to its own rules and diplomatic standards. It had frontiers nobody was allowed to cross, and it had powers to help or harm those it needed. It had the stars, the writers, the musicians, the directors, and the producers. It controlled radio airtime to make sure its clients worked. It packaged everyone from chorus members to stars for Broadway shows, and producers often thought it easier to accept an MCA package than risk the displeasure of stars that the agency represented. It dominated the band business by its careful exclusive deals with bands and with dance halls. Throughout show business everybody could expect to have to deal with MCA at some point, some day. The agency commanded respect.

It was not just size or tactics that won Stein that respect. It was also skill as an agent. When James Stewart returned from World War II, MGM tried to hold him to the years he had promised on his contract. It was inequitable, a penalty for war service, but it seemed inevitable. Stein and Wasserman thought otherwise. With their links to the East Coast band business it was simple to bring pressure on MGM, whose parent company needed MCA's help to fill its theaters. Stewart broke free of his contract. When Universal wanted him to appear in *Winchester '73* in 1949, MCA refused a flat fee and demanded a percentage of the profits of the movie. They won, since Universal thought Stewart essential to the project. For that single movie Stewart made $600,000 and MCA its commission of $60,000. Since in his peak years a superstar like Clark Gable had never earned more than $300,000 a year for making three films, MCA's strategy was convincing to its other clients. The agency delivered.

The Stewart deal had other significance. It changed the balance between studio authoritarianism and star anarchy. Instead of orders issued to contract employees, studios began to make offers to artists who might be interested. Star salaries soared. William Holden made some $5 million for his part in *The Bridge on the River Kwai*. By the 1960s, salaries were computed as an advance against a percentage of either a film's profits, or the money the theaters returned to the distributor—the gross. A Paul Newman or a Steve McQueen need not approach the cameras without $1 million down against, say, 10 percent of the profits or gross. As the fees grew, the stars took on the powers of shareholders in the projects they graced. If they chose to defer their fee on a movie, they considerably helped the chances that the film would be made. They had the bargaining position of financiers because their fee was so large a part of a movie's budget. Star power may have been invented because MCA and other agencies wanted to inflate star pay and take a fatter 10 percent, but its impact on Hollywood was extraordinary. It helped wreck studios in the 1960s. More important, it helped make possible movies that the studio system itself would never have considered. Star enthusiasm could now get a project off the ground. It was a revolution.

In radio and later in television the package idea provided work for MCA clients and a fee for MCA as producer. Sometimes it helped reinforce the star ascendancy promoted by MCA in the movies. If a radio star had a show of his own, he would take home a weekly fee and return most of it to the Internal Revenue Service. If he arranged to take the show and sell it as a property or a corporation, he would pay the substantially smaller capital gains tax on the sale, and the show could continue to pay him a salary. The device was immediately popular. William Paley at CBS liked it because it allowed him to raid the talent of his rivals at NBC: NBC liked it, since it offered some guarantee of loyalty. Networks bought star corporations, and with the corporations they bought the authority of the star as producer. In time, especially during the lulls in movie production of the mid-1950s, MCA also organized corporations for its movie clients, often making the star the production company, contracting his services to a studio.

Stein's money machine was simply better at this sort of strategic thinking than most other agencies. MCA was like a calculating businessman looking at the essentials of his business, ignoring the glamour and fuss. It thought while other agents schemed. It paid to be with MCA, usually. When it failed to pay, there was nothing to gain from complaint.

LEW WASSERMAN WAS PERHAPS Jules Stein's most remarkable creation. Stein had built his machine on principles; in Wasserman he found the ideal man to run it. He was an unlikely power figure, a onetime candy butcher in a Cleveland burlesque house who had risen to manage a theater-nightclub. At the age of twenty-two he asked for a job writing publicity for MCA clients, and he was hired. On that day, December 12, 1936, he went home rejoicing and told his wife that his chances were very good indeed. "Stein's an old man," he said. "He's forty."

For two years he wrote press handouts, but he proved to be, in Stein's words, "the student who surpassed the teacher." In 1938, he was sent to Hollywood; two years later, he was the head of the motion picture division. At the end of World War II, when MCA had absorbed Leland Hayward's clients and the CBS list, Wasserman became head of the whole operation, answerable only to the owner and strategist, Jules Stein.

Wasserman was the warmer man, the confidant and helper to stars. He was supportive while Stein was remote. He came to hospital bedsides and worried about details; he arranged the shipping of contact lenses for Marlon Brando and the forming of corporations for Alfred Hitchcock. His personal friends were also clients. Yet he was also the man who imposed MCA's house style. He was fierce about the agents' uniform, the dark gray suit, the white Sulka shirt, the thin tie. Stein thought that standard dress might produce standard thinking, but he kept his worries to himself. Wasserman, like Stein, insisted on secrecy and discretion in everything. Nothing was ever committed to paper unless it was essential. Memos were rare. It was forbidden to leave messages on a desk overnight where even rival agents within MCA might see them. In public the agents refused to discuss the business of MCA on the grounds that it was really the business of their clients, and they had a duty to be discreet. Under the secrecy there ticked a meticulous intelligence service. Every major studio had an MCA representative. His job was in part to make sure that clients were happy, to handle any complaint or dispute that might suddenly flare up on a set. His other job was to know people and get them to tell him things. He had to know what movies would be made and when and by whom and what casting was still open. MCA handled shooting scripts almost before they returned from the typing pool. Small agencies were at a grave disadvantage; one man can take only one lunch a day and reach a handful of meetings across the sprawl of Los Angeles. MCA was everywhere, and each morning, early, studio men and agents came together to pool information.

At the heart of it all was Wasserman. He was the ingenious tax expert at times, the man credited with deals that sent clients working outside the United States for eighteen months to escape a hefty slice of their tax bill; with Stein he was the architect of the deals that made stars into corporations, and salaries into capital gains. He was also the aggressive negotiator, the man who raised the howling anger of studio heads and made them feel their domestic stars were listening to wild siren songs. He invaded the lives of clients and shaped their careers, not always as they wanted. He knew when to strike and how. Raoul Walsh, the director, remembers the high-flying success of Errol Flynn's work as Custer in *They Died with Their Boots On*. Jack Warner was overjoyed. "That is one of Flynn's best," he said. "If Custer really died like that, history should applaud him." Wasserman heard the tremors of success and hurled himself into Warner's office, taking Flynn along. "When they came out," Walsh remembers, "Errol was all smiles. His salary had been doubled."

For Bette Davis, Wasserman had to go to war. She had become a monstrously rich woman and an unquestioned superstar. She had her Oscars. In 1947, the U.S. Treasury Department listed her as the highest paid woman in the United States, earning $328,000. The next year she earned $364,000. She had everything except her freedom.

Her Warners contract trapped her in a line of dreary melodramas, and the contract had ten more years to run. She was desperate. She made the scenes for *Beyond the Forest*—the film's sole distinction is the immortal Davis line, "What a dump!"—but she refused to do the recording necessary afterward. She would not do it at all, she said, unless she was released from her contract. Warner was furious. The movie was expensive, and there was no chance that the studio would simply write it off. He scented desertion. He claimed Davis had been "caught on the fly by Lew Wasserman and his associates." He remembered that his star had appeared for discussions with MCA men at her side, that she had asked for copies of scripts so that Lew Wasserman could read and judge them. In his anger, he barred all MCA men from Warners lot. His brother, Harry, warned him that it would be like "bucking a stone wall," and he was right. Davis felt protected by MCA. She was close to Jules Stein and she respected Lew Wasserman. She held out, MCA supported her, and Jack Warner had to grant her release.

Unlike Stein, Wasserman dealt in the details of careers, teasing, grooming, and protecting. Sometimes the star was grateful and unconvinced. Montgomery Clift was always to Wasserman a star on the model of Tyrone Power or Rudolph Valentino, a grand romantic. Clift thought otherwise, but he had no grounds for objecting to the deals that Wasserman brought him. At Paramount, for example, Clift was offered three movies, freedom to work at any other studio if he wanted, approval of scripts, and a promise that he would be directed by nobody except Billy Wilder, Norman Krasna, or George Stevens. But in return for such spectacular arrangements, Clift was manipulated. It could be petty. Before he was to appear with Elizabeth Taylor in *A Place in the Sun*, Wasserman insisted that he escort Taylor to a premiere, that he be seen with her. It was good publicity for the picture in which they would play lovers and for his career. It also revolted him, because of its cynicism, and Taylor was none too keen. By the time of *Raintree County,* Clift had plunged into debt with MCA. He owed them money, but also the organization of his life— they had found him a cook, chauffeur, and home in Hollywood Hills.

When he was involved in that hideous car crash that changed his features, Clift's first visitor at the Cedars of Lebanon Hospital was Wasserman.

Sometimes the MCA men were the ones manipulated. Marlon Brando always seemed deeply unimpressed with the power and authority of his agents. Wasserman was left to tell Darryl F. Zanuck of Twentieth Century-Fox that Brando had no intention of playing opposite the newly discovered Bella Darvi in *The Egyptian;* he could not stand the lady. Wasserman's task was not enviable; Ms. Darvi was very much the protégée of Mr. Zanuck. When shooting began on *Viva Zapata!,* Wasserman found himself involved in making sure the production rolled on time by deputing an MCA agent to take the contact lenses Brando had left behind to Texas. For Brando's sister Jocelyn, blacklisted because of her husband's supposed radicalism, he was required to hunt work. Those services kept Brando content, but they were only a small part of what the agents did for him. They made him into a company, Pennebaker Productions, backed his films, and eventually bought him out. For his movie as a director, *One-Eyed Jacks,* it was an MCA agent who found the script and the unknown screenwriter: MCA produced Sam Peckinpah.

There were moments when the cunning of MCA came close to the surface, a shadow in the water. Both Brando and Clift were involved in one case that disturbed Hollywood. Fox was preparing to film Irwin Shaw's novel *The Young Lions;* Clift was signed first and Brando was sold later to work off a commitment to the studio that dated back to *Viva Zapata!* There was one other major role, and for that Tony Randall had been cast. Randall was not an MCA client. Four days before production was due to start, men from MCA went to talk with the producers. At the end of their conversations, Tony Randall was abruptly removed from the project and he was replaced by Dean Martin, a singer who had made frantic comedies with his partner, Jerry Lewis. Martin had a singular virtue: he was a client of MCA. Studio executives at the time thought the casting curious and said so. Rumor said Clift had taken against the idea of working with Tony Randall. Whatever the true reasons, it is remarkable that

MCA could change the casting of a major picture at a major studio with so little apparent effort or trouble. By this time, the agency's list and influence were such that it would only have been necessary to hint that the film's main stars might turn malcontent if MCA's advice were not followed. For once, MCA allowed its powers to be seen.

Not all the cunning and the muscle were quite so negative. MCA was good at extricating its clients from terrible messes. Jules Stein was still available at times to help. During the fall of 1955, Judy Garland was hankering after her wartime glory, when she had toured vaudeville theaters around America to loud and friendly welcomes. She wanted to go on the road again. It seemed there might still be enough large theaters left to justify the tour, and her husband and manager, Sid Luft, set about recruiting them. At first he seemed to be doing well. He had a list of twenty houses where Garland could play. The catch was that only seven were prepared to guarantee minimum earnings from the appearance. The other thirteen were eager for the show, but unwilling to put up money that would pay orchestra, technical crew, and overheads even if the shows were not a success. Luft was now trapped. If the tour went ahead it could lose heavily on those thirteen theaters where there was no guarantee. Expenses would be heavy; the investment was considerable. But if he canceled the tour, there would be seven furious houses quite prepared to sue Garland for breach of contract. Her reputation was already erratic. It would suffer more if the tour were suddenly to fizzle out and die.

Jules Stein intervened. "I think," he told Luft, "we can get you out of your misery." In the small print of Luft's contracts was a clause that reserved to Garland an important right: she could cancel the deals if a bona fide sponsor called her for a movie or a TV special, and she could do so at forty-five days' notice. At the time, Stein was working on a sponsor and a special, a CBS color spectacular for the Ford Motor Company, part of MCA's massive drive into television production. All he had to do was to book Garland and persuade Ford, which he did.

MCA's failures were rarely public, but they did happen. There were stars who simply did far better with other agencies and were handled with more imagination and skill when they left the octopus behind. One was Deborah Kerr. She arrived in Hollywood trailing glory from her British film career, and foundered for years in sweet, inoffensive, inescapable roles for MGM. She remained loyal to Stein himself: "He was an extraordinarily intelligent and nice man," she says, "but it wasn't really him I saw or dealt with." Her career was sinking under a dead weight of gentility. When she did break with her image and scamper lustfully through the surf with Burt Lancaster in *From Here to Eternity*, she had already left for another agent. Men from MCA, she said, would come to visit and they would ask after the health of her children. "Their concern was touching, but not actually worth ten percent of my earnings."

AMERICA WAS COMING HOME. While Stein and Wasserman set their power high and firm, a society less gaudy and extreme than theirs in Hollywood was changing radically. In the inner chambers of the studios, in the inner councils of the music business, it would have been easy to miss the symptoms. War had ended. Money from war work left millions with riches that had seemed only a dream during Depression years. Couples who had never had the money to marry while America was in the grips of slump, who had waited with patience during the long years of wartime separation, could now start families. They chose to live in suburbs that spread like stains from the heart of old cities. New roads were punched out across fields and woods to build new communities. Where once work had seemed all-desirable, it was now a commonplace. Work had been the moral necessity, the condition of taking leisure; every pleasurable moment had its price. Now, work was a nuisance, something swiftly performed to make possible the all-important life at home, the new children, the new gardens, the new neighbors, the marriages that took place thousands of miles from old-established families and parents and made the new couples independent, home loving, centered around the hearth. This was more than a revolution in how and where people chose to live; the ranch house and the neat lawns were its least interesting symptom. It was also a revolution in attitudes. Now that a mended economy made it possible, home was the center of life. Television, like a hearth, animated the home.

"There is nothing so permanent as change," Stein says. "Had I stayed in the radio business, I'd be out of business today. We went into television when the movies could have taken over the television business. In the early days of television, the movie business could have owned the stations. But those men were too sure of themselves. They were too smug." In the late 1940s, helped by curious alliances, MCA moved into television. The core of its product was film for television, especially filmed series, and especially those with guns. Just as the great American homecoming made television viable, Stein and Wasserman took their agency into the business. Social change made the medium work. The networks needed help with programming. MCA stood ready, the assembly line of slick, reliable, homogenized product. Because it was first, and because it contrived unique advantages, it came to dominate the field. It owned a studio and filled it with "General Electric Theater," "Wagon Train," "Ironside," "Marcus Welby, M.D.," "Kojak," "The Rockford Files," and "Baretta." It was a factory so little concerned with creative quality that soundmen on the studio floor were authorized to stop the action if directors or actors broke the rules by overshooting. It produced analgesic drama, the sort that soothes without healing. It had all the talent that was needed, and it guaranteed a product that would not offend or overstimulate. It was as though the factory were some robot device that had never been programmed to consider the quality or the ideology of the material it produced beyond a bland homogenized approach. Because the shows were made only for MCA's convenience, with no higher aim as distraction, they were made to satisfy networks' basic needs—time-fillers. They were so good at their job that in 1977 MCA had sixteen hours of programming a week on the three major American networks and could seriously plan to establish a fourth network of its own—an ad hoc collection of disgruntled stations who might take the rest of MCA's overflowing product.

Within the agency there is dispute over who first thought production for television would be a fine and prosperous business. Leland Hayward was inclined to take the credit. Jules Stein was certainly interested in television from the start. But the initiative was taken by a lowly vice-president, Karl Kramer. He had the idea of putting MCA clients into a filmed showcase to be called *Stars over Hollywood,* an idea not unlike the radio packages that had kept MCA clients in work during the 1930s. His colleagues were skeptical. Film for television was still rare; moving into full-scale production was a radical move. The formula for the show was dated. Still, the show would produce cash and it would give work to the clients who were beginning to suffer a little from the cooling of Hollywood's wartime boom. Lew Wasserman gave his approval. Kramer had to find a sponsor; he persuaded Armour, the meat-packing corporation, to back the show. In 1952, it became the first show that MCA sold through syndication to stations fending for themselves outside the networks.

Something was missing. What MCA wanted as usual was an exclusive. It came through the good offices of their client Ronald Reagan, and a panic that made the guilds of actors and writers in the movie business take a monstrous risk. It proved an exclusive as satisfactory as anything Jules Stein had invented for himself.

RONALD REAGAN WAS A FLAMING LIBERAL in those days. He was a labor organizer, president of the Screen Actors Guild. He gave MCA the exclusive they wanted. Its essence was simple, its implications vast. In radio, the unions had agreed to stop agents from acting as producers only if it seemed their members' interests might be harmed. In television and movies, the Screen Actors Guild made a fixed and implacable rule: no agent could produce. A handful of agents who had made movies before the rule was made in 1939 won waivers. Most had to kick their heels, unable to expand. "Imagine," says Chester Migden of SAG, "if an MGM had suddenly decided to go into the business agency. Imagine, and you will see why we had the rule."

What Reagan gave MCA in a letter dated July 23, 1952, was a waiver. "We agree," Reagan wrote, "that for a period commencing with the date hereof and expiring October 31, 1959, if any contract rule or regulation made by us prevents your engaging in both businesses we hereby give you waiver thereof for such period." Reagan had noted: "At the present time you are engaged in the motion picture and television film agency business and in the television film production business; you expect to continue in both. You have explained to us your reasons for so doing." On June 4, 1954, John Dales, then executive secretary of SAG, wrote again to the agency. This time, the waiver was confirmed and extended. Even if the union were to change its rules, MCA was now allowed to continue as both agent and producer until all its current commitments were met. (The waiver had to be renewed, since the agreement it broke was revised in 1954 and expired in 1959.)

"You have to remember that in the early 1950s there were no major TV film production companies," Chester Migden says. "There were a few pioneers like Gene Autry and Hal Roach, but I remember we could barely find a production company when we had hearings once on employment conditions. What changed our minds about the agents rule was simple—the economics of the business and growing unemployment. The board of directors and Reagan thought it was worth giving MCA the waiver to make jobs for the membership. It was a blanket waiver, but it was only unlimited because there was so little production that it didn't occur to anyone to put limitations on it. It was open-ended because hardly anything existed then. Nobody dreamed it would blossom as it did."

The exact text of the waiver was always elusive, although no SAG member could have been ignorant of the principles involved. They were allowed to work at Revue, MCA's television production subsidiary. If they were MCA clients, they had to find other representatives for deals with MCA; they did not pay commission to the agency side if the television production side was employing them; MCA had to pay at least as much as it would have demanded from some outside producer. Those were the conditions of the waiver, and they could not be hidden. Like any MCA arrangement, it was a private matter, even if it affected the entire membership of a union. The obstinate discretion added to the fury of other agents who could not get so generous a deal. Herbert Seigel, chairman of General Artists, wanted to buy the studios of Desilu and go into production; he could not get the blanket waiver. "I've never run across anything like this in all my years in the business," he spluttered. "MCA and we are playing in the same ball game, but there is one set of rules for them and a quite different set of rules for everyone else." When the Famous Artists agency wanted to absorb Seven Arts Productions, the waiver was refused again. "Let's get it straight," Chester Migden says, "nobody was ever denied the right to do a series. People got their waivers, project by project." But no agent except MCA could make a business out of it and plan ahead, secure in the knowledge that there would be no union objections whatever they did. MCA had sanctuary in a rough business, and more and more of its rivals became curious about exactly why, and on what terms, so profitable a privilege had been granted.

The precedents for the waiver were limited. Charles Feldman, an agent with Famous Artists, had been in movie production before the first formal agreement between SAG and the agents. He was given a waiver picture by picture for movies he wanted to produce. "An individual agent, after all," Migden says, "couldn't go into production on a very big scale." Other agents had occasional, limited rights to act as producers. Nobody else had so general and generous a bill of rights. "MCA," Migden says, "turned out to be not only the biggest agents in the business, they became far and away the most successful TV-film producers. It was frightening."

SAG members were edgy about the deal, and outsiders were downright suspicious. An attorney for the Federal Communications Commission, Ashbrook P. Bryant, finally went to the offices of SAG on Sunset Boulevard in Hollywood and asked to see the letters that established the waiver. To his surprise, they were produced immediately. He used them as the basis of cross-examination of SAG officials in later FCC hearings. He was first assured that the guild had never varied its principles: "As a general rule, one who is a producer of television film may not be a franchised agent." He went on asking questions of John L. Dale, the SAG official who confirmed the extension of the waiver in 1954.

"Did you give any other blanket waivers?" he asked.

"Blanket waivers, no," Dale admitted. "We have a number of waivers, but I don't think it would be proper to term any of them blanket waivers."

Bryant wanted to know if any other agency had been as privileged as MCA and Revue Productions.

"No," Dale said. "In the main all waivers granted with respect to production by agents are set forth with respect to specific productions or a specific series of television pictures or a specific number of pictures."

The waiver was now public knowledge. SAG was acutely embarrassed. It had made its concessions long before there was an industry in television film for MCA to dominate. Now it seemed as though the actors, and the Screen Writers Guild, had helped MCA come to power. "We would have been delighted," Chester Migden says, "if the Justice Department had moved in earlier."

AFTER OTHER PRODUCERS, MCA came as a relief to the networks. They were businessmen, not artists. They understood the needs of programmers and supplied the product. In a business whose main problems were selling time and holding audiences, MCA did the messy part with commendable efficiency. With them to help, a programmer could isolate himself from ideas and ambitions and actors and writers. They made television infinitely less awkward. "I guess NBC got in the habit of relying on MCA and MCA practically controlled their programming," William Paley of CBS remembers. "We were always much closer to the product."

CBS took its star comedians from MCA in the 1940s; NBC took a startlingly high proportion of its programs from MCA in the 1950s. In 1958, for example, MCA produced one third of NBC's prime-time programs, eight and a half hours out of the weekly twenty-four and a half. They sold at least two series for 1959–60 without troubling to make a pilot film, the usual calling card of a series; the two were "Riverboat" and "Laramie." Rumor had the head of NBC summoning Sonny Werblin of MCA and saying, "Sonny, look at the schedule for next season. Here are the empty spots—you fill them in." Rumor, as usual, exaggerated, but only in dramatic terms; the meaning was true, even if the exchange never happened. Anonymous men, once employees of MCA, told lurid tales: "They talked as if they owned the television networks and in a way they did. They had friends in positions of power throughout TV. They had gotten them their jobs, loaned them money, and controlled them by giving them MCA's big-name stars or withholding them, as they pleased." The power was notorious, the influence pervasive, and the organization impeccable.

What MCA delivered was rarely original; it liked others to take the risk on pilots. It wasted nothing. A disastrous drama with Ernest Borgnine misfired so badly that it was withdrawn from its planned position on "Alcoa Theatre" and turned into the pilot for a comedy series, to be called "McHale's Navy." Robert Altman, the director, was enticed to the MCA factory with the promise that the company had developed a new interest in serious and substantial programs. Six out of the eleven scripts he prepared fell foul of MCA, Kraft, and its advertising agency. Neither sponsors nor the MCA factory could accept drama built around a black soldier in World War II, a man afraid of the dark, a convict, and capital punishment. Wasserman summarized the rule: "We don't want to have the company manufacture programs in bad taste."

Taste was an elastic concept. MCA at one point prepared a tasteful series called "The Breakdown." Its heroes were troubleshooting psychiatrists who would, each week, solve cases of nymphomania or schizophrenia or plain hallucinations. The series emerged through

Bing Crosby Productions, a subsidiary of Cox Broadcasting, as "The Breaking Point," a spin-off of "Ben Casey."

MCA'S METHODS OF MAKING MONEY from television were naturally not limited to profit on individual shows. If a network was prepared to pay $40,000 for each episode of a series, a reasonable price around 1960, then MCA would arrange to keep at least three quarters of that, even if the show were nominally owned by a star client of the agency. The mechanics ran as follows.

Out of the $40,000 MCA as agency was naturally entitled to a sales commission. That was 10 percent, or $4,000. Cynics suggested that the fee was for "putting the film in a can and shipping it to New York." Out of the remaining $36,000, MCA would take at least 20 percent as studio owner for "overhead," leaving $28,800. Out of that, MCA would probably charge $20,000 for the use of the studio, the camera crew, and the film stock. The remaining $9,000 went on artists' salaries. The unfortunate star who thought he owned 50 percent of the show would now discover that in its first year on network MCA's accounting would ensure that there was no profit to be divided. The star would have to be content with his fees from the budget. MCA, meanwhile, kept $31,000 in cash and probably made its own profit on those fees; if the profit margin were the same as MCA's overall profits, then each show would make MCA $5,500 automatically, whatever the fate of the show in its later, more profitable reruns. The Stein machine organized itself impeccably to avoid any distressing leakage of money.

Besides the shows produced for television, MCA also controlled the movie library of Paramount Pictures. MCA bought the films after other studios had released their blacklist to television; stations were hungry for new movie material. Paramount's movies before 1948 were bought out by an MCA subsidiary called EMKA for a price that was dependent on the television rentals they earned. Other MCA companies did the releasing to television and took a fee. It was a spectacularly profitable business, since the main expense was amortizing the films' cost and that was done at roughly 70 percent of gross television rental income in a given year. It was a neat device for handling a desirable property. It also broke any pattern of alliance with NBC that might have formed; half the movies were sold to CBS affiliates and a quarter each to associates of NBC and ABC.

"IF YOU SUDDENLY COULD NOT DEAL with MCA, could you continue to cast your movies and remain in the entertainment business?" Justice Department lawyers put the question to Stanley Kramer. His answer, unhesitating, was no.

It is hard to overestimate the power and ambition of the empire Jules Stein had built. It dominated the agency business, with perhaps 60 percent of the star business worth having in music, movies, and television. It dominated prime-time television. Its influence spread through Broadway, Hollywood, and the networks because of its client list and its meticulous business practices. Even in the 1950s, when its main activities were on the screen, MCA still dominated the music business. When Hover of Ciro's nightclub in Los Angeles, once the inevitable watering place after some sumptuous premiere, brought unsuccessful suit to prove that MCA was depriving him of the attractions he needed, he did succeed in extracting from several Los Angeles hotels some lists of the stars who played their ballrooms. The Terrace Room at the Los Angeles Statler reported Victor Borge (at $4,000 a week), Xavier Cugat (at $7,500 with band), Nelson Eddy (at $3,000), Tony Bennett ($3,000), and the then stellar Celeste Holm (for $4,500 a week). Of eighty-two acts presented between October 21, 1952, and May 21, 1955, only twelve came from any agency other than MCA.

Lew Wasserman, as the operating head of the agency, was regarded by consensus as the most powerful man in Hollywood. His approval was crucial even when his direct involvement was limited. When Dalton Trumbo was writing the script of the epic *Spartacus,* the producers hired special publicity men to see if they could devise a way to use Trumbo's real name; since the days of the witch-hunts, Trumbo was an undesirable element, a Leftist and a non-person.

Through Trumbo's letters, there emerges an extraordinary picture of how Wasserman's approval was vital to the restoration of Trumbo's name. He is told the name of the scriptwriter and does not disapprove; Trumbo is hopeful. Later, Wasserman's knowledge is seen as a protection. "The most powerful single person in the business," as Trumbo calls him, could easily sway the rest.

From as early as 1942, the Justice Department had been taking an interest in MCA. It was clear that its power was now qualitatively different from that of any other agency. By pursuing its 10 percents with ingenuity and skill, it had actually succeeded in rewriting the power structure of large parts of show business. Agent power was established, and MCA was the most powerful agent. Jules Stein says: "You don't have to be dishonest to be smart." Much of MCA's success can be explained by sophistication and skill. Justice, however, began to hear other stories—stories which suggested that MCA could be unscrupulously tough in pursuit of a deal, could manipulate and coerce others because of its unique authority. MCA, Justice thought, was almost the kind of trust that antitrust law was established to break. There had been a string of civil cases after Larry Finley's success, but the results had been equivocal; no criminal case was brought. In the business, most people thought MCA was invulnerable. "They can't control MCA," one man said. "They're like a foreign power. The best you can hope for is to make a treaty with them."

Public information on the company was scant. The first prospectus for the company's shares when they were offered on the New York Stock Exchange in 1959 gave three thin pages to the history of the business. A company reorganization in 1959 conveniently limited the history of MCA, Inc.; it was incorporated as a kind of holding company in Delaware in 1958, and absorbed the rest of the MCA businesses just before the flotation. The accounts were exact, brisk, and as uninformative as the law would allow. Obvious parts of the company's history emerged. Jules Stein had been sole owner until 1954; he had parted with shares to his associates in that year. The company's methods and logic were admitted by one firm of underwriters to be largely a tax convenience of the Stein family. The annual meetings, held in Chicago, rarely lasted more than fifteen minutes. When MCA later went shopping—for the Columbia Savings and Loan Association of Colorado and for larger firms—the prospectus never gave more than the barest outline of what MCA was and how well it did at it.

The networks were not likely to dispute MCA's powers; the assembly line suited them well. Independent producers bottled up what grievances they felt, aware that they might soon need MCA again. Actors who claimed MCA had done less well by them because it was both agent and producer would find it hard to establish their exact market worth in other circumstances, especially when MCA so dominated the market for television film work. Often the grievances that emerged, usually anonymously, were no more than an instinctive feeling that MCA was too big and too uncontrolled. "In Hollywood," said one insider, "I don't think you can go to the bathroom without asking MCA."

In January 1959, Music Corporation of America heard from the Department of Justice. The talent agency business was under review. Justice would like to see the files. What emerged in the investigations, and before a later grand jury, was this: of all the agencies, the one that most set the rules for the business was MCA. Investigating the business meant looking at MCA.

BETWEEN JULES STEIN AND SHOW BUSINESS, the links were fraying. He had been sick and was tired; his wife, Doris, a formidable and graceful woman, was telling him constantly that he had done enough in business. He no longer needed it. The agency and its offshoots had helped make him one of the ten richest men in the United States. It was time for him to do something else.

The corporation was in good shape. MCA still borrowed money without security and at prime rate, a privilege that was unknown to firms with AAA credit ratings. Its business was diversifying. It had bought money management with Columbia Savings and Loan. It sold its bank with uncharacteristic razzmatazz. Jack Benny, on television, thought aloud: "If it's all right for my money . . ." A cast of Rodin's

The Thinker toured Colorado colleges on a truck and came to rest in Columbia's headquarters in Denver. It stood on a revolving stand because, Stein says, "we never could decide if the head or the backside should face the administration." Moreover, in February 1959, MCA bought the vast Universal studios, a site that eventually covered 408 acres. It gave Revue Productions a factory. It made money, since the facilities were leased back to Universal. It was also a mass of land with value as real estate for some general development beyond the making of movies. It had advantages. Because Universal lies between counties, on an administrative island all its own, the studio operations were hampered by no noise regulations and development by no restrictions at the local level. Universal was answerable only to itself, and MCA owned the site.

The least relevant part of the business, now, was the part that had once been its whole foundation—the talent agency. Between 1957 and 1961, the agency barely seemed to grow; indeed commissions dropped a few thousand dollars between those years. In 1961, it was barely 10 percent of MCA's gross income, but Stein wanted to organize the agency in his own way. He did not want to be pushed. In 1961, the main corporate move that MCA was contemplating was the buying of Decca Records and its subsidiary Universal International Pictures; Hollywood already whispered that MCA was going to make theatrical movies, but it wrongly believed they would be released only by Universal. If MCA made the Decca deal, no union would tolerate its dual role as agent and producer. Members of the Screen Actors Guild were already unhappy about it. The bitter years of unemployment without hope among SAG members had ended. Now, film for television was the second largest part of an average actor's income, second only to commercials for television.

SAG told all agents in the spring of 1961 that all waivers were to end. "That was before the Justice Department got in on the act," Chester Migden says with strict truth, since the case had not yet gone before the grand jury. "MCA began to realize that we meant business." In October of that year, SAG rewrote its deal with MCA, under George Chandler's presidency. There were acrimonious discussions with MCA's attorney, who once had represented SAG. "He got fat," Migden says, "and went over to the management." The new deal laid down that MCA would automatically cease to be agents within a month of any deal that left them in control of more than 50 percent of a record or movie company. MCA agreed, but with a reservation: even when clients had other agents, MCA wanted to keep commissions on contracts that MCA had negotiated. "We wanted people released from MCA at once," Migden says, "so they could find other agents, and other agents wanted the full ten percent. In the end we agreed that MCA could keep half the commission—five percent—since they did the deals originally, and the new agent got the rest for servicing the contract."

In those talks, MCA's professional reticence was broken for a moment. "They did admit to us," Migden remembers, "that they were considering the Universal deal." But before the Federal Communications Commission hearings, which were considering MCA's power, at the time of the SAG talks, the agents remained obstinately quiet. They refused to give a list of programs they sold or represented, although all such programs were identified by the MCA logo at the end. They refused to divulge any clues as to how they did business. They would not discuss the packaging of a program, or why they took 10 percent of the fee the network paid, or how stars came to make series for MCA, or how much influence MCA would bring to bear on a series in which the star happened to be an agency client. MCA said nothing and went to court for the right to say nothing to the FCC, a right that was refused, although the court did concede that MCA's trade secrets should be kept confidential. "Over the years," said an MCA statement, "MCA has built up a vigorous and effective business organization, the success of which has been largely due to the very policies, practices, and knowledge which the Commission now seeks to make a matter of public record."

Justice came closer to a sense of discovery. The FCC was snarled in appeal and counterappeal. And Lew Wasserman sat in Hollywood Hills talking business with Milton Rackmil, head of Decca Records. The final farce of MCA, the agency, was about to begin.

NOBODY EXPECTED REVELATIONS from an MCA prospectus. Yet the one issued on March 27, 1962, in connection with the marketing of the shares MCA paid for Columbia Savings and Loan, dropped definite hints. It reported the deal with SAG: "The company anticipates that similar agreements will be required by directors, writers, and other artists through their respective guilds and unions." MCA "has under consideration plans for the continuation of its present activities in television and other possible various courses for the further development and diversification of the Company's activities." It mentioned the prospect of acquisitions within areas where SAG would forbid the agency to tread, although such plans were "not sufficiently definite to be included in this prospectus." If they materialized, "the company's artists representation business would be terminated."

Rumor linked MCA to Universal. From that, it was an easy step to assume that Universal was to be more than an ally. It was to be an acquisition. The prospect troubled some shareholders in both Decca and Universal. Milton Rackmil told Decca's stockholders at their annual meeting on April 11, 1962, that an offer was "imminent" and would come "any day." Walter Reade, Jr., the theater owner, spoke from the floor. He wanted to know if anyone had yet asked the Justice Department about the legality of a merger. "We have not," said Rackmil. Reade was astounded. "You have had no exploration with the Justice Department?" he asked again. "We're doing nothing," Rackmil told him, "until an offer has been made."

It came within days. On April 17, 1962, MCA, Inc., filed a registration statement on Form S-1 with the Securities and Exchange Commission, covering a proposed share-exchange deal with the stockholders of Decca Records.

The formal announcement put the Justice Department in an unreasonably difficult position. It appeared that their quarry was about to dispose of its main questionable activity; yet there was no statement about where the agency would be sold, or to whom. Justice worried that it might be sold as a unit, and any abuses that had been detected within MCA would be continued under new management. Moreover, the Decca and Universal deal would give MCA a spectacular power base in the industry. It would mean, for example, that MCA, owner of the Paramount movies made before 1948, would now acquire the Universal list as well—all the television pickings from movies like Douglas Sirk melodramas, Ma and Pa Kettle comedies, Audie Murphy Westerns like *Cimarron Kid,* and the works of Abbott and Costello in which they met, among others, Dr. Jekyll and Mr. Hyde, and *The Killer Boris Karloff.* Even if MCA sloughed off its agency, the men who made it work would still be in business. If MCA bought Decca and Universal, there would be a whole new superpower in show business that raised quite new issues of scale and responsibility.

Justice prepared to take its case to court.

"We say, that MCA Artists is the crux and leverage on which MCA has made its violations." Leonard Posner led the case for the Justice Department. He argued that the agency made possible the various sharp dealings that he alleged were MCA's way of doing business. The agency had to be broken up to prevent MCA from selling it as a going concern. He had to file suit before Stein and Wasserman could make a move. Justice started to ask questions of MCA in August 1961; the SAG waiver was rewritten in October 1961; but now the process speeded up. The Decca and Universal deal was to be consummated on June 23, and that would leave MCA only thirty days to get out of the agency business under their new deal with SAG. Privately, MCA lawyers had written to Lee Loevinger, assistant attorney general, on July 5. They told him the ownership of MCA's talent agency would be transferred to various current employees of the corporation, "who upon the transfer being accomplished will no longer be employed by or connected with MCA in any capacity." They would take the title of Management Corporation of America, sell their MCA stock or else put it in trust, and for the business they would pay "not much more than fees due." Posner was suspicious. Why was MCA giving up its agency "without taking a nickel for it"? He suggested the veterans would simply continue business as before. The judge in the case said, wryly: "They may turn over a new leaf."

Justice was under pressure. Hollywood assumed that the Democrat friends of Wasserman and the Republican friends of Stein would between them be able to stop the investigation and force the case to a halt. In the courts, progress became chaos. On July 13, Justice demanded that MCA give up its link with Decca. On July 16, MCA found itself going to appeal against an order that would stop it from leaving the agency business, precisely what Justice wanted to happen—on its own terms. On July 17, MCA failed in its appeal. On July 23, there was agreement in court and MCA Artists was quietly dissolved. It was the first of two consent decrees— agreements between Justice and defendant whereby the case would not be pursued in court, but the defendant would make concessions. A consent decree does not amount to a confession of guilt, or anything like it; it is a compromise and it suspends criminal proceedings. It also takes off the public record the case against the defendant.

The official letter went out over Lew Wasserman's signature. "Effective immediately," it said, "MCA, Inc., and all of its domestic subsidiaries have surrendered or will surrender all of their guild, labor union, and other franchises and licenses with respect to their talent agency function. MCA therefore is no longer engaged in the representation of talent in the entertainment industry and you may seek representation by anyone you desire." MCA was forbidden by the consent decree to influence the choice of any client. "Each employee of MCA regrets that the pressure of time and events has made it impossible to thank you personally for the privilege afforded to them and to the company of serving you in the past and wishes you every possible success in the future."

The agency was dead.

By poolside and golf course, at dinner party and cocktail party, the other agents of Hollywood seethed and chivvied and wheedled. Half the business was suddenly up for grabs. Studios realized that they knew neither numbers nor addresses for their stars; they had always called MCA. Lines to the Screen Actors Guild were jammed with worried actors. Newcomers who had barely passed their MCA audition and were looking forward to work now had to start again from scratch. Major stars made sad announcements, flaunting their loyalty like a banner. They seemed to think that by sitting tight they could reverse a consent decree. Tony Curtis said he was confused; Warren Beatty said it was "a bum rap"; Billy Wilder saw the bright side. "Isn't it marvelous," he said. "I'm going to be ten percent richer every week."

At the MCA mansion two armed security guards from Burns stood over the agents as they removed their papers. Only personal papers could leave. Out on North Kenwood Drive, a man named Jaik Rosenstein prepared the next issue of his 50-cent newsletter, *Close Up*. Across the front he streamed the headline: MCA STILL GOING FOR NO 1 AS H'WOOD COPS OUT IN BUM BEEF THAT STAGGERS ENTIRE BIZ. He wrote of naked muscle, FBI calls at midnight, anonymous denunciations, all the evocative terms for a secret investigation. He claimed Hollywood had done nothing to save its savior. All around him the various employees, employers, clients, and victims of MCA showed the same confusion.

"We are all," Stein says, "Republicans now." The MCA probe was not launched by the Kennedy brothers; it was launched under Eisenhower as an investigation of the talent agency business in general that two years later came to concentrate on MCA. The point is worth repeating. Just as MCA's political friends could not stop the questions, it seems unlikely that politics had much to do with the choice of MCA as target. It was, of course, convenient for the Kennedys to pursue a showy antitrust case, and show business was a glamorous target to prove that they were not as unconcerned with business delinquents as they might have seemed. But MCA was the target that presented itself once the good Republicans had gone to work on the industry. The surprise is only that the case took so long to arise.

MCA's agency business was divided among veterans of the firm and outsiders. One shred of evidence suggests that Justice was right in thinking the agency would not be spun off too far from the mother corporation. The day the law divorced MCA from its agency, the California Labor Commission received a set of fresh applications for state licenses to act as a talent agent, the first stage to union approval and to work. Two of the applications, never pursued, were in the names of Lew Wasserman and Jules Caesar Stein.

"WE HAVE DONE what other agencies did or tried to do," Lew Wasserman said. "Only we did it better, I think." Although their case never came to court and remains sealed with the grand jury transcripts, the Justice Department obviously thought there was something more than a standard set of agency ploys at work in MCA.

Details emerge. There is Leland Hayward handling a signed contract with Alec Guinness, an MCA client, which happened to give Hayward the unlimited right to run tapes of Guinness's performance on television. Despite the signature, Sonny Werblin of MCA suddenly asked that the contract be reworded. Then Hayward had a proposal for a television series set in a military school for boys and MCA remembered that in their Paramount library was a movie called *The Major and the Minor* which had something to do with a military school. True, the movie had Ginger Rogers and the television series was to have "an officer having the characteristics of the actor Paul Ford." MCA still wanted a royalty of $500 a week, on "moral" grounds. Their zeal to protect clients was admirable, but their demands and tactics seemed harsh.

Justice, however, was concerned with more fundamental issues. It argued that MCA "represents a very large percentage of the name talent in all categories of the entertainment industry." Nobody denied that, but MCA did try to dispute it. As Jules Stein had done in 1946, it produced a list of stars that the agency did not represent, a device spoiled only by the fact that several of those stars had once been on MCA's roster until squabbles or wars made them leave. MCA pointed to Cary Grant, Doris Day, John Wayne, William Holden, Glenn Ford, Maximilian Schell, Audrey Hepburn, Lee Remick; and also Marilyn Monroe, who had briefly been a charge of Wasserman himself, and Frank Sinatra who had been a package sold by MCA until he began to question whether the agency was entitled to 10 percent of everything the network paid for the whole show, or 10 percent of the much smaller amount that Sinatra took home each week. Most important, performers on MCA shows, MCA said, were not all their clients. In shows like "Wagon Train" and "Alcoa Theatre" they cited fourteen clients alongside twenty-four stars who paid commission to other agencies. They never asked more than 10 percent commission for any show they sold; they most particularly did not own— yet—any part of the phenomenally successful "Alfred Hitchcock Presents."

There was no sensible way for MCA to deny its size and power. It had swallowed so many agencies with so many clients, from ice dancers to concert pianists to superstar movie actors and television heartthrobs and ladies from the soaps. It represented writers and directors and producers. If its power had been limited to giving advice to the men and women it represented, it would have been incomparably the most powerful agency in America. Justice said it did more. It said: "Since at least 1938, MCA has offered talent, programs on condition that others were bought." It said: "And since at least 1945, MCA demands to represent all packages or programs owned by talent they represent."

The first charge was the less conclusive. In its big-band days, MCA always wanted an exclusive. That was the basis of its business. It wanted to be the only agent to a band, the only supplier to a hall. Exclusives meant assembling packages, selling bands together. A hall might take a year's entertainment from MCA and have no choice about the bands that came: on the other hand, before the hall learned to run scared of the agency, it could count on MCA's reputation to produce the star names that a dance hall wanted. In that sense, halls bought small-time bands to be sure of the star attractions. MCA also packaged radio shows from announcer to star singer, and with the star attractions it sold minor clients. It serviced Broadway shows, providing all a management could want, just as Jules Stein in his early days had offered everything a cabaret could need from hatcheck girl to cigarettes to favors, drink, and music. That was the legitimate packaging, the part that depended on the will of the customers to buy the package and not on the simple power of the agency. Later, MCA did exclusive deals and worked against the rivals of its customers; the Finley case in Mission Beach showed that. It had so powerful a list of clients that it needed only to hint at malcontent among its stars to persuade a producer to hire the men or women MCA named. A large element in that persuasive power was the caution of producers who knew they would need MCA again. The agency did not need to threaten. It merely suggested. Producers thought it wise to accept suggestions. Stein had played off MGM's movie needs against Loews's need for bands in its East Coast theaters; in the same way, his agency could span so many fields and offer so many names that it was always possible that a buyer would decide it was wisest to keep MCA happy. MCA did not usually need to articulate the implicit threat. It merely made sure its power and scale were known.

The second charge had more bite. MCA put its clients into packages much as it offered them advice on fees or found them colleagues. For Alfred Hitchcock, MCA thought it had a duty to pursue an elusive model glimpsed on a television commercial and present her to Hitchcock, thereby satisfying his curiosity. The girl was Tippi Hedren. MCA provided a writer when Hitch wanted to quarry a film from the undistinguished Robert Bloch novel, *Psycho;* he was a success, Joseph Stefano, and he made a script that was black and funny. It was natural, also, that in 1955 Lew Wasserman should be looking for ways to capitalize on the name of Hitchcock, then at its height despite the relative dimness of *The Trouble with Harry* at the box office. Directors rarely amounted to much in the Hollywood hierarchy, and Wasserman wanted to change that. At a conference concerned with the shows Revue should make, he said suddenly: "We ought to put Hitch on the air." Hitch himself was reluctant, not snobbish about the smaller screen but simply too busy with the larger. It took persuasion and time before he took Wasserman's advice as friend and agent. The result was a package: "Alfred Hitchcock Presents," and a private web of book publishing and television sales. MCA took its cut, but it could hardly be said that Hitchcock suffered from the packaging. In 1964, MCA decided to buy him out and offered shares. Hitchcock accepted and became the corporation's third largest stockholder.

Jack Benny reaped similar rewards. His J&M Productions, Inc., went to MCA in 1961 for $2,745,000 in stock. His was the most vocal defense of MCA as packager. "They put me in a position where I could pay terrific taxes and still keep some money for myself. . . . They called it giving an actor an 'estate.' " MCA made a company called Amusement Enterprises for Benny that could be sold to CBS; Benny moved from NBC to his new network with a hefty capital gain on which he paid relatively low taxes and received a continuing salary as star of his show. Then, they created J&M which sold CBS shows in which Benny did not appear; and, in time, they took over that second corporation for themselves. "That," Benny said, "was one of the attractions of MCA."

Sometimes stars, less content, felt trapped in the packages, as though in webs and honey. MCA was always taking its cut—as agent, as salesman, as packager, as studio owner, as distributor. Its 10 percent take from the total fee a network paid for a show could leave the star, as we have seen, far away from profit at least for the first season, while his corporate partner, MCA, had a solid return on the fees built into production costs of the show. MCA was not foolish; stars might have to be patient. Their sadness was that rival agencies were not as good as MCA, or at least were less privileged, since they lacked the blanket waiver for TV production. The rivals were no answer. Jules Stein's empire was so solid that people would not take a chance on challenging it.

THE LADY IN THE MADISON AVENUE OFFICE now speaks respectfully of "Doctor" Stein. He has taken back his title and returned to medicine, this time as fund-raiser and philanthropist in the cause of research to prevent blindness. It is fine, generous, proper behavior of a mogul. A massive and beautiful center for eye research at UCLA bears his name. He has touted and bullied to make other rich men help his cause. The anonymous Mr. Stein, mysterious and remote, becomes the visible Dr. Stein, posing in foolish spectacles alongside Elton John. There is visible luxury in his life now, a party that the Astors might envy to launch his hotel at Universal City, his movie

Sweet Charity, and his own charitable concern. To that party flock proper persons, registered in some social list as proper. Columnists who write about society and women with grand and empty titles come to visit. A daughter's wedding takes the roof of the St. Regis Hotel in New York; a celebration, partly tax deductible no doubt, requires the whole of the Universal Sheraton. Now the corporation has a life of its own and runs with only faint guidance. Since 1973 the man has left and keeps as his serious title only the word "founder"; he has more and more become the mogul in the old and stylish sense. He wants his dignity back. Moguls had in their public persona a certain fearsomeness that would pass for dignity. He pursues that hope.

Twice in the 1960s Stein tried to organize deals that would have put MCA within a far larger corporation—first Westinghouse, and then Firestone Tire. His motive, presumably, was simple. Jules Stein could hardly play the market in MCA shares, nor could he easily sell any large parcel if for any family reasons he might want to do so. As the owner of a mere 2.3 percent of Firestone on the merger terms proposed, he would have far more flexibility.

Sometimes the magic seemed to have gone from MCA when the agency ended. Banks made the company pay interest above prime rate and asked for collateral. The New York Stock Exchange valued Walt Disney at six times the price of MCA. Universal Pictures had an erratic record, with times when it seemed likely to abandon theatrical film altogether. That great party held in 1969 for the hotel and for *Sweet Charity* was missed by Lew Wasserman, who, while at home sick, heard the rumors that he was to be replaced, that Stein had suddenly decided his record on movies was so poor he could not be trusted with the company. The brief, internal crisis was much magnified. It was a rare case in which MCA's hierarchy seemed at odds with each other. Usually, the top men sat to watch the struggles of their underlings, whether at the melodramatic nighttime meetings the agency had organized or in the run of business. Wasserman and Stein, it was assumed, had almost identical interests in the business and were together on all major issues. Their brief estrangement, more talked about than real, was not significant. In

1973, Stein in effect bequeathed the corporation to Wasserman, some forty years after he had hired a pushy publicist from Cleveland who thought Stein was old and would not long be in the way.

Stein was left in the shadows now, but MCA's ambition never stopped. In 1977, it planned what was in effect a maverick alternative network, with MCA programs only. It was offered to independent stations and to affiliates of the established networks. It was part of a scheme to program an entire weekend of television, all the product of the MCA machine.

The last of the true moguls began to be troubled about his name. He saw his other enterprises forgotten, his dealings in land, antiques, and stocks and shares. He wanted his investments, or at least their shrewdness, known. He hired a string of writers to tell his story, to make the four careers a matter of public record on his own terms. He wanted recognition even as a doctor, although his work was now fifty years passed; it seemed he would more likely be remembered for his crusade against blindness rather than his career as a businessman. Businessmen do not become immortals.

He sat in his dark wood office, a dry man with a tongue flickering over thin lips, boasting a little about a remarkable life and asking for dignity. He had lived through power, glamour, and riches. Dignity was the last thing that he needed, and he needed it fiercely.

3

WILLIAM S. PALEY: NETWORK

THE MACHINE IS THE NETWORK, and William S. Paley invented it. In his offices at CBS there are the trappings of a rich man's taste, a fine collection, colors that are subdued, exact textures. It is the style of a man who has had at least a million dollars since more than fifty years ago, a man who has had time to relax with his money. The walk to the executive offices is almost as famous for its classic and slightly bland style as the building that surrounds it, all soaring black granite and glass; or the corporate notepaper, clean-cut, elegant, and as standardized as CBS executives sometimes are; or even as famous as the network whose earnings support it all, the top television network for more than two decades that was rarely the innovator and rarely challenged public taste. It was the network that raided others for its talent and success, the one that let others take risks. It was the largest advertising medium in the world, a gigantic commercial machine that ran by the rules William Paley devised. Now, he claims to feel trapped by the madness for ratings, the lists published weekly in newspapers, the hysterical concern for which shows have edged their way in and out of the top ten, the top fifteen, the top twenty. He thinks that ratings and the logic of competition between three huge networks have made it impossible to take the wilder chances on programming that might not win a monstrous, passive public, but would assure more quality on American television.

This could work only if each network would agree to provide such programs on alternate evenings, sharing the commercial disadvantages.

It is a seductive argument, with one flaw. What makes impossible the broadening of programs on American television is the nature of networks. The man who invented the network in its modern form, took the gamble and made the fortune, handled the deals, the concessions, and the compromises, who staved off government, and brought in advertisers and stars who were skeptical at first; that man, at the top of the network tower, is William Paley. He is trapped by the machine he made.

THE FIRST MEN IN AMERICAN RADIO came from different worlds. There were eager amateurs out on the rooftops with baseball bats, thin wire, and Quaker Oats packets, the essential equipment for making transmitters or receivers. And there were the corporation men, defending patents, arranging cartels, signing private agreements that tried to control broadcasting. There was a fine, wild anarchy; against it was an implacable machine.

The amateurs knew how to broadcast long before stations existed. They knew how to steal headphones from the telephone company. They knew which small New York shop would produce the minerals they needed—galena, silicon, iron pyrites, and perikon. In the harsh years of World War I, their messages were tumbling into the air, blocking and baffling official military communications. Nobody was sure how the amateurs could be controlled. Under laws established in 1912, the secretary of commerce had the right to issue licenses, but he did not seem to have the right to refuse them. The Senate decided that since the navy seemed to understand radio, the regulation of the shore-based amateurs could be left to a committee dealing with the merchant marine and fisheries. Radio licenses were a topic alongside the end of keelhauling and the future of the Maine lobsters. The amateurs were unregulated and untroubled. All they needed were call signs to be radio stations.

The other tradition was less amiable. Vast corporations had interests in radio. United Fruit wanted to link isolated Caribbean plantations and deploy its cargo ships efficiently. General Electric developed Edison's incandescent tube into radio's essential vacuum tube. Westinghouse and AT&T had relevant patents. American Marconi had the most impressive service of ship-to-shore messages, but its stations were in the hands of the American government; rank nationalism was not likely to hurry their return, since Marconi was a British company. It needed to change flags. No single one of those five corporations could dominate radio. Together, they had all the powers and patents necessary. They decided to collaborate.

On October 17, 1919, the five formed Radio Corporation of America, dividing the radio business among themselves. Marconi became part of RCA, gained American nationality, and was handed a monopoly of "telegraphy." "Telephony" was reserved for AT&T along with the manufacture of transmitters. Set-making was divided, 60 percent to General Electric and 40 percent to Westinghouse. Those two companies would have a monopoly on vacuum tube production; if outsiders wanted to build sets, they would have to buy the tubes from a part of RCA in the end. The partners decided, with some regret, that they could not quite claim a perpetual monopoly of actual broadcasting in America.

But they did do their best. America's first commercial radio station opened in 1920. KDKA Pittsburgh was owned by Westinghouse, and its purpose was more to sell radio sets than to turn a profit itself. It had a pioneer quality. The studios shook and reverberated too much for bands, so music had to be moved outdoors. Outdoors, the sulphur rain of a steel town drowned out the music. Most of KDKA's music had to be transmitted from a tent on the roof of the studio.

Inspired by the KDKA ballyhoo, other stations began to open. At the start of 1922 there were suddenly more than 500 of them on the air. Herbert Hoover, then secretary of commerce, said the explosion of radio was "one of the most astonishing things that have ever come under my observation of American life." Regulation was impossible. Stations resented suggestions that they might keep to allotted hours and a fixed wavelength. They preferred to wander. The evangelist Aimee Semple McPherson snarled at such suggestions. She cabled Hoover: PLEASE ORDER YOUR MINIONS OF SATAN TO LEAVE MY STA-

TION ALONE STOP YOU CANNOT EXPECT THE ALMIGHTY TO ABIDE BY YOUR WAVELENGTH NONSENSE.

The early constituency of radio was wide. Among those 500 radio stations, 72 were owned by universities, colleges, and schools. The University of Nebraska charged listeners $12.50 for textbooks, an examination, and, if they were successful in completing the school of the air, two college credits. Sixty-nine stations belonged to newspapers. The Scripps chain in Detroit put a radio shack on the roof simply for prestige and beamed messages to a handful of amateurs. Twelve stations belonged to religious organizations. Several belonged to cities or theaters. Department stores, 29 of them, had radio studios operating between departments. It was a thrill that customers came to take for granted. Even in 1912, the two Wanamaker stores in New York City had been linked by a Morse radio line. For seventy-two chilling hours, the operator became the only link between shore, the foundering *Titanic,* and her would-be rescuers like the *Carpathia.* He was a radio buff with "a good fist for Morse" called David Sarnoff. Later, he became the president and moving spirit of Radio Corporation of America.

Among all this diversity of ownership and programming, tinkling music and heavy lectures, religious bombast and thin news, not a single advertisement sullied the airwaves. Radio was thought to have dignity. Church billboards in Louisville, Kentucky, proclaimed: GOD IS ALWAYS BROADCASTING and His messages came through without interruption. In New York, however, AT&T was planning to change all that.

For years the company had seemed none too keen on selling transmitters. The City of New York wanted to buy one; instead of welcoming the prestige, AT&T stalled. An enterprising salesman eventually found second-hand equipment in Brazil to sell to the city. The reason for reluctance now became clear. AT&T had plans for a station called WEAF that transmitted from 463 West Street. On August 28, 1922, between 5:00 and 5:30 in the afternoon, WEAF New York became the first American radio station to sell advertising time. AT&T insisted the new development was "radio telephony," well within the monopoly that the RCA agreements granted them. Their radio station, they said, was like a telephone. Anyone with the money could send his message through the microphone. The only difference was the size and scatter of the audience.

The first user was Queensboro Corporation, selling apartments in the Jackson Heights area of Queens. The message spoke of the works of Nathaniel Hawthorne and the joys of living outside Manhattan. The next month, American Express and the Tidewater Oil Corporation became the first big corporate advertisers on radio. To build an audience for the messages, AT&T provided programs—live football games, for example, between Yale and Harvard or Princeton and Chicago. The outside broadcasts were made possible by the landlines owned by Bell, part of AT&T. The same lines made it possible to sell time in more than one station and link separate cities into a rudimentary network. With landlines and advertisements, the network that centered on WEAF began to look radically new. Friendly stations were given free programs to fill any unsold, empty hours—"sustaining programs." Airtime was filled with material designed to attract attention like the ringing of a telephone does. Excited by the prospects, AT&T now went to its partners in RCA and made demands. The telephone company wanted a monopoly of broadcasting on the grounds that radio was indeed "radio telephony," that is, sending sounds long distance. The partners were cross and flustered. Their resentment grew when AT&T played its trump card— the original RCA agreements. If the partners stood by those agreements, and gave AT&T what it wanted, all would be well. If not, then the Justice Department might be interested to know how radio had been divided between the corporations. The threat was not idle. The first investigation into radio trusts had started barely a year after the first radio station went on the air.

Moreover, AT&T had a way of engineering such outrageous deals. It already took a licensing fee from any station operating with a transmitter not built by AT&T. It had told stations that it held all the patents for making transmitters. It was distressed to see those patents broken. Payment of between $500 and $3,000 a year, according to the size of the station, might soften the blow. The first courageous resistance collapsed when it became clear that AT&T

was implacable. It would go to the law. It would wait. It would do anything necessary, but it would win. After that trick, nobody ever believed that AT&T was bluffing.

The RCA partners needed help and found it from within. David Sarnoff had risen from storefront operator to Marconi's confidant, and a power in the cartel. In February 1925, he prepared a memo. RCA should, he said, "put all stations of all parties into a broadcasting company which can be made self-supporting and probably revenue-producing, the telephone company to furnish wires as needed." Even AT&T liked the sound of that scheme. It provided steady fees for landlines even if the stations made no money. RCA, stealing out from beneath the oppressive weight of its original partners, now broke for freedom. The means would be NBC.

The word "toll" was never mentioned. It had been attached to WEAF. It was thought to lack dignity for NBC. Money was a vulgar subject. A president, Merlin H. Aylesworth, was hired for the new network. He was a crass man, a propagandist from the National Electric Light Association who had spent years persuading America that public ownership of electricity, gas, or water would lead inevitably to the end of civilization. His arguments were rarely understated. On November 15, the call sign of the first advertising station, WEAF, became officially WRCA. America was promised in full-page advertisements "national radio broadcasting with better programs permanently assured. . . . Every event of importance may now be broadcast throughout the United States." RCA assured its audience that it was not "in any sense seeking a monopoly of the air . . . if others will engage in this business, the Radio Corporation of America will welcome their action whether it be co-operative or competitive."

Competition seemed unlikely. Outside NBC, all was anarchy. It need cost no more than $3,000 to set up a radio station; it was hard to spend more than $50,000. Conservationists thought radio used airwaves that were a precious national resource; it should be regulated. In practice, radio was open to any private interest, however outrageous. These were the finest years of Doctor Brinkley, a quack who founded a station and a fortune on promises of new life through goat glands ("note the difference between the stallion and the gelding. . . ."). RCA's power over more organized broadcasting seemed absolute. AT&T controlled the landlines essential to linking stations into a network. There were, in any case, rather few available. NBC could afford to be magnanimous in its first announcements.

THE WALDORF-ASTORIA WAS MOBBED. Crowds circled the hotel as they would some Hollywood premiere. They were out to catch glimpses of stars and socialites, dowagers and financiers, all stepping out to the Grand Ballroom for a great event. It was November 15, 1926—the christening of NBC.

The event was magnificent, if economical. Stars gave their services for tiny fees for the sake of having been there when radio arrived. Will Rogers imitated President Coolidge and brought the house down. There was only one sour note. Arthur Judson, agent and promoter of concerts, was extremely cross.

Judson had thought he had a deal with the new network. He thought Sarnoff had agreed that he should supply programs and talent. Sarnoff thought otherwise. In a temper, Judson told Sarnoff he would found a network of his own; Sarnoff, comfortable in his knowledge of RCA's power, told him simply that a new network was impossible. If Arthur Judson was to recover his self-esteem, he had to prove Sarnoff wrong.

It was not easy. By January 1927, NBC had the only competition it truly approved of: itself. Red and Blue networks ran alongside to give some variety to radio. Outside competition seemed even more remote. AT&T told Judson it would take at least three years to find free landlines for another net. Backers were scarce and doubtful. The commercial prospects seemed dim, and the government was taking a new interest in radio. The newly formed Federal Radio Commission had powers that far exceeded those of the 1912 act. The Columbia Phonograph Record Company invested in radio, but only briefly; the company wanted publicity for its records, put up

$163,000 to match the network's debts at the time but eventually withdrew, leaving the network to pay off the investment in advertising time.

Arthur Judson had a sense of grievance. He had to start a network, but a network was the last thing he wanted. His idea was to supply programs, not sell advertising and run a corporation. His strongest ambition was to find a buyer for the network. Atwater Kent refused it. Adolph Zukor at Paramount Pictures was interested, but for only $80,000. The Victor Talking Machine Company had disappeared into RCA's hands before he could finish talks. In September 1927, the new network, United Independent Broadcasters, was due to go on the air. It had its own orchestra, sixteen stations, a brave facade but no sponsor. The first program of music had been devised for a furniture-maker, and the tunes all made some reference to wood. The company withdrew and left UIB to open transmissions with a curiously wooden medley.

There was nothing promising about that first evening. There was no Waldorf-Astoria and no celebrity. There was no studio clock to monitor time. The control room was the men's lavatory, the only soundproof space in the building. Some Fridays there was no money to pay the wages. UIB tactlessly ran up a debt of $40,000 to the watchful AT&T that had to be paid off by a desperate phone call to a seaborne Mrs. Christian Holmes, friend to the New York Philharmonic Orchestra and its agent, Arthur Judson. She was a brave woman, and a rich one, and she arranged for payment.

Most irritating of all was the lack of sponsors. The better UIB sold the idea of radio, the more likely were those potential clients to go straight to NBC and book time. Losses mounted. In its first year, UIB spent $396,803 on making programs and sold only $176,737 worth of advertising. Some advertisers were loyal; Bromo-Seltzer was a regular, and so was the magazine *True Stories,* which provided sanitized radio versions of their more lurid tales. The problem was the birds of passage. They could seem so promising and go so swiftly. Congress Cigar, a Philadelphia company, spent $50 with Station WCAU for airtime to boost La Palina cigars. It was a small account, but it had some potential. The buyer, a young man named William

Paley, seemed keen enough. But then his father and uncle returned from a trip to Europe and checked the accounts. They saw the radio payment and stopped it. The Congress account seemed lost.

THE LIFE OF WILLIAM PALEY was good. He earned $20,000 a year from the family business for buying tobacco in Puerto Rico and Amsterdam, overseeing production in Philadelphia, and dabbling in advertising. He liked gambling to the point of threats from gangsters if he changed his casino. He liked Bricktop's club in Paris and his grand Hispano-Suiza car, until its splendor brought too much attention. He had a small suite in the Warwick Hotel. Once he reached it each evening he could wash his mind of work and concentrate on the high good times of the 1920s. "I was very happy," he says, "and I loved the business I was in and I had a good relationship with my father. I wasn't restless at all." But he did have one quite exceptional characteristic among the bright young men of Philadelphia. In the bank he had $1 million of his own. Congress Cigar went public in 1926; that was his share of the proceeds.

"Radio came as an intrusion in my life," Paley says. "I don't think I had ever heard of it until one day a friend put earphones on my head and I discovered that there was such a thing." It fired his imagination. "I heard something that was able to speak to the whole country at the same time. I saw that it could entertain and inform a lot of people, maybe even educate them, people who wouldn't otherwise be educated. I didn't see it in any more specific terms. I just knew it was a great communicator—of information of any kind." He had some little say over how La Palina cigars were advertised, so he bought radio time while the senior members of the family were away. It was an experiment, soon stopped, but his father discovered that the idea would not die. Weeks after the show had been cancelled, he said to William Paley: "Hundreds of thousands of dollars we've been spending on newspapers and nobody has ever said anything to me about those ads, but now people are asking me—what happened to the 'La Palina Hour'?"

The Paleys knew Jerome Louchheim well. He was rich and

grand, a substantial citizen of Philadelphia, builder of roads, sub-ways, and bridges. He had become, without quite meaning to, a pi-oneer. He had invested $135,000 in Arthur Judson's radio network. UIB had by now become the Columbia Phonograph Broadcasting System, but the company that loaned its name was edgy and wanted to get out. Louchheim had been the main investor after Columbia left; he had been, as he saw it, trapped now for ten months. His judgment on his investment was unshakable. "It is," he said, "a lemon."

Louchheim turned to his friends the Paleys and asked if they would buy advertising time on the struggling network. He even of-fered his shares. He reasoned that Congress Cigar at least had a product to offer on the air. A building contractor could hardly land a contract with a series of one-minute spots. The Paleys considered. Because he had been so obviously infected with radio fever, Wil-liam Paley was deputed to oversee a new show on radio. It was to be called the "La Palina Smoker," with a comedian, an orchestra, and a singer called Miss La Palina. It went out once a week and was a startling success. Sales of La Palina cigars doubled. Paley went north to New York and watched the workings of radio. He was fascinated, excited, in love with the city once again. It was true, as he had painfully discovered in adolescence, that lovely ladies of sweet nature and fine family did not tumble into a young man's arms along Fifth Avenue quite as he had once expected; but there were compensations. When Jerome Louchheim began pressing his point about the network and offering his shares, it was not the sen-ior Paleys who responded. Out of enthusiasm over radio and New York, William Paley went to see Louchheim on his own.

Paley stood in awe of the man. He knew him to be abrupt in manner. He now had to ask, directly, to be sold a network. Louch-heim's terms were none too generous. For $40,000 he would give Paley a ten-day option on his stock, 60 percent of the company now known as the Columbia Broadcasting System. His price for the stock itself was $503,000 for half the company, $200 a share. For his money Paley would get little more than hope and furniture, but that did not matter. The price was less than the money he had in the bank, and he made the deal.

He went nervously to his father to seek approval. He had always regarded the million dollars from Congress Cigar as in some sense a family asset, to be used only if the family approved. It was his money, but he felt it to be in trust. To his surprise, his father was enthusiastic. His private reasoning was this: if William failed, it would be good experience and Congress could not suffer; if he succeeded, he would be in a business more promising and infinitely more interesting than cigars.

On September 26, William Paley arrived at the network's New York offices, young, bright, and incongruous. He now owned control of America's third radio network with all its problems. His own problem was more pressing. The office boy barred the way to his president's office on the grounds that Paley looked young and unlikely for a network owner. It took minutes of arduous proof before Paley could enter his empire.

"I KNEW NOTHING ABOUT SHOW BUSINESS," Paley says, "unless you count that little experience supervising the program my father's cigar company was putting out." There had been no flirtations with theater or early gambles on a show. There was only a new owner inspecting a new business. Paley was formally on leave of absence from the family firm. He did not expect to stay long in New York. He settled in the Hotel Elysée for the sake of its restaurant and sampled the night life of Manhattan. But his main job was to learn the radio business quickly, settle the network's troubles, and pull it out of the bleak, red position the ledgers showed. Once he had learned, he expected to leave. Radio was a sideshow in his life.

"I wasn't alone in being ignorant," he says. "Everyone going into radio in those days had come from a very different background. It was very exciting and it was very difficult and at times it was very discouraging. We were losing money, and we could have gone broke very easily. We had to get on the right side of the ledger. We had to enlarge our network, which was very difficult at the time—we had only sixteen stations. I was head programmer and head salesman and head accountant and my principal function was to provide business. We needed business very badly.''

He had some luck in the earliest days. In 1928, Al Smith and Herbert Hoover were up against each other for the presidency. They poured millions of dollars into campaign advertisements on the new, brash, popular radio. NBC took the largest share, but its two networks could not absorb all the money they were offered. The overflow, hundreds of thousands of dollars, went to a grateful CBS.

That helped, but Paley found the structure of CBS itself to be the worst of the immediate problems. In its first year CBS had been desperate for affiliates, stations to take the network's service regularly. It promised to pay each station $50 an hour for ten hours of time each week, whether or not the network could find sponsors to pick up the bill. The drain was intolerable. Sponsors came only occasionally; the checks to the affiliates had to go out regularly. Next, the old management of CBS tried charging the affiliates for programs to fill the hours that did not have sponsors. Still the equation was wrong. The network had to expand to attract advertisers. If it expanded, it simply had to pay out more to more stations. If CBS tried to grow, it would go bust.

What Paley did was to invent the network. AT&T had linked stations by landline and charged advertisers for time on all of them. NBC offered programs across the nation, but it was CBS under Paley that wrote the rules for the power structure of the modern network. The deal was ingenious. It was designed to make CBS viable, and it changed broadcasting. ''It just hit me once,'' Paley says, ''while I was in bed with a cold.

''What bothered me was that we were putting out a lot of programs that weren't being used. It was a waste. I wanted our affiliates to carry those programs, but at that time they had to pay for them, and they weren't about to spend that money. So I created this new system of payment. We said that everything we did would be theirs for free. They could take and use it all. In return for that we wanted some special privileges. We wanted to have an option on time throughout the network, so we could sell any hours we wanted. We also wanted the first five of those hours free of charge. We would take the revenue from those first five hours to get our money back.'' After those hours, the network was paid $50 for each hour that carried commercial broadcasts. His deal meant, simply, that the networks could dictate programming and the local stations would be grateful. Madison Avenue would run the main, glossy, prime-time shows for Seattle and Kansas City and Baton Rouge and Atlanta and Richmond—when CBS had stations there. It would also have an option on all a local station's hours of broadcasting. No station now needed to tell its own story on the airwaves or even sell its own time too hard. The networks provided. The shows were better; the advertisers and the public liked the deal; the stations and the network liked the deal. Each call sign now was a collection box for money. The networks held the grand responsibilities, and by becoming networks in this careful way, they made themselves custodians of the mass audience, the mass appeal.

First, Paley had to find the stations and the audience and the advertisers and the stars. Existing affiliates signed the deal quickly. Paley began enticing independent stations to his net with the same offer. In a single crucial meeting at the Ambassador Hotel in New York, CBS signed twelve new stations and broke into the South. In New York, Paley bought a flagship station, then call-signed WABC. He paid $500,000 for $25,000 in fixed assets and an inventory of jewels, saucepans, and live chickens—payments in kind by less than eager advertisers. He eased Arthur Judson out of the network's inner councils; Judson's classical taste would not match the coming era of the brash and breezy. He offered advertisers discounts if they would buy the whole network at once. ''The income was obviously larger for us,'' he explains, ''and the advertiser paid less. But the stations also loved it. They were getting more programs from us, and they were getting money when we sold the whole network.''

In January 1929, CBS was informal, frantic, growing, and already within range of 87 percent of the population. It did not have the wattage of the two rival NBC networks, but it already had forty-nine stations spread across forty-two cities. With strict truth, if less substance, Paley splashed his claim that CBS was already the largest radio network in the world.

THE SUNSHINE YEARS after World War I were fading, but Hollywood was not to know. The movies boomed. The stock market raced ahead. For three years now, shares in solid, basic companies had wilted along with confidence in basic industry. It did not matter. What investor could care about the price of a share in Celanese when the movie companies soared away? It was better to look on the bright side, while you could.

Sound brought the movies a brilliant present and apparently a brilliant future. Money spilled from the studios. Warners' profits soared from $2 million to $14 million. Mergermania broke out. In March 1929, William Fox bought a controlling stake in MGM. Adolph Zukor of Paramount wanted to merge with Warners, to make a power much greater than Fox, MGM, Loews, and RCA. With the help of Joseph Kennedy, not yet settled in respectable control of the Securities and Exchange Commission, RCA itself was talking marriage with the Keith, Albee, and Orpheum theater circuits to produce RKO Radio. The studios were rich, ambitious, and buying. As they looked around for new acquisitions, CBS was uncommonly attractive. It was manageably small, but growing dramatically, selling advertising at an annual rate of $4 million a year. It seemed available. The studios began teasing explorations to see if CBS wanted new money and a new home.

William Fox arrived first, a head-on assault that fitted a mean and graceless operator. He learned his business in the garment trade, and made his money from a film exchange in Brooklyn. His moguldom, uncertainly based, was then at its height. He told Paley that he could "make him into something." He sent his men to check the books of CBS and named a price. For half the network he offered exactly what Paley had paid months before. It was insulting. Paley walked out.

The next was Adolph Zukor, who knew a suitor's ways. He had known the CBS business when it was weak and ramshackle. Now he wanted to know if the network might be for sale. He sent his messenger to Paley's office, in the Paramount Theater in New York, and asked about price and terms. Paley knew Zukor's worth; at that time Paramount had almost a thousand theaters to play the movies made by a roster of stars. He was ready. "I don't want to waste any time negotiating," he said. "I've got a price, and if Paramount wants to meet it, fine. If not, don't bother talking about it." The messenger, assuming that Paley was bluffing, asked what the price might be. "Five million dollars," said Paley. "For a half interest." It was ten times what Paley had paid; even allowing for the cost of the new flagship station in New York, it would mean the worth of CBS had grown sevenfold in less than a year. That is, if Zukor paid.

Paley's fellow shareholders grew nervous. They wondered why $5 million was so significant a figure, and not, say, $4.5 million. Zukor thought the price a bargaining position. He came back with other offers. Paley would not listen; he got his price. In the final deal, Zukor paid in stock. Paley told Paramount that he expected CBS to earn $2 million in profits in the next two years. If it did, he wanted Paramount to buy back its stock at $85 a share. Zukor thought him foolish. Paramount stock was already at $65; Zukor expected it to be above $150 within two years. At $85 Paley would surely be cheating himself. Paley said that he would take that risk. He was right. When CBS did indeed earn $2 million, Paramount had to buy back its stock, which stood on Wall Street not at $150 but at $10. Paramount was heading for receivership. (William Fox also suffered. In 1936, he went bankrupt; in 1942, he was jailed for a year, convicted of bribing a federal judge.)

While the sunshine lasted, Zukor took Paley to Hollywood and let him look down on a gaudy promised land. He promised a salary of $450,000 with regular bonuses if only Paley would come to "the Paramount family." He was flattering, seductive. "One of the reasons I want to buy your company," he said, "is not just because of broadcasting. I've heard a lot about you." Paley could be Zukor's right-hand man, or run a skein of leisure companies for him. In the meantime, there were grand estates, beautiful women, spectacular parties, and constant flattery. There was Hollywood at its grandest and most baroque; there was Zukor's estate on Long Island, a caricature of luxury.

Paley resisted. He had sold part of CBS as a cold decision. It caused him no hurt. The shareholders deserved a reward; the company needed capital. But he would not divorce himself from his new, demanding business. "CBS," he says, "was my life."

ON THE S.S. *EUROPE* there was time to walk while you made your business trip to Europe. It was a usual, graceful way to travel in the early 1930s. It led William Paley to discover Bing Crosby.

The chase for stars and advertisers was constant and hectic. The discovery of Crosby was luxurious only at its start. Afterward, it was trouble. On the decks of the *Europe,* a teenage boy was playing a Gramophone record over and over again. The tune was ordinary, but a single sweet voice stood out from the chorus. Paley borrowed the record, checked the label, and cabled impetuously to his office: SIGN UP SINGER NAMED BING CROSBY. By the time he returned to New York, Crosby and his sharp West Coast lawyer understood the score. So did NBC; the rival network knew that Paley himself was interested in the signing. The market was rigged. Unknown singers performing on unsold airtime were lucky to touch more than $100 a week. Perhaps for some star attraction, the network might pay $500. Crosby wanted $1,500 for a start; should his show find a sponsor, he wanted $3,000. Paley had to be very certain of his shipboard inspiration, but he paid. To match the cost, he proposed a splendid launch for Crosby, a fanfare on the air. The catch was Crosby himself. "Not the most responsible person in the world," Paley remembers. "I had been warned." It came to the night of the Crosby premiere and everything was set. Broadcasts were live then; CBS did not allow taping by singers until well into the 1940s. The fanfares sounded, but there was no Crosby. He missed his own debut. "I am happy to say he straightened out awful fast," Paley adds. "I never saw success do more for a person than it did for him."

Paley had a string of discoveries—Kate Smith, the Mills Brothers, Crosby—but he also needed established names. He needed the stars who would attract the powerful advertisers, the handful of men and women who already controlled disproportionate amounts of commercial radio programming. He went wooing wherever he had hopes. Like a sad-eyed lover he would besiege his object. He followed the band leader Paul Whiteman with a string of proposals. "Young man," said Whiteman, "you don't think I'm going to do a regular program on radio, do you?" Paley nodded. Whiteman was known as an innovator; his soft-toned band made room for jazz stars, played vaudeville houses before that was usual, used its own arrangements, had a full reed and brass section, and even made the voyage of discovery to Europe. Radio, Paley was sure, would eventually appeal to Whiteman. He was right.

He set out to woo Major Bowes and his "Talent Hour" away from NBC. For that, he even went to rehearsals in the rival camp. He was supportive and helpful. At Major Bowes's parties he was always there, grateful and insistent. By sheer persistence, he won. Bowes changed networks; the question was whether his sponsor, Chrysler cars, would follow. Bowes had a fierce and general following, but CBS was a less known quantity than NBC. Paley looked and sounded like the urbane businessman that he had been; he fitted in boardrooms. He went directly to Walter Chrysler, and sat hiding his nervousness as he was raked with sharp questions. Finally, he was invited to hear the decision. Chrysler had a taste for torment. He made Paley sit down and he said, lugubriously: "I have bad news for you, Bill." There was an infinite pause. "I've decided to put Major Bowes on CBS." Paley, ecstatic, leaped up from his chair and hugged his newest sponsor. The technique of the talent raid, vital to CBS radio between 1935 and 1936, was vital again when Paley was preparing for television more than a decade later. Sometimes, it seems almost to be a philosophy. Paley also took the "Lux Radio Theater" from NBC, dropped the Broadway adaptations that had been its staple, and moved the show to Hollywood, where, introduced by Cecil B. DeMille, it helped allay the movie companies' dark suspicions of radio as a rival. The shift had another significance: for the first time, broadcast production moved to California and its eventual home.

Before those grand days, Paley was deep in bluff and counter-bluff. He wanted the comedian Will Rogers, but Rogers hated the cold mechanics of radio. He said he did not know how to time a joke without a live audience in front of him. Paley talked and talked; he talked to Rogers and to his influential wife. Rogers finally agreed, after Paley promised that all his shows with CBS would have a live studio audience. The delays were heart-stopping. While Paley was bluffing Will Rogers onto radio, he had already promised the show to Squibb pharmaceutical company. It was the one show that interested them in CBS.

Advertisers had to be wooed. Some were content to come to the studio for live auditions. They sat and listened as the show was piped from a neighboring studio. If they liked what they heard, they might buy. Paley has a warm memory of the system. "In television," he says, "the lead time is enormous and the whole method of selecting what you think will be successful has changed. You have to commit yourself to quite a lot of money, and you can't do it just by saying let's have an audition next Tuesday." Everything then was flexible. "I was young, I didn't need much sleep and I had fun. Once I thought a guy was drunk on the air and he was, and I rang up to say take him off. Think of it. I could even change a program while it was on the air."

More senior advertisers required more delicate wooing. George Washington Hill of American Tobacco, makers of Lucky Strike cigarettes and Cremo cigars, always had to be persuaded that ideas were his alone. It required great subtlety. For Hill, Paley made dents in the dignity of radio. Cremo cigars were loudly said to be all machine-made; "There is no spit in Cremo," said the voice. When Hill discovered some rogue manager had introduced hand-rolled cigars with the Cremo label, cigars that might well contain spit, Hill was so embarrassed he cancelled his sponsorship of the Bing Crosby show and could not bring himself to tell Paley why. He was the most persistent campaigner for the right to mention price on radio. Both CBS and NBC thought that improper at the start. "These clients neither describe their product nor name its price," said Aylesworth of NBC in 1929, "but simply depend on the good-will that results from their contribution of good programs." By 1932, at Hill's urging, Paley made concessions. "When I told my people we were going to allow the advertisers to name the price of their products, they were aghast," Paley remembers. "We were sort of on a high plateau. We took our responsibilities very seriously." In a public statement in 1932 he had named as the specific CBS contribution to broadcasting "the permitting of price mention."

Social contacts brought programs as well as stars and moneymen. Paley kept as close to the Hummerts as that spiky couple would allow. They were the architects of dozens of soap operas, the agency team that placed those dramas on the networks, the creators of raggedy story lines that fascinated a nation's housewives. They invented the women who drank only water and always refused cigarettes, who stayed calm, pure, and resourceful in the face of gangsters and lechers. Their characters never had colds; they were subject only to amnesia, temporary blindness, paralysis, and false accusations of murder. Paley took lunch with the Hummerts behind the screen of ferns that Frank Hummert insisted be placed at the end of the dining room at the Park Lane Hotel. There, a few times each month, he would make conversation as Hummert digested his vegetables and Shreddies cereal. Anne Hummert would mention, perhaps, some new idea with which they were toying. From that social link, Paley took soap operas like the classic "Just Plain Bill" (the life and times of a small-town widower with family trouble and a barbershop) and "Ma Perkins" (the life and times of a small-town widow, swiftly labeled by *Variety* " 'Just Plain Bill' in skirts"). By the 1940s, there were fifty soap operas on American radio, and CBS had some thirteen of the more successful ones.

"THERE WERE RATING SYSTEMS," Paley remembers, "but they were not very reliable. Done by telephone calls. They would call somebody up and ask what he listened to last night, hoping he'd remember. It was not a very scientific way of doing it, but numbers came up.'' The system was Archibald Crossley's Cooperative Analysis of Broadcasting. For a while, in 1930, it came close to destroying the credibility of CBS.

Crossley's early reports made Sarnoff and NBC content. They showed that NBC's blackface comedy ''Amos 'n' Andy'' reached 53.4 percent of the radio owners of the nation, and so had a 53.4 rating. Rudy Vallee, under presidential orders to continue singing America out of the Depression, had a 36.5 rating. But only two CBS shows crept above a 10 rating. Most were below a derisory 3.3. Either Crossley was wrong or else William Paley was less of a showman than he thought. He imagined the network was doing respectably. ''Vocalists were very important in those days, and we could tell by what happened to them when they went out on the road. And there was all that word of mouth about radio. You had a pretty good feel about whether you had a success or not.'' The figures said otherwise; Paley set out to disprove them. Instead of Crossley's method, CBS asked the accountants Price, Waterhouse to run a survey. They sent out postcards to listeners across the nation asking them to name their favorite radio station. In the ten largest cities, CBS won. It had a five to four lead over NBC Red, a seven to three lead over NBC Blue. CBS kept a tatter of credibility.

Before ratings, there was no science of programming in the manner of a Fred Silverman and the major networks. ''We didn't learn the great secret about helping a show which follows a popular show for some time,'' Paley says. ''We didn't have real control of our schedule, either. Sponsors decided which programs went where, and they weren't alive to all the benefits of following a popular show. It was sort of a hit or miss thing. If a show was good, we reckoned people would tune in and the best would win out.'' That was, he admits, optimistic. ''There simply wasn't enough regard to the importance of placement.''

Slowly the two cornerstones of a modern network began to develop. Paley himself in battling the Crossley ratings had shown that the circulation of his network would be the deciding factor in the battle with NBC. He could not afford always to be second or third. To fight back he would raid talent and buy shows from his rivals. In the 1934–

35 season, the five top shows were on NBC. In 1935–36, four of the top five were on CBS. Paley had simply bought the shows. There was excellence on the air, excellence in comedy and music as well as solemn discussion and heavy drama, but it was exceptional. There was the daytime educational service, American School of the Air; the New York Philharmonic played, thanks to Arthur Judson's influence, and CBS narrowly lost broadcasts from the Met to NBC; there was the drama created by Orson Welles, on radio and in real life, by shows like his adaptation of *War of the Worlds,* which brought anxious citizens and furious police forces out into the streets. "Mercury Theater," long unsponsored, was distinguished radio. But Paley was developing his belief in radio as the massiest of mass media, and he was also building the network machine that would reinforce that belief at every turn. He was constructing the network trap. "We have a mechanism which is all over the country, and it is a very expensive mechanism," he would say in 1979. "To maintain that and afford it, we have to satisfy the mass audience, and to do that you bring an awful lot of pleasure to an awful lot of people." He always wanted something more out of both radio and television; he could rarely deliver it. "At the same time, you have to say that broadcasting can do other things and put them on. Once in a while, we've had big surprises by doing that." But for the most part, radio and television were dedicated to offending nobody and winning the largest possible audience. When people do what they think will achieve those two ends, they rarely do much that is odd, salty, exciting, or fine. They take easy, predictable, well-trodden ways. They do so, not through indifference, but because of the constraints they think the network machinery puts on them. The network has certain demands for results; network employees demand even more of themselves to be sure of success. The result is the blandness and the wasteland of American television. The machine makes that inevitable, and the machine knows well how to protect itself.

"IT HAD BEEN a very mixed-up business and not highly regulated at all," Paley says. "No hearings or anything else. If you wanted a wavelength, you went down and signed a piece of paper and you got your wavelength. That's the way most of the broadcasters got started." It was obvious that radio had long since ceased to be an affair of excited amateurs shouting their private messages into the void. It was business—centralized and powerful. William Paley knew that Washington would be watching, and he shrewdly set about deflecting any attack.

He proved to be a good diplomat and that was just as well. His opposite number at NBC lacked tact; in 1934, he told a startled *Chicago Tribune* reporter that he would rather leave the country than see Roosevelt in power with the New Deal program. His White House links became unsurprisingly distant. Paley did better. He hired Henry Bellows, a Harvard man who had been close to Roosevelt, away from the Federal Radio Commission and put him in charge of government relations. From the FRC he also took Sam Pickard to handle relations between network and affiliates. Even now, there is a faint sense of defensiveness when Paley talks of hiring Pickard. "We had a function which we called station relations, and I wanted somebody who had come in contact with stations and could represent CBS properly. Pickard was resigning from the FRC, he was a very attractive man and very intelligent, and he was one of the few men around who knew stations. Remember, none of us knew too much then; we were all groping and learning. Of course I hired him."

The boardroom allies were convenient. Paley wanted radio as free from regulation as Congress would allow. He was prepared to offer self-denying ordinances and good deeds. He kept a careful eye on the content of broadcasts, whether the issue was one of taste (with great to-do, he banned laxative advertising) or substance (he removed from the air Father Coughlin, the proto-Fascist priest). Any attempt to write rules for radio appeared, by Paley's alchemy, as a threat to freedom. Somehow, in later years, criticism of the amount of music played on local stations became a violation of the First Amendment. The rhetoric was sometimes overheated, but the device had class.

"I went down to Washington as a witness often," he says, "and I found them very interested and, I must say, not hostile at all. I think they were beginning to see the magic of radio. I had some pretty concrete ideas about the importance of freedom. I was on my guard at all times against anything that might be said about the government having the right to intrude, to tell us what to do and what not to do. Right from the beginning I was a fervent advocate of freedom to the nth degree." Conservationists still had a faint voice in Washington, arguing that the airwaves were a national resource that should not be handed over thoughtlessly to a major cartel and its rival. Paley helped drown out those voices. "I think those early fights did more than anything else to keep us free. There was a tendency to say radio might be very powerful, to ask if it was right to put it in the hands of private people, and whether the government shouldn't place some restrictions on it. I had to plead the case for freedom of the medium, comparing it with the Press. There is more competition in practice in broadcasting than there is in print and that ought to be enough to provide safety." In 1945, four out of ten American daily newspapers had no competition in their area; in 1961, the figure was almost six out of ten; and at the same time, newspaper ownership of radio and later television stations became a particular source of alarm for Roosevelt, who had felt their massive, stinging opposition from all around him. "We never got what we really wanted, which was the full benefit of the First Amendment, freedom of speech and what that really means, which is the right to be wrong."

Paley was always firm in his conviction that his own news bulletins and current affairs programs should have no fixed, overt position. Of course, they could not be neutral, since the selection of news items implies some system of values that allows the news editor to decide which items he values more highly than the rest. "Objective" news summaries are actually the institutional form of a dozen men's individual hunches about what viewers want to see and what matters; in that form, they often reflect a clear position that is disguised to many people by the lack of obvious partisanship in the news shows. There are no slogans, but there do not need to be; the show itself is a statement of values. Given that, Paley's position was a little weak. In 1931, he spelled out what he meant. "We must never have an editorial page," he said. "We must never try to further either side of a debatable question." That meant some degree of self-censorship.

Father Coughlin was a rogue priest and a speculator who started his radio career with a sweet devotional stream for children. He soon found a touch of raw drama and a line on politics could keep the offerings flowing even faster. CBS had the ill luck to be chosen as his network. He began to denounce international banking, to warn of the "red serpent" of communism, to demand that silver be made the basis of money again. At meetings he called silver "the gentile metal." He savaged President Hoover. CBS was more and more embarrassed. The priest became more openly anti-Semitic. The network began to demand scripts in advance. Coughlin promised that he would drop all his usual subjects, and on January 4, 1931, he did just that. Instead of the usual stream of political troublemaking, he turned on CBS. He asked listeners to write to the network and say if they thought Father Coughlin should be censored or not. The letters of support for Coughlin flowed, but Paley decided that he was now far too dangerous and awkward to be allowed to stay. Quickly, a Church of the Air slot was devised, and each week a preacher of a different denomination held sway. Thus radio acquired a concept of religious balance.

Coughlin found other radio stations willing to take his speeches, now openly Fascist in their tone. At Manhattan rallies he told about the "British propaganda from these Tory bankers"; he supported Roosevelt and ranted that inflation was just "a trick word to scare us." He continued to campaign for the money value of silver rather than gold. It took some time before a Roosevelt aide discovered exactly why Coughlin and his Shrine of the Little Flower were so keen on silver. A list of speculators in the metal included the names of both priest and mission.

Political debate took time to soften and be limited. "There was a great sense of responsibility along with the great opportunity," Paley says. "We had to develop a sense of balance. The law didn't say that we had to, but I think it was just my good common sense that said if you're going to have the freedom you want and be left unmolested, you have to be sensible.'' It was the age when George Washington Hill could urge America to dance its way out of the Depression. Serious analysis of the appalling economic state of the nation was quite missing. No voice dared suggest that perhaps the economy had become radically unsound, unable now to provide employment and riches for all, whatever spurts of consumerism might come. The ''Ford Sunday Evening Hour,'' by contrast, offered classical music broken by the authentic, cruel voice of Detroit capitalism. Its spokesman was William J. Cameron, a Ford executive who deplored surplus profits tax and unemployment insurance and all the other minor dressings that were put on the broken economy. He may have spoken only for himself; if so, then Ford would no doubt have found another speaker if company and executive diverged too far. His words were apparently not in Paley's view an editorial page. Nor were the views of the various industrialists brought to the ''Forum of Liberty'' by Bernarr Macfadden, the aging publisher of *Liberty* magazine, who allowed his guests to speak their minds and later took his reward in plush corporate advertising for his magazine. It was thought only mildly scandalous when, in 1935, Alexander Woollcott spoke slightingly of Adolf Hitler, and had his show removed from him forthwith by his sponsor, Cream of Wheat. Such displays of corporate position on a range of issues were thought acceptable for a time. The networks came to fear interference, though. Organized labor found it nearly impossible to gain a hearing because it had no product to sell. The Ford Motor Company could say what it wanted because it could have been using the time to sell Ford cars; or perhaps its views were taken as an inducement to go buy the products of a right-thinking corporation. Balance arrived because the corporations' freedom of speech became an outright scandal. Self-regulation was too important to lose.

Serious debate faded from the air. Politics died down. Time was sold for outright propaganda only in the election season. Something besides the drama and the music had to act as the public purpose, the conscience of radio. That something was news.

CHARLES A. LINDBERGH, JR., was twenty months old when he was stolen from his parents' home, and twenty-two-months old when he died. His story proved the opening of the news war between press and radio.

The baby Lindbergh was stolen from a house in Hopewell, New Jersey, on March 1, 1932. He was the child of a hero, and the kidnapping had a peculiar horror. A Newark newspaperman tipped off the CBS newsroom in New York. The network broke into its program to give the story. A location team laid siege to the house, waiting for developments. On most of them, radio beat the press easily. Since radio was doing its own reporting, the newspapers had no easy way to retaliate. They nursed a sense of injury and waited for revenge.

"If I had not been a broadcaster," Paley says, "I would have liked to be a journalist." As early as 1931, while radio was still developing, CBS notepaper for press releases was headed: COLUMBIA—THE NEWS NETWORK. Spot news broke into programs far more often on CBS than it did on NBC's channels. The CBS news operation irritated the newspaper proprietors. It stole their commodity and, worse, they found themselves giving free advertising space to the rival by listing programs of the medium that seemed to be draining their advertising dollars. Like most good capitalists faced with actual competition, they howled for government help.

There were skirmishes during the presidential campaign of 1932. Radio was good at capturing the immediate atmosphere of the convention floors; the nomination battle between Democrats Alfred Smith and Franklin Roosevelt was a natural radio story. But radio newsrooms needed help to cover all the speeches in all the towns of the nation; for that, they turned to the wire services whose owners and customers were the newspapers. Abruptly, in midcampaign, United Press cut off its service. On election night, UP tried to renege on its contract to supply the results as they arrived. Its twelfth-hour sabotage would have broken the networks' coverage except that UP's rival, Associated Press, had also agreed to send the results. AP did not know what UP had done and sent the figures chattering into the network newsrooms. It was too much for UP. They did not want to help the radiomen in any way, but they wanted to cede advantage to their rival AP even less. The AP machines started to chatter news. CBS had a triumphant election night. It had the results and, much more, it had the immediate drama of the President-elect speaking live to the nation from Hyde Park.

Newspaper proprietors were furious. In 1933, the annual meeting of the American Newspaper Publishers Association made belligerent noises. AP and UP would break links with the radio networks immediately. There would be no more free listings of radio programs; if the networks wanted advertising space, they would have to pay for it. The *Washington Post* noted that CBS had set up its own, active news-gathering service and promptly refused to carry CBS listings, although the two NBC networks appeared as before. Newspapers threatened to stir up their congressional lobbies. They would demand that radio be forbidden its private trade of finding and disseminating news. Since radio was directly subject to government regulation, and newspapers were essential allies for most politicians, the threat was appallingly real. Sarnoff at NBC wanted peace. It was not an issue that greatly disturbed him. Paley had little choice but to follow. Together, they marched into the Hotel Biltmore in New York on December 11, 1934, and hammered out the so-called Biltmore Agreement.

It was worth slightly more than the paper on which it was written, but only slightly. The newspapers demanded that radio should not report a story until they had a chance to get it onto the streets. They insisted that there should be only two radio news bulletins each day. Only news of "transcendent importance" would be transmitted at any other time. Paley wanted to use radio for fast spot news; he argued that newspapers would benefit, since listeners would want the fuller account and the analysis that would only be possible in print. He lost his case. Columbia News Service had been prohibitively expensive to run. In the days before frequent news bulletins, it made little sense; radio news more easily rested on the great wire services. Paley oversaw the ending of the news service and the networks' brief obedience to the new rules.

Within months the deal collapsed. Newsmen still tipped off radio stations when something startling happened, and the stories appeared instantly on the air as news of "transcendent importance." Most stories, it seemed, could be of "transcendent importance." Within eighteen months, AP itself had gone back to selling material to radio. It was not a glorious victory for the networks, but it was sensible.

Its historic importance was twofold. The commercial consequence was the choice networks faced in 1950, when radio began its long decline. CBS could either go for news or for music, and it chose news. It was the public service element most demanded by the FCC, the successor to the Federal Radio Commission. It also made money and gave radio a peculiar value, a reason to survive. Before that, however, CBS owed much of its reputation to the excellence of its news and current affairs programs. In wartime, there was the voice of Ed Murrow telling America how London looked under the dripping fires of the Blitz; there had been live reporting when the Nazis moved into Austria; there would be continuous reporting from the battlefields of Europe and beyond as the war spread. Moments of comment or fact mattered out of all proportion to their length, cost, or splendor. It mattered, for example, that the radio commentator H. V. Kaltenborn could tell his audience that mention of Soviet Russia had been cheered in a public meeting; it was a time before the grand alliance against the Nazis was either settled or popular. It mattered more that Wendell Willkie, a conservative Republican radicalized by contact with real life, was allowed to broadcast in 1943 his Open Letter on Race Hatred. Since many of the rules of network operation that Paley wrote led straight to the banal and undemanding, it is worth telling the story of one program that went straight against that trend.

The Letter was the story of the Detroit race riots. Its most remarkable section was Willkie's own message. He warned his audience that fascism was not to be found only on the other side of enemy lines. Taking away economic, civic, and political rights in America had exactly the same basic motives as Fascist attempts to dominate whole peoples and nations. "It is essential," he said, "that we eliminate it at home and abroad." He even asked open questions about the West's new alliances with Third World countries, the two thirds of America's allies who were not white. He asked if the white man's promises would mean anything when his allies' help was no longer vital.

It was brave and it was advocacy, banned by the rules that Paley himself had made. It had to be checked and checked and checked again. Paley summoned the writers and challenged their facts; the CBS man in Washington had been told privately that Detroit blacks had started all the trouble, and he wanted to know that the very different broadcast story was definitely true. He heard the program through twice, suggesting that parts were excessive, that the show as a whole needed more caution and care. Before it was broadcast, the show was previewed on blind landlines to southern stations; many refused it. Checked, previewed, and amended, the program went out. It was rare, indeed, but it was honorable. Radio could do things finer and more substantial than its usual diet. Sadly, it did so only sometimes.

CBS WAS ALWAYS A NETWORK; it was also becoming a corporation. Since Arthur Judson's days it had been an agent, one of the largest in America; now it also moved into the record business. The first uncertain steps to the corporate world were under way.

Both CBS and NBC ran talent agencies. They were both buyers and sellers of talent. The Justice Department looked askance. "We knew the pressure was going to come," Paley says. "I knew we would lose and to be frank I thought we ought to lose. Things not only have to be good, they have to look good." Paley sold the agency to MCA; it became one of the biggest building blocks in Jules Stein's castle. He sometimes regretted it. "We had taken four or five of the biggest talent agencies in the business," he explains. "There wasn't much money in it, but the concert business was going down the sewer and there was a strong economic reason for consolidation to happen. After the merger, somebody—I didn't invent this, somebody else did—started the idea of having concerts in towns that never had them before. We had a separate organization for that. An advance man would go, say, to Oshkosh and find the so-called social leaders and say to them: 'How would you like to have some culture in Oshkosh?' And he'd explain they should form a group or an organization of some kind and we would supply the culture. You can laugh, but it was important. Usually they couldn't afford the big artists, so it gave work to hundreds of lesser artists and it worked like a dream.''

Next came the record business. Columbia Phonograph had left nothing but its name in CBS, and after it quit the network, it had fallen on hard times. Competition was tough. In 1934, Decca had turned the record business upside down. Usually stars and hits sold on 75-cent records, and has-beens and newcomers appeared on 35-cent labels. That was how Columbia ran its business. Decca thought otherwise. It put stars like the Mills Brothers and Bing Crosby out at 35¢ a time. Established companies stuck to the prestige 75-cent record, but it was a losing war; coffee, for example, was 20¢ a pound. Columbia's own 35-cent artists were a lackluster crew who could offer no competition to the likes of Crosby. In the year of Decca's assault, American Record Company bought all of Columbia for $70,500. For that, ARC took a trademark, a catalog that went back three decades, the label's European connections, and even a manufacturing plant in Bridgeport. The next few years brought little improvement. RCA Victor revived its interest in recorded music and began to sell aggressively. By 1938, Decca and RCA Victor sold three quarters of the 33 million records bought in America. Columbia was sinking fast. "I wanted to expand," Paley says, "and there was a natural affinity, I thought, between records and broadcasting. Besides, the thing was so cheap." The price tag was $700,000.

"One of the reasons for the record business going down was that there was so much music on the air. That was the cheapest way to fill time. Now, I knew it was not going to keep on that way. We were developing variety acts and dramatic acts and comedy programs of one kind and another, and they were all coming up. I knew we were going to overcome this tremendous reliance on music and the most natural thing would be for people to go back to buying records.'' Into Columbia he put a bright executive from RCA, Edward Wallerstein, who contrived quickly to sign Benny Goodman, Duke Ellington, Count Basie, the Cleveland Orchestra, the Minneapolis Symphony, and even the All-American Youth Orchestra, whose conductor, Leopold Stokowski, had long been associated with RCA. The catalog regained some of the luster it had once had. It improved, but not enough to turn Columbia from a derelict label to the biggest maker of records in the world. Paley had other plans for that transformation.

On August 6, 1940, he halved the price of records. At that time a new recording by an American orchestra would cost perhaps $2.00 for each 78 rpm disc; to own Beethoven's *Pastoral* Symphony, some forty-two minutes of music, meant buying five records for $10. Paley's coup was to cut the list price of the entire catalog to $1.00 a disc. The *Pastoral* now cost $5.50; for the album in which to store the records, free at the higher price, the collector now had to pay 50¢. Wallerstein's careful repairs to the CBS repertoire paid off. ''Pretty soon people started to buy records like mad,'' Paley says. ''The response was overwhelming.'' It proved a qualitative rather than quantitative change, a radical change in the market. RCA Victor, smug in their traditional place as the only substantial label for classical music in America, were frightened into dropping their own prices. ''Columbia was way down at the bottom of the heap,'' Paley says, ''but we really gave RCA Victor a run for their money. Now, of course, we're the largest manufacturer of records in the world.''

RCA smarted from the blow. It had been quite bad enough that CBS went ahead in radio. In the early days of competition, Aylesworth of NBC answered Paley's calls for a meeting with stonewalling silence. Like some imperial power, RCA felt that to acknowledge the presence of a rival would give CBS special, magical powers. If they ignored the upstart, it would not exist. Despite their rivalry, the two corporations came to have some common causes—working against regulation, negotiating union contracts, defending their news services. More important, however, were the war games. The record battle had only begun with Paley's price cuts. There was the saga of the long-playing record to come; the battle of Jack Benny; and the violent feud over television that almost wrecked CBS. At the center of the rivalry were Paley, the urbane, sophisticated, subtle showman, and David Sarnoff, the remote, ruthless, formal technician. The war of the networks, already fought out over ratings and stars, was about to turn vicious.

"HE WOULD TELL ME THINGS I don't think he would have told his children, and two weeks later he would be goddamning me all over the place. He liked me very much. I liked him very much. We would have weeks or months of battle and then suddenly there would be calm again." William Paley remembers his relationship with Sarnoff as "sort of intimate. He was a man with an exaggerated ego, a little jealous of a young snip who had come along and made progress at a pace which was greater than his."

Sarnoff was an established power. In 1932, RCA had struck out for its own identity and independence; it would no longer be the outward visible sign of the sizable, invisible cartel that formed it. David Sarnoff led the fight for independence. He was a cold, reserved man, an autocratic manager, and the overseer of a corporation seething with rivalries. Sarnoff had clawed his way to the top, the poorboy Morse operator come to be the king, and he expected others to do the same. He would deal only with the survivors. "Of course," says Paley, "he had no interest at all in the entertainment side. His interest was the hardware and at that he was very good."

Sarnoff, the poor boy, was against Paley, who started in radio by buying a network. The hardware merchant was against the network chief whose worst decisions were always to do with hardware, and whose genius lay in a mixture of showmanship and building the machine to make showmanship pay. Paley was not gentle, but he was certainly not the ice monster in a distant lair; Sarnoff was. The two complemented each other. Their differences made the battle more fierce.

In the early 1930s television was a dream. "It was always in the laboratory being worked on," Paley says. "We started experiments in 1931. We put a signal on the air from a little transmitter on top of 485 Madison Avenue. But television wasn't something we worried about.'' RCA had a television system, a black-and-white receiver that was almost ready to be put into production. CBS wanted to wait for color. Other inventors around the country complicated the issue. They produced other television technologies. They also devised an alternative use for the very high frequency (VHF) wavelengths that RCA wanted to use for television. As television was developed, so was FM radio. One offered a new medium; the other would improve existing radio beyond recognition. Both needed the same wavelengths. It was inevitable that the battle should come before the FCC, the government body responsible for allocating space on the air.

RCA backed television staunchly. They hired judiciously. Sarnoff took the chief engineer of the Federal Communications Commission in 1936. In 1947, when the FCC had made up its mind about the use of the VHF frequencies, he even hired the head of the commission, Charles Denny, and made him vice-president and general counsel. This time RCA would not lose for lack of tact and contacts. The reasons for delay were the Depression and war; not until wartime production got into full swing were most people likely to want such expensive consumer durables as television, and when war was declared, factories were needed for other goods. RCA was ready to do battle in 1946.

CBS was unprepared and trapped by its own sense of self-confidence. William Paley had been off to war, a distinguished civilian service in propaganda and psychological warfare. He had dined with Churchill to explain Americans. He had soothed the monstrous ego of de Gaulle when the Free French leader refused to broadcast on D-Day because Eisenhower had failed to mention his name. In liberated Paris he worked eighteen hours a day while the rest of the allied forces, heroes by reason of a uniform, played in the city. Nine days after the Japanese surrender in 1945, Paley considered his war was over. He returned to America. His mind danced with the horrors and stimulus of war, and he needed a little time to turn his thoughts back to the troubles of CBS, which were considerable. The network was consistently number two. It had only two shows in the top fifteen, while NBC Red had twelve. NBC Blue had been divorced from its family in 1942 and made independent as ABC; the stepchild network was the irredeemable number three, with only one show in the top fifteen.

Paley had little reason to be happy. Matters were worse when he caught up with company policy on television. Inside the company there was a brilliant inventor named Peter Goldmark. Paley speaks slightingly of him now, but he was in some ways a genius. He was simply not a commercial genius. He could pursue ideas, but not tell when to stop. He could devise new techniques, but he could not examine the market for them. In 1946, he had invented color television. The trouble was that it was expensive, and it was incompatible with the monochrome system devised by RCA. The set manufacturers did not want two systems. They wanted a launch in black and white with color coming later. They wanted to milk both markets, and they certainly did not want to have to choose between the two.

CBS had put its corporate ego into color. Frank Kesten, Paley's surrogate during the war, had promised that color was coming soon in 1944. He urged America to wait; nobody, he said, should settle for the inferior black-and-white product. Paley claims he had cold instincts that Kesten and Goldmark were wrong, but he said nothing in public. By now CBS had to tailor its public actions to a solid faith in the coming of color TV. It could not be caught applying for a black-and-white license on VHF. That would imply doubt. It counseled its affiliates to opt for FM radio for the time being, until color came on ultrahigh frequency (UHF). In short, it could not hedge its bets. In the event, CBS could not find a fifth television station to buy and complete its legal allowance—five stations of its own—until 1959.

Paley had been away too long to reverse decisions suddenly with any grace, but he did display an expensive patience. In the summer of 1946, RCA put television on the market. Sarnoff promised the FCC a compatible color system within six months; he was asked why he was so sure his engineers could manage that and he said, without a trace of irony, "Because I told them to." By fall, there was a color television system, crude but workable. In 1947, the FCC denied a CBS petition to introduce commercial color television. They ruled that the system was not yet well enough field tested, which, since RCA had been experimenting publicly for ten years, was a fair point. When in 1951 CBS went on the air with a color spectacular transmitted by its own system, Paley calculated the number of sets that could receive the show. However he made the sums, the number never came to more than twenty-five.

Curiously, Paley did not order a stop to the work on color TV. He had no fallback position, but he did not work to create one either. In his opinion, there was time. During the Korean War the expansion of television stations was frozen, partly to free manufacturing capacity and partly to allow the FCC to sort out technical problems of allocating wavelengths. When that war ended, boom followed and the factories hummed. There were 23 million television sets in America, all on the RCA system, and that meant 23 million reasons why the incompatible CBS system could not be introduced. Still, the work went on. In March 1955, Paley was more than usually anxious about his investment. He called Goldmark and a dozen network executives to a small New York theater. On the stage stood two television sets. One took pictures from an RCA color camera, the other from the Chromacoder, Goldmark's latest development. For fifteen minutes, tense and awkward, the men watched a live audition of a CBS program. At the end there was silence. Paley broke it. "Gentlemen," he said, "I'll be glad to speak first. I think the RCA camera has us beat."

CBS left color alone after that. Paley had more pressing questions to consider. He looked at the ratings when he returned from war and was profoundly unhappy. In radio CBS was number two. It had to do better. Moreover, it had to have reserves—ideas, performers, formats, producers, writers—for the time when television was launched full-scale. Paley looked back to the technique he used in the thirties. He went raiding.

Those raids became industry legend. They did nothing to improve relations with Sarnoff and NBC. They were too successful.

Like many other shifts in show business, the talent raids had their origins in the American taxation system; otherwise they might not have worked. Every star had reason to stay with NBC. It smelled successful. Its studios were grander. Its ratings were infinitely stronger. Stars like Crosby and Sinatra, who started their careers on CBS, would see their move to NBC as graduation. There had to be some compelling reason to bring them back.

Lew Wasserman found one and sold it with the help of William Paley's ambitions. At that time income tax was stiff; an MCA client paid 70 percent tax on all earnings over $70,000. However, if a star owned a show and sold it to a network like a corporation, then he or she would pay only 25 percent tax on the price agreed—capital gains tax was less crippling. The star could continue to earn from the show, but he would have in his pocket a substantial sum of capital that would have attracted rather little tax in the earning. The scheme was obviously attractive for the stars. It also stirred Paley. He was worried about program standards on CBS, concerned that the shows were simply not good enough to move his network up to number one. He wanted to upset the absolute power of sponsors and advertising agents who then provided completed shows and told CBS when to air them. CBS had to be in production for itself. Its shows would find sponsors, the advertising agents would still collect their 15 percent commissions but would be relieved of the problem of packaging shows. By the end of 1947, Paley had introduced thirty-six radio programs and fifteen had sponsors. A year later two of the CBS shows were in the top ten and there were twenty-nine sponsors. There was "My Friend Irma," the very archetype of the dizzy dame situation comedy, and Arthur Godfrey's "Talent Scouts," a successor to Major Bowes and the amateur hour tradition. Now that CBS made shows for itself, it needed strong shows that would bring new sponsors and new audiences, and it was prepared to buy them. Wasserman had them for sale.

The first show sold by MCA, bought by CBS, and mourned by its longtime host, NBC, was the blackface comedy program "Amos 'n' Andy." In the business it was as though the Statue of Liberty had defected. CBS had never been able to program successfully against the seven o'clock start of "Amos 'n' Andy." During daylight savings time, factories in Charlotte, North Carolina, closed early each evening so that nobody would miss a moment of it. It was a national institution. Its creators imagined that the show, white actors mimicking droll blacks, presented a "thorough understanding of the colored race"; black males were shown as lazy, quaint, amiable outsiders, jolly folk who were a welcome relief from the serious business of white life. Black children were said to love the show. Their smiles faded when they realized the clowns were meant to represent them.

No deal could have made a stronger impact on network politics. "Amos 'n' Andy" would go to CBS at 7:30 on Sunday night. Paley, newly aware of the finer science of programming, wanted another show that would make his Sunday night impregnable. He chose "The Jack Benny Show" because it was on offer from MCA. He almost lost it.

Lew Wasserman had proposed the Benny show in the same month as "Amos 'n' Andy." CBS would buy a corporation called Amusement Enterprises whose main asset was Jack Benny. The talks were hard and fast; both sides knew each other well enough to set a price quickly. Benny would be sold for $2,260,000. The deal seemed set. Wasserman suddenly appeared in person at Paley's office in New York. He had flown from Los Angeles to announce that the deal was off. Benny's sponsors had warned NBC; NBC had entered the contest. "I thought," Paley says, "we were close to making a deal." For a moment when Wasserman arrived he had thought the deal could be done there and then. Now, Paley nursed feelings of betrayal. He felt Wasserman had shown bad form and bad faith. He had to find some exact, fast escape from his disappointment.

There was only one significant person who had not been involved in the talks. That was Jack Benny himself. Paley thought for two weeks about what he could do and placed a call to Benny. It was dinnertime in California, and the contact was brief. The next morning, Paley and a lawyer arrived in Los Angeles. Benny had gone to rehearsal, but Wasserman was in his office. On the desk was the contract selling Benny to NBC. It was still unsigned.

Wasserman explained that the NBC men had arrived to sign the deal, but that Sarnoff himself had telephoned from New York and demanded that they return for further consultations. He had spotted a clause that disturbed him, a matter of the precise status of Jack

Benny's corporate tax position. Wasserman passed the contract across the desk. Paley's itinerant lawyer read it through and approved it. The situation was now extraordinary. Paley said he would sign on the terms in the contract. Wasserman took a pen. He struck out the words National Broadcasting Company and put in CBS. Jack Benny changed channels. "It was as simple, as complicated, and as close as that."

There was a catch. By law, Paley could buy only the physical property of Benny's corporation. The comedian's services were already sold. They belonged to his sponsor, American Tobacco, and the sponsor had the right for several more years to decide which network Benny would grace. They were not convinced that the second network, which was behind in the ratings, was a good idea. Their advertising agents were anxious; on NBC Benny was a certain winner, but on CBS there would be doubts and uncertainties. Paley faced obstacles ranged in a course by Benny's associates. He had to stage a showdown. Lawyers for American Tobacco challenged his certainty that Benny would do well on CBS. They wanted nothing less than cash guarantees that Benny's ratings would be at least as good on CBS as they had been on NBC. In logic, it was a fair challenge to Paley's confidence; in practice, it was cruel. Nobody could be entirely sure that the alchemy of network, show, and star might not go wrong, that Benny himself might not lose an audience in time. Yet Paley could hardly refuse the guarantee. He had only minutes to think. Audiences might be fickle, but the lawyers, ranked opposite him, were implacable. He agreed to pay a penalty for every rating point the Benny show might slip on CBS. He never had to pay.

After Benny, Crosby returned. He had opted for ABC, the only network that would allow him to record his songs in advance and choose the best performance. Paley changed the rules at CBS to allow recording. He touted sponsors. Chesterfield cigarettes bought the show for $20,000 a week and a promise that Crosby would carry a pack of Chesterfields, even if, as he complained, they spoiled the line of his suits. Stars crossed over enough to change the balance between networks. By 1949, CBS had sixteen of Nielsen's top twenty programs; twelve out of the first fifteen in Hooperratings; and an average audience rating 12 percent higher than any of the other networks. Paley had shown signs of nervousness about his network. On an eastbound train journey on the Chief he told the writer Norman Corwin he should write for a broader audience; "That's what we're going to need," Paley said. "More and more. We've simply got to face up to the fact that we're in a commercial business." He knew the network wars would be vicious. He now started with the best advantage. CBS was number one.

THE DREAM HAD FAILED in 1904 with the Nephone. In 1931, RCA Victor priced the machinery out of the market. In 1948, it happened at last. CBS and Peter Goldmark had lost heavily over color television to Sarnoff and RCA, but now, with the long-playing record, they added downright injury to the insult of the talent raids.

Goldmark's record ran at 33⅓ rpm. It was light and unbreakable, made of Vinylite, with 224 to 300 grooves per inch instead of the usual 80. The technology was less startlingly new than the simple fact that this long-playing record worked, and converting any record player would cost only $29.95. The innovation made economic sense. "I had called Sarnoff over some months before we introduced the LP," Paley says. "I didn't want a record war. I wanted to standardize things. It was obvious to me that the long-playing record was going to take the place of those little shellac 78 rpm records. I offered it to him. I think we wanted quite a small royalty fee on each record sold—not much at all—and he was very interested. He was also a little chagrined that we had achieved so much on our own." Sarnoff came to lunch and heard the LP; two days later men from RCA crowded the CBS boardroom for a demonstration. It seemed so simple.

"All we got," says Paley, "was a message saying they weren't going to do anything about the LP. Sarnoff just called it all off and came out with the 45." RCA had been working on its own extended-play records which, being shorter and faster, were more suited to popular music. Paley accepted that. Meanwhile, CBS had the ideal vehicle for RCA's huge classical list, he thought. The abrupt refusal shocked him. Only one thing had changed in the relationship between the two companies, and that was the only motive Paley could discover. "I'm practically sure," he says, "it was the taking away of Jack Benny and a few other people that embittered him."

The public launch of the LP was spectacular. The wondering Press was confronted with two piles of records—eight feet of ancient shellac against a mere fifteen-inch stack of LPs containing the same music. The public was less convinced, fearing a long war of systems. RCA's 45 was then incompatible with the CBS 33⅓. Record collectors bought cautiously for fear of ending up with the wrong records and the wrong equipment. After a year of suspense, Decca opted for the 33. RCA crumbled. Sarnoff salvaged the corporate ego by firing those executives who had been wrong, or at least who had voted against the LP. On January 4, 1950, RCA came into line. They also issued a statement that pointed out that the public would find the 45 the ideal way to buy popular music.

Columbia was ready for the LP. For years, their recording engineers had made unbroken tapes of performances that were issued section by section on the old shellac 78s. That way, there were unbroken stretches of music without the irritation of boundaries between one 78 playing surface and the next. Classical music labels had been the first to opt for the 33⅓ record; popular music remained on 45s for singles and extended-play records. In the long run, CBS built another industry on the LP. Because it was light and unbreakable, it could be mailed. It could be sold directly to customers through a club. The Columbia Record Club started business in 1955 and made CBS the largest manufacturer of records in the world.

"IT WAS SICK," Paley says. "It was one of most difficult periods we ever had to deal with." CBS was the number-one network; it had a brilliant technological leap; it had pulled ahead of its rival, NBC. It was also in turmoil. CBS was questioning its employees about their political affiliations, watching shows go off the air under Rightist pressure, worrying that it might have been infiltrated. It was the years of paranoia, and CBS helped the blacklist.

A child star was put out of work because a sponsor feared her father had once been a ''premature anti-Nazi.'' A star actress was removed from a series under pressure from lobbyists who threatened supermarket pickets and embarrassment to sponsors if ''Stalin's little creatures'' stayed in work. It was wrong to have hated Hitler, or honored Russia as a wartime ally, or to have any liberal view at all on race, a predictable sensitivity of the vocal, vicious Right. Sponsors and advertising agents wanted quiet. It seemed foolish to employ anyone who was on a blacklist if there was an alternative. Networks, having ceded so much power to sponsors by the mechanisms that men like Paley had established, could do little to protect their own. They were networks of inertia, while the Right went trumpeting out against civil liberties.

Paley knows it now. ''There were not many people,'' he says, ''who said this is a load of tommyrot and to hell with the son of a bitch.'' CBS, with its care for news and its occasional, dramatic concern for liberal values, had seemed the exception to the corporate mania that supported Senator McCarthy and his allies. Its drama had sometimes concerned itself with ideas about fascism or liberty. Its current affairs programs had tackled subjects like Detroit race riots in the 1940s. Now, it was investigating its staff. ''The people handling it were liberal-minded,'' Paley insists. ''They weren't zealous. But our people recognized the need for certain protections to be instituted so that at least we could say we hadn't completely ignored what was to many people a very important danger.'' Paley saw some veiled menace. He worried about the ill publicity the network might earn from employing some notorious Leftists, but he also thought the Left might pose a threat. ''We felt we had to do something. After all, our wavelengths were a wonderful means of communication. We were supposed to have a lot of influence. Everybody would tell me—my God, if they got into your place and started monkeying around, think how much damage would be done. We thought we had to protect ourselves.

''I don't know how many people suffered because of the questionnaire. We said whatever we did, we would do it in the open. I suspect the other networks were doing the same thing less openly. We did turn up some people including one man who said he had been a Communist and still was. We didn't do anything to him and he disavowed the affiliation. Three or four people were severed, I think. One man resigned on principle rather than answer the questionnaire. One man is still working for us, and he was an out and out Communist. He went down to Washington and we got word from a senator on some congressional committee who had interviewed him, and the senator said, 'You do anything to this young man and you'll hear from me.' '' Paley shrugs. ''The advertisers were more concerned about the problem than the networks because there was direct retaliation against advertisers who didn't comply.''

He feels some sense of shame now. ''You look back on that period,'' he says, ''and realize how little there really was of a danger—practically nothing. It must have pleased the Russians a lot.''

It was a CBS program, a cold-eyed report, that helped destroy McCarthy. It showed the lists he brandished at his audiences, changing the numbers and the places, the menace and the victim. It was a fine hour. If Paley and CBS failed, as they did, to be brave and knightly during the blacklist period, there is little point in suffering moral indignation now. There is a more fundamental issue. McCarthy and his threat to civil liberties could exercise so ferocious a hold upon network attitudes only because the networks thought they had a duty not to offend. Paley had proposed that duty, not anticipating a consensus of silence in face of an articulated minority fury. The McCarthy era is the extreme case of the ideology of blandness that already permeated the networks. The same desire to evade issues and debate would recur again and again in network broadcasting; so far it has never again involved so much human misery. But the blacklist was possible because the networks had deliberately chosen to live by a philosophy most chillingly articulated in 1959 by Robert Foreman, a manager at the advertising agency Batten, Barton, Durstine and Osborn, testifying at FCC hearings. ''A program that displeases any substantial segment of the population,'' he said, ''is a misuse of the advertising dollar.''

"MR. FLY," SAYS PALEY, thoughtfully. "I devoted a large percent of my time to combating Mr. Fly." James Lawrence Fly was a lawyer veteran of the Tennessee Valley Authority. He came to Washington at Roosevelt's request to be head of the Federal Communications Commission. Previous tenants had seen themselves as program vigilantes, ready to ride out against foul language or mistakes of judgment. Fly was interested in the structure of broadcasting. He represented the last sizable obstacle to network power. He even won some of his points.

There was a strange distance between the public rhetoric and the private sociability. In 1941, Fly proposed reforms that Paley publicly proclaimed to be "a wrecking operation" that would reduce broadcasters to "impotent vassals of Washington." In private, Paley says: "We were pretty good friends." The two might drink together after a Washington battle, talk over the debate, find themselves in a bitter shouting match before the second round of drinks because some careful compromise had already come unstuck. Their battle was political, and they fought it by means of political ploys; but it turned serious. The 1941 Report on Chain Broadcasting tried to undo what was a clear scandal in radio—that men in two boardrooms determined programs for a nation.

For three years the FCC looked at monopoly. It came to conclusions that the networks found hard to answer. It told NBC to sell one of its networks; CBS had always survived with only one, which undermined NBC's corporate case to keep its radio empire whole. NBC controlled an overwhelming majority of the nation's high-powered stations at that time. The report told NBC to follow the example of CBS and sell off its talent agency. CBS undermined the case for linking "artists bureaus" and networks by selling its own operation to Jules Stein and MCA. Then the report turned to CBS. It wanted to end the option system which Paley had made the whole foundation of the network's success. CBS affiliates gave the network the right to take whatever hours it wanted, whenever it wanted them. To Fly, this was a nonsense. The FCC existed to regulate individual broadcasting stations and took no legal note of networks. Its order to NBC to sell a network had to be issued obliquely, as an instruction to stations: "No license in future shall be issued to a standard broadcast organization affiliated with a network organization which maintains more than one network." Now the CBS scheme meant that those regulated stations were ceding the power to program to some remote and irresponsible power that had no legal existence within the various federal acts on broadcasting. Moreover, CBS could not claim that broadcasting could be done no other way. NBC considered some hours belonged to network, some to station. CBS would have to follow suit. In the final compromise, the day was divided into four segments and the networks were allowed to take no more than three hours in each segment. The most lucrative time spot was 6:00 P.M. to 11:00 P.M., and the network's three hours became "prime time." The present mix of local news between 6:00 P.M. and 7:00 P.M., a half-hour program not presented from the network, and eventually the major entertainment hours to follow is the direct product of that FCC ruling against CBS.

"It was full of limiting rules," Paley says. "It was the beginning of the end. The fight was worth it. Even though we lost the battle, in defending himself, Fly had to deny all the threats I'd seen in what he was trying to do. He did it with such vehemence that anything I feared he had the right to do under that particular language just was never practiced. His public statements were so strongly against, it never could be."

The campaign against Fly and the FCC turned ugly. In 1943, congressional hearings opened on the commission itself, headed by Representative Eugene Cox of Georgia. Cox had links to radio that he found hard to explain when photostats of the checks were produced, but for the moment, the hearings were set. Fly was threatened with impeachment for heading "the nastiest nest of rats in Washington." The radio industry was said to be "so purposefully terrorized by [the FCC] that it is enslaved and lives in an unremitting state of fear, as a result of which it acquiesces in every whim and caprice of the Commission." Fly was accused of "reputed Communistic techniques"; these were said to be a "menace to national security"; he was said to be the leader of a group "commonly called the Gestapo for the purpose of unlawfully dominating the radio industry." Representative Cox, unfortunately, had spoken often for WALB Albany to the FCC, and for his pains he had been paid $2,500. The *Washington Post* was presented with photostats of the cancelled checks. The hearings lost fire, and their decline amounted to a vote of confidence in Fly. He retired with honor, to become chairman of Muzak.

The issue behind the rhetoric was this: should the FCC or the military monitor marine messages? It was a warning of the stridency of speeches when the FCC turned its attention to the quality of local broadcasting in 1946 with the so-called Blue Book. The issue then was whether the FCC had the right to examine a station's programming at all. If so, there would be violent protests about infringement upon the First Amendment right to freedom of speech. If not, the commission could do little except check on a station owner's bankbook and technical expertise. Trade papers like *Broadcasting* howled about "stooges for the Communists" who wanted to grab power "like Goering." The FCC was dazed at the violence of the response, although after 1943 it might have expected almost anything. It equivocated, delayed, and lost. Nothing effective would be done about the wasteland of local programming on radio, and after that battle little would be done in the future about local programs on television. Occasional gestures by the FCC fell foul of the organized might of networks and precedent.

The FCC conceded, in the aftermath of the Blue Book affair. Stations were allowed to editorialize, provided they maintained balance. Wavelengths and channels that were clearly public property, subject to public licensing, became as good as private property. FCC rulings allowed would-be buyers of a radio station virtual freedom from interference. Wavelengths as well as equipment could be sold, and the FCC was limited to examining the credit of the buyer that had done the deal. It could neither suggest alternatives nor take initiatives.

The weakening of the FCC, even from its faded position under Fly, allowed the power of the networks to expand unchallenged. If there were objections, say, to sponsor power in radio or television, they came usually from network executives worried about their own authority. If there were worries about the content of programs, the program practice department of the networks was the effective censor. Government had been made irrelevant, and public accountability limited to stockholders and conscience. The political balance remained in the networks' favor all through the early years of television. In 1952, with the Korean War ended and Eisenhower in the White House, there were no more obstacles to the nationwide expansion of television. Americans, snug and secure in suburban homes, wanted entertainment by the hearth, friendly stars who would pretend they were visitors to each home, an easy evening at home with children, family, and something anodyne on television. William Paley had the stars, the capital, and the stations. He had helped construct the rules and logic of network power, the guiding principles that created American television. Nothing could stop him now.

Still he was not keen. He had taken a sabbatical in Washington, working on a report for President Truman on matériel. He was fascinated there, alert and hard working. Back in New York, his attitude changed. He became sluggish when faced with the problems of CBS. In the morning he would ask his chauffeur to drive once more around Central Park so that he could sleep a little. He worried. Perhaps CBS was no longer his life. Perhaps television was not so attractive and radio had lost its charm.

He discovered the reasons for his malcontent by accident. Each morning a servant gave him a tablet of vitamin B_{12}. In Washington, that was what he took, and he thrived. In New York, a new man was confused about Paley's tablets. He was stunning his master each morning with a hefty dose of the sleeping tablet Seconal.

BEFORE AND DURING THE TELEVISION AGE there were corporate matters to organize and resolve. Radio had to be organized in its declining years. There were more innovations from the unfortunate Peter Goldmark. There were experiments in manufacturing that did not work and massive acquisitions that did. CBS was already a substantial corporation, but it was establishing its business beyond broadcasting. "I was ambitious," Paley says. "I wanted to grow. I suppose

I had more at stake than anyone in terms of stock ownership, and I would hear a lot of people say: 'You have all your eggs in one basket and it's subject to government regulation and how do you know what they might do?' Personally, I had no fears, oddly enough. But it gave me an excuse for growing.''

First, there was radio's future to settle. The last great year of radio was 1950. It took and made more money than ever before. On the air there were signs of more desperate clawing for attention. Comedians moved to quiz shows. Singers, even Frank Sinatra, acted as disc jockeys. Old stalwarts like Fred Allen and Bob Hope began to fade in the ratings. Soon there would be factory space to start mass manufacture of television sets, and radio would be pushed into second place. Paley had to find a strategy that would keep radio profitable even though it had to cede its position as the nation's top entertainment.

In 1951, he slashed the cost of advertising on radio in the afternoons and evenings, the time slots where television did the most damage. The other networks claimed to be shocked, but they saw the logic. Within weeks they, too, had cut prices. Radio could no longer afford the big, brassy show with superstars. It was officially demoted. Just because all the family was no longer listening, some old taboos were broken. Venereal disease was seriously discussed. Black humor about do-it-yourself surgery was allowed. That minor freedom aside, there were two obvious strategic choices for the radio networks. They could choose news—or music. Paley chose news. It gave him a service that the public actually wanted, of which the FCC approved; it also gave him magazine programs with advertising conveniently divided, segment by segment, at prices much more affordable than sponsorship of an entire show. Radio's survival seemed assured.

It was just as well. CBS was about to make mistakes that were public and humiliating. The last years of work on color television still continued. The work cost money and it complicated the coming of CBS television. It also produced Hytron, Paley's experiment in making television and radio sets. The firm seemed logical competition to RCA but, Paley says, ''It wasn't just that we didn't know much

123

about the business. It was that we didn't care about the business."
Distributors complained about the quality of Hytron and AirKing
sets. Paley was embarrassed for his careful CBS image of style and
value. Hytron was a small firm in a competitive business; by 1956,
the first boom in television sets had already ended and there was not
yet a market for replacements. It was vulnerable, and its standards
did not fit the CBS style. "Sheer inertia and false optimism kept us
in it for ten nagging years," Paley says. When the exit came, it was
messy and out of character.

On May 24, 1956, Frank Stanton, now Paley's second in command, announced to the world that CBS had no intention of going
out of the set business. It did, however, want to close its old-fashioned plant on Long Island. Times were hard. The industry as a
whole was praying to its disparate gods that the party conventions
would bring back viewers. General Electric had walked away with
17 percent of the market by launching a $100 portable set. Stanton
admitted that CBS was hurting. Days later, it became known that
CBS-Hytron factories at Danvers and Salem were staying shut "to
reduce inventory." The trade buzzed with rumors. On July 8, the
radio lines were shut down forever and the dies sold to Trav-ler Radio Corporation. All the stock was unloaded. Nobody could believe
any longer that the Hytron experiment would continue. On July 10,
it became clear that CBS branches in distribution centers were col-
lecting outstanding accounts, clearing out stock, and preparing to
close. There was still no official word, but the reality could no
longer be concealed. On July 12, CBS finally spoke. After a
monthly board meeting, there was a terse official statement; the TV
set business was at an end. CBS-Hytron remained in the electronics
business until 1961, when William Paley began to ask how much it
would cost to shut down the whole operation. "It's even harder to
say we failed, to shut it down, put a stop. You always think of all
the people involved. You wonder if you're wrong, if maybe in another six months. . . ." Paley made up his mind, decided to accept the
$12 million cost of closing Hytron, and CBS withdrew from the
unrewarding electronics trade in the same shambles that had char-
acterized the business all along.

During this time Peter Goldmark had not been idle. He invented a video cassette player before its time, a visual record player that operated on black-and-white film instead of the more sophisticated tape. He called it EVR and it was launched with much enthusiasm in 1967. Major studios promised their films. Educational libraries backed the idea. Dealers were promised a whole new market. Paley was faintly surprised to find that this miracle was being developed not with the help of electronics firms, but with partners like the chemical giants ICI in Britain and CIBA in Germany. It seemed an unlikely alliance, but he refused to panic. "We also had some difficulties with the system itself. There were still some bugs left in it," he says. "But the real trouble was the market. Too late, we discovered that it did not exist. I started extensive market research when I saw some of the projections and I realized we had overshot the goal by a wide margin. I lost faith."

With hindsight, Paley diagnoses the faults as these: "You couldn't record yourself. You had to buy material. People talked about how you could get the ballet, you could get the opera, you could get lessons in tennis and golf, all kinds of things that we suddenly discovered had no market at all. There was only one thing that people wanted and that was feature-length films. And our machine wasn't good enough for them." EVR was abandoned, a costly failure. It finally soured Paley's relationship with Goldmark. It was hardly Goldmark's fault; the mistake was commercial.

There was one last failure, a program of feature films that CBS made for itself. They are only now moving into profit, through television sales. "We were dependent more and more on the large studios and we wanted to let them know they weren't the only source. It's always good to have the ability to produce some of what's basic to your business yourself." It was strange and difficult territory despite Paley's Hollywood apprenticeship in the 1930s at the side of Adolph Zukor. The movies died at the box office and the program was abandoned.

The failures changed Paley's philosophy. Most of them came from within CBS. They reflected corporate ambition, products of a clever research department not under commercial control. Paley had wanted a sizable expansion in CBS into areas traditionally dominated by RCA. He wanted to play the Sarnoff side of the business as well as his own. He failed, and he was left with a more coherent approach. "We are in the software business and we'll make software for any hardware that comes along and is taken up by the public. There'll be no more hardware. That's not our bag. We're not a conglomerate; we don't buy something just because it might be a moneymaker. We like to have it relate to what we do." He bought publishing houses— educational, trade, paperback, and magazine; Pacific Stereo shops and Fender guitars, a harp-maker, a flute-maker, and Steinway pianos; firms that made miniature furniture and plastic rockets and Filmore, the large stuffed puppy. Records, the record club, and radio in its new and more meager form all contributed handsomely. But there was one product on which Paley's career had risen, one line of profit that opened because of all the decisions he had made from the start of United Independent Broadcasters and CBS. He laid the necessary foundations for it; he created its ethos; he beat off government attempts to regulate it, and made its structure so firm and profitable that the power of CBS was assured for as long as the technology did not change. William Paley made most of his money out of network television.

NOW, THE EMPIRE of the networks justified itself. It must be the only way to run broadcasting in America, because it was the only way anybody knew. The money logic of networks might limit the quality and ambition of programs, and the architects of networks might regret the fact, but it seemed too late to tamper with the structure itself. Networks and broadcasting seemed the same idea.

Look now at what Paley had made out of radio. Stations depended on networks. Networks delegated powers to advertisers and sponsors. All shared a common instinct for the safe, the comfortable, the anodyne. Government failed to use the public licensing of the airwaves to change the ownership of stations or influence their programming. Prime time was everything. Those men who first exploited wavelengths now had everything ready for the television age—stars and

126

capital, advertisers and formats, rules and ideology. All television needed was the pictures.

There would be great events, tantalizing glimpses of the sort of challenge television could present if the rules and the logic were different. CBS presented a conversation with J. Robert Oppenheimer, the scientist who helped form the atomic bomb and had his security clearance abruptly revoked. It was not a political talk. It was cool, clear, and direct, and it dealt with science and responsibility. Paley was enthusiastic, and the show did the network honor. But when he talked of the broad public for television and the costly machine of CBS, he had other things in mind.

There were quiz shows, the bad money that drove out the half-good. Big-money prize shows cascaded onto the networks. Revlon backed the "$64,000 Question," inflated successor to the "$64 Challenge." The least consolation to a loser was a Cadillac. Trust officers from major banks held the answers to questions in buried vaults until the last possible moment. The ritual, the trial by questioning, was mesmeric. Las Vegas casinos emptied on the night of the ultimate gamble. Sales of Revlon lipsticks soared. Hazel Bishop, Revlon's nearest rival, said in its annual report that the slump in sales of its products was due to the fact that "a new television program sponsored by your company's principal competitor has captured the imagination of the public." It was too good to be true, a perfect marketing strategy perfectly played. It depended on a touch of artifice, enough to count as rank dishonesty. Before the questions went to bank vaults, they went to the more appetizing contestants. Dull personalities lost early. Brighter hopefuls were coached in how to fluff a simple answer, how to stall, look baffled, and time a final, triumphant, correct answer. Even distinguished guests accepted help; Xavier Cugat said, "I didn't want to make a fool of myself." The scandal became known and Paley ordered investigations. They showed wrongdoing and Paley took all quiz shows off the air. "We had given very little attention to them," he says, "because they were so successful and trouble-free." When they were removed, the network president who devised them went too. Paley believed him innocent of wrongdoing, but a proper sacrifice was necessary. In the pages of *The New York Times*, Revlon's other major rival, Coty, took gloating pages to talk of honesty in business.

After quiz shows, the network cast around for a savior. Paley thought he had found one in James Aubrey, a network technician at ABC whom he hired to be president of the CBS network. It was a stormy time. Paley had been sick and remote. The schedules needed help. CBS was number one; the magic had to continue. Aubrey was younger and more glamorous than the run of CBS executives. Hints of scandal hung around his private life. He was ruthless and ambitious and his colleagues called him the "Smiling Cobra." That was nothing new in television. But he lacked the indefinable characteristic that Paley had given to CBS, a public seriousness about quality. Aubrey produced a schedule for 1960–61 noticeably lacking in those cultural events that Paley liked to promise. There was no Olivier, no Orson Welles in Shakespeare, no Pablo Picasso explaining pictures, or opera by Menotti. The schedule was too naked for Paley's taste; it lacked the necessary stylish dressing. In an internal memo, Paley told Aubrey sharply that CBS had "maintained the kind of balance which, on the one hand, gave most of the people what they wanted and enjoyed most of the time, while, at the same time, produced enough product of outstanding merit to gain for itself a reputation of quality, responsibility, etc." Aubrey never understood that balance or realized that to Paley it was the justification he needed for the way CBS was run.

Aubrey did supply some culture, but he ruled far more by the principle of "broads, bosoms, and fun." In a memo, a colleague said: "You remember Jim Aubrey saying: 'Put a sexy dame in each picture and make a "77 Sunset Strip"' if that is what is necessary, but give me sex and action.' " Aubrey oversaw the last decade of true mass television, the years before advertisers started to demand particular segments of the viewing public rather than an undifferentiated mass. He offered, mostly, comedy. Eight out of the top ten television programs in the 1962–63 season belonged to CBS, and seven were comedies. Most were rooted in rural tastes, in the incongruous "Beverly Hillbillies" playing strangers to affluence, or

Eva Gabor exiled to a mink-lined farm on "Green Acres." Paley insists he enjoyed all those shows very much. They certainly delivered huge audiences. The numbers were not enough, however. Those huge audiences were growing older every year; young viewers did not have the same taste for rustic farce. The big numbers and the big success were the start of a problem that CBS has not yet properly resolved.

Aubrey was acknowledged to be Paley's picked successor, even by Paley himself. He built the audiences and the profits. He was bright enough to be the extraordinary man that Paley would some day have to approve of as his heir. Paley always hunted for some other Paley, a mirror image who would be younger and who could take CBS further along the same road. On close examination, all candidates had failed. Aubrey was no exception. Paley heard the rumors about his private life. He heard the scandal over gifts that Aubrey was said to have received from a company that made movies for television. He found Aubrey too public and too awkward. Privately, Frank Stanton complained of late-night telephone calls in which Aubrey would abuse him wildly. "I think CBS was too dependent on me for too long," Paley says; he half hoped, half feared to find his successor. One Friday afternoon he knew quite suddenly that Aubrey was not the man. He walked down the executive corridor to Frank Stanton's office, flung open the door and said, simply: "He's got to go." Stanton knew precisely what he meant.

Such palace revolutions left Paley again in effective charge of programming at CBS. His ultimate authority was never much in doubt. "You always knew the old man was watching," said Michael Dann, head of programs at CBS between 1963 and 1970. "If you saw something lousy on the set one night, you were scared. You'd know you'd get a call the next morning. He always went straight for the jugular, asking who wrote the script or who directed." Now Paley was back, molding the network's schedule; he has, in his own words, as much experience of that art as any man living. He says CBS is "a consensus organization," but he admits, "I guess my voice has more weight than anyone else's."

One reason is Paley's developed instinct for placing and nursing a program. He saved "Gunsmoke" when that Western series had lost all its drawing power on Saturday nights. "It was a program I liked very much," Paley says. "A quality program, well done and beautifully cast, but it had run its course on Saturday nights and the people who wanted to cancel it were quite right. I just suggested that before throwing a thing as good as this away, we should try for a new audience. We moved it to Monday night and it ran for another seven years. Of course, we couldn't be sure that we would get a brand-new audience. It was a gamble, but it worked. We had the same kind of thing with the Dick Van Dyke program. It was on for a whole season and barely made the grade. It should have been cancelled, but it was a quality program, beautifully written, and I said let's give it a chance." He put the Van Dyke show after the all-powerful attraction "The Beverly Hillbillies," and it leaped swiftly to number nine in the ratings. Such decisions confirm the stolid picture of America preferring to slump with a single channel rather than changing to find something fresh. But they also require a certain flair, to play on the known proclivities of the more passive television audience and win the loyalty of the channel-changing few.

Paley has such flair. The mistakes that he chooses to remember are those where he underestimated success. "I thought 'The Waltons' was going to be a failure," he says; it was a rural, family program that CBS put up against the powerful "Flip Wilson Show" on NBC. "But that had emotional schmaltz and caught on—and drove Wilson off the air." He never believed that "60 Minutes," the CBS current affairs magazine program, had any power to hold a top-ten audience. He took a chance in keeping it on. Now the show is rarely out of the top ten. Mistakes in series or timing can easily be buried; a network chief has a duty to his stockholders to remove a flagging show before it pulls down the network ratings. But Paley has a record of remarkable success.

It is mysterious, what instinct a rich man in a Manhattan office needs to play with public taste. Paley's life is led between a grand office on Fifty-second Street, high in a black granite tower, and homes in Manhattan and Lyford Cay in the Bahamas—a world where paintings that Matisse sold to the young Paley hang alongside sculpture from Giacometti. It is a world of privileged taste. Average opinions of the average man do not bulk large; yet they are the foundation of the business. Paley admits his remoteness. "Of course, we do a lot of testing," he says. CBS has Little Annie, an ingenious system for wiring the audiences at previews of shows to test their reaction minute by minute. "But public taste goes through a very funny period sometimes and I don't understand it at all." He thinks back over shows that foundered in other media but triumphed on television, over movies that died in theaters but prospered on television. He puzzles over why certain women, "very funny and very appealing," should have the faces or talent or style that suits only TV; he cites Lucille Ball and Mary Tyler Moore, "a terrific piece of talent." He breaks his musings: "But we don't get on a bus and go across country and stop at certain places for two or three days at a time. That's the way to do it." His one certainty is that when he started in radio, taste differed region by region; "A song that was popular in New York could take four or five months to reach San Francisco. Now the most important divisions aren't geographical at all, they're a matter of age. There are some things which still do better in rural areas than in cities, but it is age which is the great divider now."

At the end of the Aubrey era, that point came crashing home to Paley. "We had an audience which was just older than the other networks and we knew we were headed for trouble." Advertisers had recently grown skilled at deciding exactly which part of which age group and social group they wished to reach. Old shows hold their audience and that audience grows even older. Known shows appeal less to the young than new shows. The advertiser wanted the affluent consumer aged eighteen to forty-nine, in quantity; the only exceptions were the merchants of laxatives, denture powders, and indigestion relief, who advertise still on news bulletins to reach a suffering older public. CBS had to provide younger viewers or lose business. The power and magic of the big, simple number had gone. "We stripped the schedules," Paley says. "We threw off some very good programs. Just in time . . ."

In their place, CBS tried some modest daring. "New concepts of realism and relevance" turned out to be medical shows like "The Interns" and comedy about a working woman in a TV newsroom in "The Mary Tyler Moore Show." Realism in the world meant something different from the same emotive word in the castles of the networks. "All in the Family" proved the point. Paley considered it highly daring: "Some would say that white people do not have black people coming into their homes, and if you, Mr. CBS, think they do, you're mistaken and we're not going to listen to your network anymore. That would have been, I think, the kind of reaction we would have received ten years before." The show's producer, Norman Lear, had to do constant battle with the CBS censors to preserve the comedy of outrage and bigotry. Suggestions that married couples might make love were considered shocking; a baby being diapered had to be shown in long shot. CBS, always decorous, was catching up with America slowly. Worse than any detail of network censorship is the point Lear makes about the whole range of comic programs that went before Archie Bunker first snarled into camera. "I don't think any subject we have touched— in all of our shows—has expressed as strong a point of view as the omission of all social awareness in all the TV comedies of the '50s and '60s."

THERE WERE TWENTY-ONE SEASONS of being number one, and when that ended Paley was in pain. "It hurt when ABC got ahead of us," he says, "but I wasn't surprised." Until the fall of 1976, CBS was the most successful network in America, the largest advertising medium in the world. It had grown through the years when a grossly heated economy needed some new effort to absorb its money and work force; it had been a prime beneficiary of the need to sell expensively in order to use money. It became one of the gigantic diversionary tactics of monopoly capital. In itself, in the apparently bitter rivalry between networks day by day and their substantial, hidden cooperation in maintaining their own structures against outside attack, television had become an industry that followed the models of monopoly capitalism. Nobody fought too much; price-cutting was out of the question; the only issues were the various premiums that advertisers were prepared to pay to be on the number-one network. Paley lost his treasured position at the head of the network battle at a more general turning point. Satellite technology was ending the dependence on landlines which had made it sensible to have only three networks and to have them centralized. Stations in Seattle and Miami and New York could now share programs with no subscribers needed in the spaces in between. The idea of a network was liable to change. Networks may be a historial phenomenon whose dying date is close.

What concerned Paley was the clear evidence that his network, his machine, had started to slip. The ratings started to tumble in the fall of 1975. He went to network headquarters in Hollywood and ordered drastic changes. He held off defeat for one more season. In 1975–76, CBS was the number-one network for the last time. "It was a management error," Paley says. "We had run out of inventory. There was a striving for a while to build up cash and cut down overhead and expenses, and we saved money in the wrong places. We suddenly woke up with some failures on our hands and nothing ready to replace them." CBS acted too much like a corporation, too little like an entrepreneur—a proper reason for decline in a corporate economy.

Paley went back to programming, back to fixing which shows go where and which should live and which should die. "I still am happy when I go to Hollywood and talk shows," he says. "I still love the business." He regrets the dearth of creative talent; "We chew up so much of this material so fast." He gave up the role of chief executive to a man whose management style was cool, precise, and technocratic, a publisher named John D. Backe whose particular and proven skills lay in areas like the calm management of takeovers. "Now I'm a problem solver to this whole big corporation, a problem solver on big issues. It's a different world for me now."

In CBS man and machine merge into one. Paley's taste, exact and good, holds sway throughout the building. Paley's mixture of caution and showmanship, political care designed to keep the networks running as commercial corporations and intuitive leaps to what would be most commercial for the corporations, becomes the philosophy of a $3 billion business. Reticence, decorum, taste, decency, and often lack of courage mark the man and the network. Mogul and machine are one.

A certain edginess begins. The mogul sees his fine machine in retreat because of the kind of corporate decisions that managers make. The mogul comes back to seize control of the machine, but knows he cannot hold on to it. He made the network, but the network corporation has the power to survive him. He matters because of his role in CBS; he has no other role that would give him the same prominence. The machine he so carefully built is now his limitation.

"It is," he says, "a different world for me now."

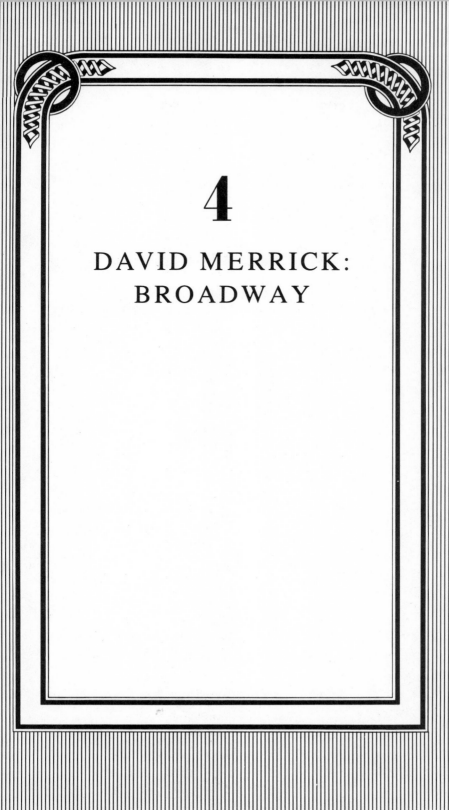

4

DAVID MERRICK:
BROADWAY

T HIS IS THE PUBLIC STORY of the formation of a mogul, and the hidden story of the business that makes it worthwhile shaping so strange and esoteric a creature. A mogul may be a marketing device. He may bluff and thunder in a blood red office, acid of wit and monstrous in his domineering ways. He may present a mask of outrage to persuade backers to give him money and punters to pay for tickets to his show. He may, like David Merrick, present his name as though it were a kind of trademark, the sign of a company. Behind that, men like Merrick are meticulous. They are working showmen, careful businessmen who allow no money to leak from their operations and cut the risk in a gambling business. David Merrick is all that, and a careful construct, marketed with skill and attention; he was also the salvation of Broadway for many years. This mogul may be an irrelevancy in the great economic game, but he made live theater work in New York when it might otherwise have died, and his management gave glossy musicals, tart comedies, and imported drama to the American audience. He built no network and changed no industry; his attempt on the corporate virtue of Twentieth Century-Fox was not a success. But his life in theater was remarkable. David Merrick, mask and businessman, plays a mogul as a mogul once was thought to be.

He stalks through the alleys off Broadway; he watches the state of the footlights, the fresh paint on a first-night stage, to avoid disaster; he is defiant, cantankerous, voluble in his feuds with actors and his war on critics. His life is theater. He told a press agent once that he was born in 1946 when he launched himself on Broadway. Later, he edited his life still further, claiming as his birthday November 4, 1954, when his first big show, the musical *Fanny,* opened in New York. He was obsessive about privacy, troubled by any questions that he had not himself prepared to answer. He set out to turn theater into a business, which was a radical and brave attempt, and for that he needed the figure of a showman, a monster who made shows happen. He took the role himself. Still, he valued the lack of identity that was possible behind that mask, the privacy that a monstrous reputation helped guard. Merrick was good enough copy in his most contrived and public moments to move attention away from his curious divorce and his miserable childhood. It was easy to see the showman with the best part of a dozen shows on Broadway all at once, and miss the hard industrial logic of what he was doing—the spreading of risk, the economies in bulk buying of advertising space and time, the overhead that was levied on a dozen shows instead of one. For Merrick the all-important mask of a mogul conceals his life and also his business, and it also helps him sell his wares.

MERRICK HAS NO CLASS, no parents, no background, and no education in the official version. He comes out of Broadway full-grown and successful. He was born a mogul.

It is not hard to see why he has worked so hard to preserve that story. He was born David Margoulis in St. Louis in 1911. His father was a storekeeper, neither rich nor successful; his mother was a fantasist, a "Blanche du Bois," he says. When he was seven their bitter little marriage, arranged originally in Poland, was taken into court and broken up. Merrick was asked to speak, but he could only stand, silent, and gnaw his nails. Through his school days he lived with scattered members of his family, a married sister, his mother, his parents when they tried a brief reunion. His fantasies were all of escape. He made money by delivering newspapers and spent it on "the sort of clothes that I imagined a gentleman would wear." He wanted to study law and go into the theater, a curious pair, since he had only a little high school acting ("A pleasant boy, but with no great skill as an actor," said a teacher) and a victory in a college playwriting contest (he beat Tennessee Williams and considered the verdict showed the shallowness of the judges) as a basis for his passion for the stage. He hated his hometown, and the law seemed a far more likely means of escape. David Margoulis grins ingratiatingly from a picture of his school debating team, only a would-be favorite who speaks well in public. His plans worked, though; he went to Washington University in St. Louis, became a lawyer, and began to found his fortune.

He distinguished himself in a legal wrangle over government claims to oil land, pocketing a substantial fee. He also married Leonore Beck. She was not rich, but she did have some capital; her mother had died recently and left an estate of $116,319.66. There was money now for the journey to New York, at first as a commuter and then for welcome exile. He watched Broadway from the fringes, fascinated. He changed his name to Merrick, taking at least a syllable from David Garrick, the eighteenth-century actor who had managed the Drury Lane Theatre in London. He entered the business as a backer.

He went to Herman Shumlin, the producer, and confided that he was interested in investing in a comedy. Shumlin pushed over his desk a copy of James Thurber's *The Male Animal;* Merrick took it away and read it overnight. The next morning he returned with a check for $5,000. Shumlin was impressed. In those days $5,000 was a substantial sum of money.

The show made profits; Merrick's share was $18,000. He ploughed his money into other lost extravaganzas, *The Willow and I* and *Bright Boy*. He contributed enough cash to be called associate producer on the billboard, but that was the extent of his contribution. It was left to Shumlin to invite him, stage-struck and new, to join the firm. Merrick said he was prepared to work for nothing; Shumlin persuaded him to draw a nominal wage.

In return, Merrick did everything. He read plays, helped manage companies, acted as assistant to anyone who seemed to need an assistant. It was his apprenticeship. He observed not just the basics of stagecraft, but also how people could be manipulated, how Broadway egos soared and fell, how backers should be wooed. By 1949, he felt ready to strike out on his own, and he left Shumlin. With a producer named Irving Jacobs, he bought an insubstantial British farce called *Mr. Clutterbuck*. He staged it and nursed it. He sold it with stunts; Manhattan restaurants and hotel lobbies were full of urgent calls paging Mr. Clutterbuck, who could never be found. The name stuck and the show ran for 218 performances. David Merrick was a Broadway producer in his own right.

He used his position quixotically. He behaved like any other Broadway producer. He was infected by a dream, a single project that ruled out all others for the moment. For three years, he tried to make a musical out of the Marcel Pagnol trilogy *Marius, Fanny,* and *César*. His first idea was to take the movie material and turn it into a straight play; he soon discovered that had been done unsuccessfully in 1930 under the title *Marseilles*. Next, he wanted to take the story, make it into a musical, and set it in San Francisco. Backers bit. Julia Clayburgh, one of Shumlin's assistants, put up $5,000; Merrick put up $2,500; other investors provided $10,000 more. There was at least a pre-production fund, even if there was as yet no rights, no script, no stars, and no show. The movie rights had gone already to William Wyler. In France, Pagnol refused to answer Merrick's importunate phone calls, letters, and cables. Money was short. Merrick decided the next stage had to be invasion.

He went to Europe and besieged Pagnol. He stayed on the doorstep and demanded attention. He bought the rights. His first attempt at a book was not successful—he used Frances and Albert Hackett, later Pulitzer Prize winners for *The Diary of Anne Frank*—and Merrick slowly realized who was the man he wanted as director and writer. His approach was roundabout. He had come to know Edward F. Kook of the Century Lighting Company while he was with Shumlin, and Kook had generously opened doors for young Merrick. One led to Jo Mielziner, then the doyen of Broadway designers. Through Mielziner, Merrick met his director.

JOSHUA LOGAN HAD BEEN at an all-night party. "I was terribly tired and terribly sleepy," he says. "I was escorted with my wife to a little studio projection room and shown a picture that Merrick thought I would, perhaps, like to do on the stage." The film was *Marius,* the first of the Marseilles dockside trilogy. "I thought it was very good and very charming and I just didn't think it was dramatic enough. Towards the end I got up and left. David was there, and so were all his backers, and he didn't dare speak to me."

Logan was a Broadway giant, maker of musicals that filled the dreams of theater angels. He was clever and profitable. He had been impressed with Merrick on first meeting, but found him somber as well as eager. "He struck me a little like he strikes everybody," Logan says. "As an undertaker." Merrick's face was chalk white with the sting of a black mustache. "Not a very happy-looking face," Logan says, "except when he was in work. He may have been limited in his credits at that time, but I've never seen a man who studied his career and prepared it as well as David Merrick had. He had seen everything that anybody ever did. It follows, you know. You can't be just a big, thick-headed businessman and do what he did."

Logan was still unimpressed with the Pagnol material. Merrick floundered for a year in versions that did not work and gratefully held to the support of Jo Mielziner. He had made enough of an impression for Logan to listen when he asked for one last favor. "He came back to me and urged me to see the second picture in the trilogy," Logan says. There was a screening. "It was *Fanny* and I thought it was the most marvelous thing I'd even seen in my life. I couldn't wait to do it. The awful thing is that David had waited a whole year and had to pay off other people. . . ."

Fanny was under way, an embryonic idea without the support of book, words, or music. "I tried to get Rodgers and Hammerstein interested," Logan says, "but David wanted credit alongside them as producer and they refused point blank.'' Merrick felt no need for coproducers; he already had the rights and the backers. Hammerstein and Rodgers apparently spluttered at the prospect of sharing credit with an unknown young man. ''Oscar Hammerstein told me just a few days before he died: 'Oh, we should have done *Fanny*. Who cares who gets the credit?' '' It would serve as a grand line from a grand producer. The neophyte Merrick needed credit very much indeed.

''As far as I was concerned, he was really starting a new concern,'' Logan says. ''I hadn't seen *Clutterbuck,* but he made a great deal of sense. We got to be very close. I don't think we ever raised voices once.'' Logan was now preparing both book and production. ''He let me go very much any way I wanted, and right in the middle of all that I had my nervous breakdown. I was a manic-depressive and I had to go to the hospital for four months. I should have known him after I took lithium. But he was marvelous, he didn't even bat an eye about my illness.'' Out on the road, Merrick had the producer's proper instinct for avoiding rehearsals—''not just because they're dull,'' he explains, ''which they are, but to leave the creative people free to do their own thing.'' He was meticulous about detail, about paint on backstage doors and rubber to stop actors' footfalls from sounding like thunder through the microphones. He also had ideas. ''Three or four days before we opened in New York, we were still having problems ending the show,'' Logan remembers. There was a sudden death that released young lovers to marry. The audience would get the point; nobody could improve on that drama. ''I remember talking to David up in my hotel room in Philadelphia and I said I just can't seem to get an ending. And he said you got an ending for *Mr. Roberts,* and I said yes, that was a letter from the dead.'' Logan thought back to the earlier show. ''I thought—could this end with a letter from the dead, too? I started dictating to Jo Curtis, my secretary.''

Fanny had the worst reviews: uninspiring. The advance sales had been good, but the prospects were doubtful. Musicals have to run long on Broadway to get back their money. Merrick was watching his first major Broadway show dissolve and melt away before his eyes.

He fought back. He took the first full-page advertisements ever for a theatrical show in *The New York Times* and the *Tribune*. He bought time on radio and television. He caused stickers to appear in a thousand men's rooms asking: HAVE YOU SEEN FANNY? Scenes from the play appeared on "The Ed Sullivan Show." Advertisements appeared in taxicabs, on wide electrical displays at Penn and Grand Central stations in Manhattan, on liners plying to Europe, and even in Paris newspapers for exiled Americans, on the assumption that the Americans would soon return home, would do so by way of New York, and might as well see a show while in transit. In forty American cities Merrick placed announcements that implied that *Fanny* was the only reason a tourist now visited New York. At the wedding of Princess Grace of Monaco, a bored and claustrophobic press corps lay and watched a small plane circling overhead, urging them when in New York to see *Fanny;* the plane was trapped by fog later near the columnist Art Buchwald, and Merrick had a serendipitous publicity coup. Merrick went walking an ostrich in Manhattan, and called it Fanny. In Poet's Corner in Central Park there appeared one morning a statue of the show's enticing belly dancer, nude; its sculptor had imagined the commission rather more serious and announced his anger. Newspapers trailed Merrick's curiously unsupported story that some wealthy Turk—a swarthy and very transient man—had offered him $2 million for exclusive rights to the belly dancer.

That was the public stunting, the vital hoopla that kept some attention focused on a show that might otherwise have stagnated. Merrick had other tricks. By contract, he had to close the show and surrender the theater to its owners, the Shuberts, if takings fell below a fixed level. But the show was making profits, and Merrick wanted to prolong the run. He culled names at random from directories for suburban towns within fifty miles of New York City, and invited the out-of-towners to see *Fanny* for free, provided they brought one paying customer. If that failed, and the gross endangered the run one week, a Merrick aide was sent out with a few hundred dollars in bills to buy enough tickets to keep the show running.

The last balance sheet proved all the stunts were justified. *Fanny* ran for 888 performances. On an investment of $275,000 it made a clear profit of $847,726.74. Merrick had arrived.

"I RUN IT AS A PROPER BUSINESS," he says, "which has always been considered impossible in the theater." His braggart pose as mogul was founded on clever and essential points of doing business in the theater. Without those foundations, his machine for making shows would not run.

He was cunning in his choice of properties—not necessarily right, but clever. He broke ranks with other New York producers when it suited him. He tried to end the threat of sudden death to a show opening in New York. He cared for audiences and acted as though it were possible to be a rational impresario.

He rarely put money behind a new American play on Broadway; the exception was the work of Tennessee Williams, which he nursed long after the first fine flame had gone from the writing. He was hated for his caution about other American writers. Poison pen letters from would-be dramatists called him "Broadway's number-one bastard." He stuck to his policy. Almost everything he staged was presold. It could be some serious dramatic production imported from Britain, a *Look Back in Anger,* a *Taste of Honey,* an *Epitaph for George Dillon.* The British past meant the show was already run in, sometimes had cheap sets for sale as with *A Severed Head,* the Iris Murdoch–J. B. Priestley comedy, or came with a name of high prestige, like the Royal Shakespeare Company in *Travesties.* There were press clippings to show the backers before opening night and an established reputation. Merrick stayed out on the road in Europe, stalking his shows. He found dozens in Paris, even in dull seasons. He brought Anouilh's *Becket* to New York after some well-wisher had the told the author that all Merrick could do was make money; Anouilh, dulled by years of half-success and flops on Broadway.

liked the idea. He always bought an option quickly on any show that had promise. For that, he was prepared to fly to Europe for openings, to haunt the cold corridors of New York airports, and pay quick money for a chance to consider a show for Broadway. Other theater men were slower. Their imports did less well.

When Merrick did an American show it was usually a comedy or else a musical. In either case, it would be acceptable to theater parties, the kind of show that would make a charity gala or a Rotary Club night out. That way there was a guaranteed audience that would start to promote the show by word of mouth. He had disastrous flops among his musicals; he abandoned a stage version of *Breakfast at Tiffany's,* the musical successor to a best-seller and a hit movie before its New York opening on the grounds that it was excessively tedious. But when he had a monstrous hit, the chances of a long and spectacularly profitable run were usually higher with a musical than with straight drama. It was a gamble, but the rewards were extraordinary.

Once he had chosen his property, he made it part of a private Merrick season within the Broadway season. The numbers dazzled outsiders. There would be a string of Merrick shows, while other producers patiently assembled a single offering every two or three years. The volume made industrial sense. It helped the backers to spread their risk; if this Merrick show lost, there would soon be another in which they might gain. He could buy bulk advertising space and even put together the Merrick shows in a special theater guide in newspapers, much to the fury of other managements who thought he was trying to pretend his shows were the sum total of action on Broadway. Their attitudes did not worry him. Other producers were a crew-cut club to which he did not belong. He did work with them on such matters as pay negotiations, but he took high-handed action of his own on curtain times. The others wanted 7:30; Merrick thought 8:00 was better, since it allowed his audience time for dinner and a civilized evening. Merrick did what he wanted and the others fumed.

Because he produced a string of shows, he could influence theaters and box-office and ticket policies as well as the style of the show. He helped start telephone bookings. Nine out of every ten arrived to collect the tickets they had booked; the system filled more seats. Other managements resisted furiously. He kept a mailing list of 65,000 names who formed the core of theater parties and charity galas, and he used the list frequently. He was fussy about courtesy at the box office; he tried to bury the familiar Broadway snarl. He also kept unusually close tabs on touring companies to make sure he could continue to make money on a show when it went out of New York on the road. Moreover, he made very sure that everybody in the audience knew how hard he had been laboring on their behalf. His virtues would be less if they were not regularly recorded.

Every management tries to control budgets; Merrick makes it near impossible for money to leak away. The guiding principle is that "I won't do a show which requires more than sixty percent in running expense." That is, if more than 60 percent of the seats have to be sold just to pay the weekly bills, Merrick is not interested. In practice, he likes 50 percent a lot better. He keeps close control of productions. Even where he is only coproducer he insists on handling management. He likes to chivvy companies to make sure they function well. He has even applied for guild permission to be his own company manager on *Promises, Promises*. Then, he keeps within his empire as much of the budget as possible. As a "general partner" in the show he expects 50 percent of the profits, and as a producer he expects one percent of the box-office takings. Then, for office space and secretarial help, Merad Productions requires a fee, $500 a week when *Travesties* came to New York in 1975; the sole stockholder of Merad is David Merrick. He may also provide lighting or electrical work and be paid for it, or even serve as press agent. All this is provided for in the small print of the prospectuses that managements must file with the Securities and Exchange Commission when they solicit money from the public for the stage. Since he concentrates the expensive effort within his own small organization, Merrick can eliminate the worst Broadway risks and spread overhead over several shows. He can minimize a loss as well as provide for a hit like *Hello, Dolly!* Since *Fanny*, he has never had to audition a show. He consults his list of backers, makes judicious phone calls, and says: "I'm ready."

He works carefully against the awful power of the Broadway opening night and the New York reviews. "I decided quite early," he says, "that the producer who could beat mixed notices was the one most practicing members of the theater would be interested in." The cost of nursing a show that has lost its audience is phenomenal; it is often better to close and take a tax loss. It follows that a producer who survives is good at helping his productions through the first weeks.

Merrick has often arrived in New York with a profit. He took the British musical *Oliver* to the West Coast, took in more than $750,000 in subscription ticket sales alone in Los Angeles and San Francisco, and grossed over $1 million in fourteen weeks. The backers had a profit before the Broadway opening; the tour defused the panic that usually follows a New York show preparing out of town. For Shelagh Delaney's fragile melodrama *A Taste of Honey*, he managed the same trick. It was a play of atmosphere and tenderness, difficult to sell despite its British success and the legend that its author, in late adolescence, had seen a play by Terence Rattigan and decided she could do better. Merrick was jostled out of the New York theater he had expected by a glossy comedy with Lauren Bacall. He waited for two years. Before a theater finally came clear on Broadway, he took the show to Los Angeles. Its direct, basic character triumphed. He could bring a hit, an established American hit, into New York. The Bacall comedy flopped in the theater he had wanted and had signed a contract for; *A Taste of Honey* ran for 391 performances.

Merrick is notorious for savaging critics. He also manipulated them. He opened Thornton Wilder's *The Matchmaker* after previews heavy with the ominous sound of shifting in seats. The play had failed once before on Broadway; it was a gamble. Merrick decided to play the critics carefully. He timed the opening night to follow the premiere of an insubstantial Rodgers and Hammerstein production called *The Pipe Dream*. That show lacked edge and distinction and Merrick knew it. He carefully invited high-minded members of his mailing list to his own first night performance so that his show would seem brave and worthy after the musical of the night before. The audience applauded; the critics took their cue from the atmosphere; the play was established. When he opened the Lena Horne spectacular *Jamaica,* he reversed the ploy. "Frankly," he says, "I got hold of a lot of rich squares, let in the out-of-towners, and they loved the show."

"DAVID DOESN'T CARE what people say about him," Joshua Logan says, "as long as he's famous." Merrick is attacked, derided, lampooned more than most Broadway figures, and each attack has a solid value as advertisement. He tries to keep rigid control over what people say about him, laying down questions he will answer and those he will refuse. He appears in *Who's Who in the Theater* with an eye-catching entry that says, simply, that David Merrick has refused to be included. Press agents produce reams of paper on behalf of the private, reticent Merrick. In the files Bill Doll and Company say Merrick is enterprising, tenacious, quick witted, and flamboyantly colorful; "Merrick's 11 Shows in One Season Make Him Man Who Owns Broadway." He is the "A&P Merchant of the Muses," and yet a sensitive man who has "presented several attractions simply because the artistic values of same seemed so overwhelming to him that he felt compelled to do the shows even though they were commercial risks." Years later, Solters, O'Rourke and Sabinson, press agents, are calling him "the prodigious producer" whose "artistic accomplishments cannot be measured in dollars as he considers the audience and Press approval of his efforts and the various awards, plaques, and citations honoring them even more satisfying than the box-office statements." The barrage of flak from the promoters and the relative difficulty of finding the man himself helped create a press agent's fantasy, an all-complaisant public figure waiting to be invented. All producers like their press agents to issue some generous, soothing statements about their virtues. Merrick took that egotism and elevated it to a business principle. In essence, he helped invent himself.

The mogul steps down: Jules Stein in retirement at his cottage gate—in
Belgravia. *Kevin Brodie/Topix*

The mogul steps out: Jules Stein (third from right) leaves the MCA mansion in Beverly Hills with assets Lawrence Welk, Louis Prima, Freddie Martin. *Gene Lester*/Saturday Evening Post/*General Research and Humanities Division, The New York Public Library, Astor, Lenox and Tilden Foundations*

Above The mogul inspects: Jules Stein (far right) looks over his Manhattan team in the mid-forties. *Harry Saltzman*/Saturday Evening Post/*General Research and Humanities Division, The New York Public Library, Astor, Lenox and Tilden Foundations*

Below The mogul makes friends: William S. Paley (second from left) with stars he bought for CBS, (left to right) George Burns, Gracie Allen, Mary Livingston, and Jack Benny. *CBS*

Mogul and machine: the pristine Hollywood headquarters of CBS towers over William S. Paley (left) and Frank Stanton. *CBS*

Above In the beginning: Paley and Miss Radio of 1929 open CBS
headquarters at 485 Madison Avenue, New York City. *CBS*

Below As he is now: William S. Paley in his Manhattan office. *CBS*

Opposite The mogul at work: David Merrick prowls backstage. *Billy Rose Theatre Collection; The New York Public Library at Lincoln Center; Astor, Lenox and Tilden Foundations*

Right The mogul at work: Peter Guber (left) with Jacqueline Bisset, making *The Deep.* Columbia Pictures

Left The mogul at work: Peter Guber (left) with Prince Charles, selling *The Deep.* Columbia Pictures

The mogul triumphs: Peter Guber with Golden Globe for the movie he nursed, *Midnight Express*.   *Casablanca Records and FilmWorks*

Left Official face: Trevor Nunn of the Royal Shakespeare Company. *Sophie Baker/RSC* Magazine

Below Human face: "In sneakers in the rehearsal room, the real Trevor Nunn comes out." *Judith Aronson*/Telegraph Magazine

Below Stigwood family: the mogul with Bee Gees Robin (left) and Barry Gibb. *RSO*

Above Stigwood spectacle: Argentina revolts in *Evita*. *RSO*

Below The mogul: Robert Stigwood in close-up. *Mark Ellidge/Topix*

He was there when his stunts happened. In the catalog of bizarre events and calculated gimmicks, the familiar face, white and mustached, recurs. See him in Philadelphia, waiting to leave a performance of the comedy *Cactus Flower*. He has taken a position against a local television station's habit of interviewing the audience as they leave the show to ask for instant criticism. A Merrick press agent, armed with shears, steps forward to cut the cables to the television cameras. Headlines rose around him. Merrick had hedged his bets. Before the shearing, a second press agent had infiltrated the line and praised the show. Even Merrick himself had gone on camera, but he was recognized in the cutting room and removed.

For *Subways Are for Sleeping* he pulled a stunt that had been long planned. He found private citizens with the names of the major Broadway critics, and quoted them in banner type, praising the show to which he had given them free tickets. It was a trick delayed some years, he said, because of the difficulty of finding anyone but the critic who had the name of Brooks Atkinson. The idea had imitators. When the British comedian Peter Cook opened his review *The Establishment* in New York, he found a Philadelphia postman named David Merrick and sent him down Forty-fourth and Forty-fifth streets in Manhattan, bawling through a megaphone. "This is the real David Merrick speaking," he said. "Take no notice of cheap substitutes. I advise you to cash in your tickets and go to *The Establishment*."

The feuds were legendary. He fought critics in order to give the public the idea that their criticism might have an edge of malice that should be discounted. The idea stuck. When he had to close *Breakfast at Tiffany's* before its New York opening, a local television station tried to stage a confrontation between the downcast Merrick and the critics who had never seen the show. "We figured," said the TV researcher calling the reviewers, "you critics would welcome the chance to get even with Mr. Merrick." It was, of course, untrue; at least one critic devoted a column to explaining how much he felt for Merrick in his time of trouble and how he should be allowed his private grief. Still, critics played Merrick's game, as eager for self-promotion as the impresario. Clive Barnes, when writing for *The New York Times,* was found at lunch with Merrick demanding a food taster to guard against poison. In that way, he played Merrick's game to the hilt, and by Merrick's rules. When a critic had been unflattering for several shows, Merrick had another ploy. "I'm an ex-lawyer," he says, "and I have a theory that if you don't invite the critics and they pay their way and the review is particularly wild and obnoxious, you might have a lawsuit. Who knows, I might prove it."

He fights actors as often as he fights critics, and for a variety of reasons. There is the obvious line in publicity. Throughout the run of a musical called *Take Me Along* he fought with his star, Jackie Gleason. Merrick, unjustified, snarled in print with mock concern: "Why do you pick on a big, fat drunken slob like Gleason who was appearing night after night virtually drunk on stage?" and Gleason answered back: "Now there's a mother for you. He's surrounded with talent and he has no way to communicate with it." Merrick sent a private detective to perch in a tree outside Gleason's house when his star reported sick. He told the world that the $3,000 a day insurance he collected in the star's absence was worth far more than the star's presence. Such headlines, column mentions, and news stories continued even through the lifeless months of a long run.

He has a professional detachment that upsets stars who require a gentle ego massage. Peter Ustinov has said that Merrick is a strange man because "he must first alienate you in order to woo you." He is notorious for paying actors no more than they demand, and turning later to them to suggest they fire their agents for not asking enough. If he is rarely cruel without purpose, he does not have a name for generosity. He dislikes actresses, which may be a product of a dozen hopeful glances at Sardi's or awkward and classic moments like his one encounter with a girl who entered his office and prepared immediately to display every talent she possessed. His public statements on actors are unflattering; he talks of running a kindergarten and arriving with enough bubble, gum, consolation, and jump ropes to keep the children happy. He says performers need to be whipped, albeit "with lettuce leaves." His range of productions makes it impossible for him to act as nursemaid to the performers in all of them, and there is a sense of edgy anticipation in the links between his casts and his office. He can seem ruthless because the show is everything. Anthony Quinn played in Anouilh's *Becket* for him, and was vital to the commercial prospects of a playwright who had never had a full success on Broadway. He fell sick. One night, Merrick put him on stage although his vocal chords were bleeding. "As long as you can talk," he said, "you go on."

The hidden reason for the bad-mouthing is often the need to prepare a change in cast or keep a show alive while its star is out of commission. Merrick staged a show called *Carnival,* whose star was Anna Maria Alberghetti. She was taken ill and hospitalized. Merrick sent her a bouquet of plastic roses and a demand for a lie detector test. When her understudy appeared, Merrick pronounced her performance "the best replacement performance I've ever seen on Broadway. I wish I had been clairvoyant enough to know at the beginning that she was that much better than Miss Alberghetti." Merrick needed, of course, to cover for the absence of his star. Slight scandal did that admirably. He also had a running dispute with Anna Maria Alberghetti. She wanted a leave of absence from *Carnival* for eight to fourteen weeks in order to appear in Vincente Minnelli's film *Two Weeks in Another Town.* Merrick had demanded, by way of compensation, that she extend the run of her contract by eight to fourteen weeks. If Alberghetti went, her replacement had to be good enough to keep the show running until her return.

Sometimes the complaints of actresses had a solid foundation. Merrick always called Lauren Bacall a "professional malcontent," although he admits her performance in the comedy *Cactus Flower* was "opening night every night." Now, in that show Miss Bacall had a star's contract. She wanted 10 percent of the gross box-office takings and the right to leave the show for fourteen weeks should anyone offer her a movie. Merrick demurred. He would concede the break, but only if Bacall settled for 7½ percent of the gross. She had to agree. No movie offer appeared. The share of box office that she lost was worth some $125,000. Her discontent blossomed.

He would put a cast in fear if he thought he could help the show that way. Kenneth Haigh had spent months playing the obnoxious

Jimmy Porter in John Osborne's *Look Back in Anger*. He told Merrick that people on the sidewalks had begun to revile him as an authentic angry young man. Merrick pondered. A few weeks later, in the third act of an ordinary performance, a woman leaped on stage and began to tear into the cast with fists and furious words. The audience was aghast. The morning papers had already gone to bed, but the evening papers next day gave the story banner headlines. It was, Merrick admits, "a rough moment for the cast." It was also a stunt. The woman was a friend of a Merrick press agent. The incident fooled newspapermen who could not believe any press agent would wait until the third act for such a stunt and miss the morning papers. *Look Back in Anger* had begun a gentle decline at the box office; its new notoriety helped it run another seven months on Broadway and five on tour.

"What the writers and directors—all the creative artists, even the actors—like most of all is royalties, the prestige of a long run, and basically that if they got mixed or poor notices (and they are all in fear and trepidation about critics and notices) then they have a hard-working, driving producer who will invent many ways of keeping the show alive." Merrick's credo is this: "I am a working producer and that is my stock in trade."

GYPSY WAS A STRIPPER and a fine one. She wrote her story and Merrick thought it could be a musical. It had a theatrical mother, bosomy and brassy, and a theater family, heartache and ambition, stardom and striptease. What Merrick did, along with his coproducer Leland Hayward, will serve to show what the "trade of working producer" can contain.

There are egos, lawsuits, threats, and walkouts, a show at stake over whether a man's name appears in a box on the posters. The producer is expected to reassure an anxious star that her proper press agent has been signed, and tell her public that the air conditioning will be fixed. He must find the money, the writers, the cast, the director, the theater, the press agents, the musicians, the lighting, the publicity, the theater parties, the preview audiences, and the ideal mixture for the first night to ensure the critics are content. At the start, Merrick was deluged with telegrams from hopeful actors and agents, names half-remembered, all asking to be noticed, considered, and perhaps cast in the new show. He had to contend with late-arriving money and lawyers' letters that arrived only too promptly. From the conception of the show to the writing of the prospectus that allows managements to approach investors, from the first meeting with the writers to opening night, the "working producer" is administering the most intensely political factory that can be imagined.

With *Gypsy*, the property itself had problems. Gypsy Rose Lee had written her autobiography, and it formed the basis of the show's book. But Gypsy Rose Lee was a real person, and it followed that an elder sister put on stage would be identified with her real-life elder sister, an uncle with a real uncle, mother with mother. The prospect of endless lawsuits was appalling. To be safe, the family had to consent to how the show would present the characters who, of course, were not to be confused with persons living or dead. Gypsy's sister was the actress June Havoc. The Press made the obvious link very early. *The New York Times* wrote about Carol d'Andrea, who "will portray June Havoc, Gypsy Rose Lee's sister." Merrick's lawyers were anxious; they even invited Havoc's lawyer, Louis Nizer, to a run-through to check that nothing had been left in inadvertently that would harm or annoy her. Merrick had to accept, for example, that no elder sister of Gypsy could ever have appeared in a talent contest. Ms. Havoc insisted she had always been strictly professional.

Egos boiled and blustered right up to opening night. Jerome Robbins was signed to direct the show on November 7, 1958. His agents, MCA, sent copies of the contract off to Merrick and Hayward, but the producers apparently did not return them sharply enough. Within a month, the deal was in trouble. The issue was billing. Robbins felt cramped with his name on a single line. He had not yet seen a book for the show, and he had no idea how much of a contribution he would have to make as choreographer as well as director. He required the authors to rely on his good faith to claim the billing he deserved. He would decide if it should be two lines or one, double credit for a double function or merely a simple "directed by." If the billing were only one line, though, he wanted a box around his name.

The authors disagreed to the point of rebellion. Arthur Laurents, who wrote the book, was especially insistent that Robbins should on no account have double credits and on no account be allowed to put his name in a box. Merrick's lawyers took these blusters with alarming seriousness. The threats were real enough to upset or even wreck the production. All Robbins's points had to be met, said the lawyers, or else there could be considerable trouble, since there did not appear to be a contract with the man. At least the authors were contracted.

That was the case until 3:35 P.M. on the afternoon of February 4, when a single phone call brought the entire production grinding to a halt again. Jule Styne was the composer; his counsel called Merrick's lawyers and asked where the indemnity was. No indemnity, he said, no music. The indemnity, giving a contributor to a show his profit participation without the duties and responsibilities of a shareholder or partner, was late. On March 24, Arthur Laurents took exactly the same stand on exactly the same principle. Since he had received no indemnity, he would not sign the first-class production agreement, the Minimum Basic Production Agreement. He would sue if his book and his words were used at a private rehearsal or a public performance. *Gypsy* was two months away from its opening night. The lawyers were saying it was illegal to speak its words or play its music.

Meanwhile, little troubles surfaced. Ethel Merman was anxious. Merrick had promised her William Fields as her press agent, the show was in preparation, and nobody had told her if Fields was free or if he would work for her. She wanted confirmation in writing immediately that a deal had been made. By the end of January, June Havoc seemed happy with the script and only one trouble remained:

Merrick was never at his desk to take phone calls, and the lawyers could not reach him to say that those problems had been resolved. The last money for the show arrived only in early February. There had been talk of a TV network backing the show because it had earlier backed another Ethel Merman show, *Happy Hunting*. But the network wanted TV rights, and the producers did not want to cede them. The money-raising had been divided, with the help of Robert F. Six, president of Continental Air Lines, Inc., who had helped fund other Merman shows. On February 13, Six wrote to his partners and told them that the last $35,000 had been found, in five 1 percent units of $7,000 each. It seemed that if the composer would release his music, the author would allow his book to be used, the director would patch up his war of egos with the authors, there might yet be a show.

During the melodramas and the shouting, Merrick and Hayward were also dealing with the more obvious functions of producers, like casting. Gypsy herself was hard enough to find. They needed a girl who could handle complex shifts of emotion, because Arthur Laurents had written a dramatic part. Singers and dancers would not be enough. There was talk of contacting the Actors' Studio for new names, even breaking Broadway decorum and contacting the West Coast. Anne Bancroft was suggested, but she was committed to appear in *The Miracle Worker* that fall. Arthur Laurents was agitated. It might be easy to teach an actress to strip, but it would be impossible to teach a nonactress to play Gypsy.

Still, the show opened, with Sandra Church as Gypsy and the book, music, and production intact. After that, the troubles were minor. Gypsy wore a leotard that was tied with a bow when the book required she give a titillating impression of being naked. Fierce ladies from Flushing wrote complaining notes to Ethel Merman because the air conditioning in the theater was malfunctioning in the sour, heavy summer of New York. Novelty acts built into the show were failing to get applause. The producers had the usual troubles, nursing a show, checking a show, making sure that the product was right.

It was a varied trade, being "working producer." Under Merrick's management, *Gypsy* ran for 973 performances until December 9, 1961. On every dollar invested it paid its backers $1.30 in profit.

MERRICK BECAME MORE PRIVATE as his public actions needed less public money. By the mid-1960s he had amassed a sizable personal fortune which he wished to invest in plays without considering the cautious interests of angels. He made himself a foundation, and the foundation invested in plays on its own account. If they succeeded, the foundation profited; if they failed, there was no band of backers to recriminate, only a brief report to the Internal Revenue Service and a red line at the foot of the accounts. By using charitable status, Merrick had the resources to pursue his own taste as he wished. The Internal Revenue Service could act, obliquely, as one of his backers.

He had kept Broadway alive during bad years, during times when the reputation of the Times Square district sank so low people were afraid of the fear they felt in going to the theater. He had kept producing, made an assembly line that could continue logically as more fainthearted producers dependent on a single show every few years dropped out of the business. By the early 1970s he felt there was simply not enough action on Broadway. He needed action. He turned to movies, fought a stockholders' battle within Twentieth Century-Fox, whom he rightly thought had given him much too much of their money for the failed movie of *Hello, Dolly!*, and later lost other studios' money on *Child's Play* and *The Great Gatsby,* tasteful and boring movies with an overliterary bent. His sole triumph of substance was *Semi-Tough,* a movie about football, male sodality, and friendship between sexes, which started from a property he had designed for the theater. As a moviemaker, and a manipulator of movie companies, David Merrick sat irrelevant in the Beverly Hills Hotel, a man nobody needed to fear.

He had been good at dealing with the movie men. Thornton Wilder's *The Matchmaker* had been on the market for sixteen years after its first disastrous Broadway production. Merrick made it into a stage hit, and only then did Hollywood pay $250,000 for the rights. Later, the studios paid again for its musical by-blow, *Hello, Dolly!* He took *Irma la Douce*—tarts, policemen, and fishnet stockings in a cardboard Paris—and made it work on stage; Hollywood ignored the play in Paris and bought it from Broadway for $300,000. His sort of material was particularly attractive to that generation of movie managers in the 1960s who lacked any particular vision, dealt only with established properties, and often had to convince banks as well as board members that they were buying the right subjects. A Broadway hit was obviously a potential film hit, or so those film men thought. Twentieth Century-Fox researched the prospects for *Hello, Dolly!* on film assiduously and still lost money. Original material would have been a risk. The high price tag and the competitive bidding merely proved that it was right to pay high. If Merrick has any importance in the history of Hollywood other than as a stockholder agitator and a minor producer, it will be as one of the main suppliers of safe material to a movie machine that had lost its nerve.

On Broadway, he had pushed up authors' advances notably; for Anouilh's *Becket* he paid $15,000 in advance, which was thought to be outrageously high. He had his own empire of subsidiary companies to mop up any money that might spill over from a production—not just Merad, but also Thespian Sound, Vidmer Lighting and Stage Lighting, David Merrick, Inc., Merrick Associates, and Merrick Affiliates. He had tried to rationalize the business and make it something more than a series of indulgent flings. In 1966–67 he proved valid his theory of a constant flow of productions. *The Lives of Cass Maguire* disappeared after twenty performances and lost $75,000; *We Have Always Lived in the Castle* crashed after nine shows and lost $80,000; Woody Allen's *Don't Drink the Water* had bilious attacks out of town and changes of heart and cast. Any of those might have meant trouble to a more limited producer. Merrick could suffer the failures, since he had so much else. He was the sole investor in *Cactus Flower,* still running from December 1965. He had *Hello, Dolly!,* which had opened in January 1964, the main product of a financing fund provided by RCA Victor that by 1968 had grossed more than $45 million and made more than $8 million profit. *I Do,*

I Do, a two-handed musical, had opened in December 1966 and survived more than eighteen months. Out of all this activity, Merrick managed a weekly payroll of some $250,000 and his shows grossed each year between 1965 and 1968 a startling $25 million. In the middle of that machine it was possible even to absorb a loss like *Breakfast at Tiffany's.*

Other impresarios have shut glossy musicals before their New York openings; however, few have done it with such grace or such enormous and sympathetic publicity. Merrick had conceived the idea of *Breakfast at Tiffany's,* a musical play to be based on the novel by Truman Capote. A movie version had been a huge success. He had hired Mary Tyler Moore to play Holly Golightly, and taken Richard Chamberlain from "Dr. Kildare." After first trying a book that failed by Nunnally Johnson, he called on Abe Burrows; when that also failed, he made a last desperate stab and asked Edward Albee to rewrite the show. He tried every means to add gloss, style, and wit, but the mixture remained leaden. In Boston, notices were disastrous: "A multi-set disaster," said the *Globe,* "a straightforward musical flop." The unfortunate Holly was shifting character like oil on the Hudson. In Philadelphia, she was a tough $50-a-night hooker; by Boston, she was a sweet girl who might generously give heart and body to any passer-by. There was $500,000 at stake in the show and most of that was Merrick's. He killed the show. "Since the idea of adapting *Breakfast at Tiffany's* for the musical stage was mine in the first place," he said, "the closing is entirely my fault and should not be attributed to the three top writers who had a go at it. It is my Bay of Pigs. I have closed it to avoid subjecting the drama critics and the theater-going public to an excruciatingly boring evening."

His faith in theater as an industry was confirmed; it allowed an impresario to make mistakes without ruin. He always was spectacularly good at avoiding total loss. Between 1954 and June 1965, the years of his most varied Broadway activity, he had only three shows that cost their backers every cent of their stake. There was Menotti's music drama, *Maria Golovin,* a worthy risk; the Murdoch–Priestley *A Severed Head,* an excessively stylized piece of sexual Gothic; and a review that came out of Las Vegas called *Vintage '60*. His shows lost some of their backers' money seventeen times and made money eighteen times. His most successful shows were both, curiously, British imports. They reveal his methods. The most successful of all was *Stop the World—I Want to Get Off*, a low-budget musical with symbols, big ballads, and a character called Everyman; it paid $4 on every dollar invested. The second most successful, rather surprisingly, was *Look Back in Anger*, also a British import, which inspired some of Merrick's better stunting to keep the show's name known. It paid $2.39 on the dollar. The Merrick method produced hits best, it seems, when applied in its purest form.

THE CLOCKWORK FURY of Merrick's pose as mogul and entrepreneur was running down in the 1970s. His production fund had long been swelled by money from RCA Victor, who had a natural interest in musicals that could be recorded; like MCA and CBS, they wanted rights to record that came more cheaply when shows were first staged. He maintained a splendid independence from his corporate backers until he went to Hollywood and found they were the men who decided if his films would appear, and how they would appear, and why. He had performed an elaborate shadow play for so long on Broadway that his near-eclipse when he dealt with the corporations was a surprise; show business was now an industry with a corporate structure. The age of the making of corporations was over; Merrick himself was almost too late for the days of a Stein or a Paley when structures were being created and powers divided. From now on, survival and success depended on the contract, the treaty that was signed with massive corporations, even governments. The illusion of the entrepreneurs was carefully maintained. The reality was managements not moguls.

There came new generations. "Mogul" meant something new.

5

PETER GUBER:
SURVIVOR

THE CORPORATIONS GREW AND TREMBLED, subject in bad times to the will of banks, glorying in good times before happy stockholders. In its new corporate guise, show business recruits its management not through their will to work with a camera or their devotion to a medium or their ideas. It hires from business schools by interviews. It absorbs the bright lawyers and accountants and professionals, the ones whose skills are abstract and, they claim, applicable wherever there is a business to manage and money to consider. The machines that were built by the likes of William Paley or Jules Stein now require constant replenishment with managers who will respect and glory in the machine itself. Stein always hired from Ivy League schools, men who went against the image of agents; Paley's associates were the careful, calm men with "a background." If Merrick contrived his operations with only a small team it is because he was a survivor, an entrepreneur in the days when such functions had not been taken over by the apparatus of corporations. Others were not so fortunate.

It is not so easy, life within the show-business corporations. The decisions remain a heady mixture of creative inspiration, guesswork, gambling, and calculation. By and large the calculation, however careful, can only reduce the losses or the failures to manageable proportions and structure a business out of chances. It cannot make hits or select them. The management men have therefore a dual and uncomfortable position. They gamble and conserve: they are responsible for decisions that are always risks and yet they are responsible for avoiding risks. The tension tells. It makes either nervy, cautious, troubled men who scuttle away from ideas, or those who survive and go on to make what they want after years inside the corporate structure. Such people are rare. The corporation trains people to its own requirements, and the ability to be an individual operator is not one of them.

Peter Guber survived one of the harshest times in one of the most troubled companies in Hollywood. He was recruited by Columbia in the late 1960s when all seemed well. The annual report had embossed on its cover a page of New York Stock Exchange prices. In 1968, the company hit all-time highs: $243 million came in, and $21 million of it was profit. Next year, the decline began. Profits slumped to $11 million on sales of $206 million. In 1970, the annual report had only company logos embossed on its front cover, and the color pictures had vanished. Instead, there was a $11 million profit again, but barely, on sales of $242 million, and there was ominous talk of rising costs, rising interest rates, and unfair competition from television networks making their own movies. Columbia seemed nervous. The next year that annual report appeared in plain and penitential brown; there was no more full directory of all the senior operating officers; there was, in fact, a loss. On income of $233 million, Columbia lost $40 million, reduced to $29 million by the simple expedient of adding back all the money previously set aside for paying taxes that would not now be levied. The next year was said to be better; banks provided a revolving credit of $180 million, the actual studios were merged with those of Warners, and the spare land sold off; the operating loss was down to less than a million dollars. The next year, fiscal 1973, was so bad that the penitential brown reappeared and a separate section was headed ''What We Are Doing About It All.'' The loss was almost $65 million, brought back to $50 million by tax provisions. The years of disaster were the product of overpriced conventional movies sent out to a deadly silence from the audiences; high indebtedness at a time of high interest rates; problems with the true value of already released movies on the books, since television prices for feature films were no longer buoyant; and a management crisis which the rest of Hollywood had already felt and Columbia contrived to stave off for a couple of years.

Through all this, from the fat annual reports to the lean, apologetic ones, Peter Guber survived Columbia. He rose whenever his seniors left. He succeeded because he was the cheapest management Columbia had. He was bustling and frenetic, sharp and exact. He spoke up for himself. He was there when in 1974 the profit and loss account again crept into the black; true, it was spoiled by taxes and a loss on selling the division that put movies on pay-TV in hotel rooms. By 1975, profit was $14 million, revenue was $332 million, and the pictures came back to the annual report. Guber stood, open shirted, on a street set and looked imposingly into camera. He had been a company man for almost ten years; having survived the fury and the storms of the decline of Columbia, he was now executive vice-president, worldwide production, and heartily sick of it all.

Guber escaped the corporation, or at least he left the inner workings, to become an independent producer. As such, he had to deal again with the machine. He wanted to make movies, but he did not have money. He needed Columbia's money. Outside the machine, he remained dependent on the machine's resources. True, he might now choose which studio he would do business with; but in practice he was new and unknown as a maker of films. He had been a maker of corporate decisions, which is quite different. Columbia proved his most friendly backer.

But then he broke through. He made *The Deep*, an adaptation of Peter Benchley's novel written after *Jaws*. He merged his company with Neil Bogart's Casablanca Records, made a disco movie called *Thank God It's Friday*, and released his own personal project—a movie that was simply what he wanted to make, *Midnight Express*. Suddenly, Guber was hot. The record side of the business had Donna Summer, Village People, an ear and an eye for disco styles. The movie side had hits. The structure had not changed too drastically. True, the European giant Philips/Siemens now had a substantial shareholding in the company Guber and Bogart had once owned outright, but that was a help. It gave financial credibility and freedom of action to back judgments in the early days of a project, always subject in time to the scrutiny of the men from an electronics firm in The Hague. Guber was now in an immensely strong position to deal with studios; but he still had to deal with them. He appeared to be an independent power, and he was. He had the sense of being almost a mogul, able to make things happen and movies appear, but he had to be constantly aware of the apparatus of corporations which was ultimately responsible for what was made, what was released.

Guber had this advantage: he had been the corporation man handling the would-be moguls. Now he had changed sides. He had lived through the atmospheres, pressures, and horrors of corporate show business, and he knows exactly how it feels.

"WEDNESDAY WAS THE ONE EVENING I didn't have school until late," Guber says. "I took interviews late in the afternoon on Wednesday." He was the bright boy from Boston, studying fiercely in New York. During the day, he was at law school. At night he worked on a Masters in Business Administration. Life was tight, since he had a family to support, a wife and a baby. School was coming remorselessly to an end and there was the real world to consider.

He wanted to be a clerk to the Supreme Court, or else some fat corporate lawyer on Wall Street, or perhaps a senatorial aide. He kept the law school happy by going to be interviewed by firms in Washington, New York, and Los Angeles. He annoyed the business school by talking about a legal future. "I wasn't doing my bit," he says. "I wasn't taking interviews with the firms that endowed the business school with a great deal of funding." The community exerted thunderous pressure, and Guber agreed, for the sake of form, to some brief discussions late on Wednesday afternoon. Only three corporations were interviewing at the right time: a lumber firm, a detergent and toothpaste giant, and Columbia Pictures Industries, Inc. "I didn't see myself,'' Guber says, ''working with trees or toothpaste or movies.'' But he felt obliged to go. It was for the sake of the school.

To his embarrassment, Columbia seemed keen. Each year, they hired one person from a business school. They seemed to laugh a lot, to share Guber's feelings and his wavelength. The next week, they phoned and offered lunch at their Fifth Avenue headquarters. ''I was not a very well-to-do person and the idea of having a free lunch uptown seemed appealing.'' He went to meet Stanley Schneider, then among the first vice-presidents of the company, and the son of the chairman. Would Guber, Schneider asked, be interested in joining the company? ''Now Hollywood had never seemed the place that my education would fit,'' Guber says. ''I was just not a theatrical person. I was a good writer, I could express myself, but never with an eye to the theatrical. Besides I had $29,000 in student loans outstanding and a baby and this law firm offered me $150 a week, and I had to start my life.'' He did nothing to check out Columbia or the movie business or the prospects; ''I had no intention of going to work for the company.'' He began to think about movies only after he had made his plans.

It was 1968, the last year when movies were a fashionable industry to investment analysts, the glamorous side of leisure-time activities. Studio corporations noted happily the huge returns from selling movies to TV. Wall Street, briefly, took their assets seriously and paid more for their shares. *Easy Rider* was to roar across the nation proving that old Hollywood could attract a young audience, once. Memories of the clangorous cash registers after *Sound of Music* still sweetened and confused the cocktail talk of executives. True, management squabbles had already torn MGM apart and made Twentieth Century-Fox vulnerable; the cost of inventory, films on the books that were not making money, was colossal; debt was spiraling ever upward, a device to make profits on other people's money which collapsed when movies made only losses. Worse, managements were growing old, stale, tired, and smug, making movies for people like themselves instead of the people who actually went to the cinema. It was a bad time, but it was generously masked with hope and rouge. Hollywood may have had an old, cracked face, but it knew how to light itself.

All that was not what persuaded Peter Guber to go out to the alien wastes of California and into the mad and maddening business of movies. "They offered me $450 a week, which is three times what the law firm offered, and they paid off all my student loans and promised they would pay for me to study for the bar and give me a ticket home if I was unhappy." So Peter Guber was found a parking space on the old Columbia lot at Gower Street in Hollywood, and the culture shock began.

Guber, a man from Boston whose brother is a doctor, became Mr. Hollywood. "I moved into a little Hollywood box in the Hollywood hills. I shopped in Hollywood; I worked in Hollywood. If three dogs got together round a lamppost somewhere in Hollywood, I would find some reason to be there." He was dazzled and insecure. His second day, a passing secretary chattered about some new guy called Guber who was to be fired. Guber dashed to a telephone, eyes filled with tears, and furiously called the chairman of the board in New York. No, he was told, there was no question of firing. "You are," said the voice, "too cheap to fire." With his ears ringing with admonitions to listen to no more gossip, Guber returned to his work, which was also his play. "Because it was a toy store," he says. "To me, I was finding my way around a giant toy store. I thought everyone was a genius. The whole profit motive, the way they saw the marketplace—everything. Of course, after six months I thought everyone was a fool, but that was development."

He was assigned to creative affairs, which meant the part of the studio where eager readers thumbed *Publishers Weekly* and *Kirkus Reviews* for the first sighting of a property, where scripts descended, and where directors, writers, and actors were, in theory, supervised. "It was hocus-pocus," Guber says. "There's a great fear among creative people that somebody will find them out, that actually there is no great grounding for their decisions. It's just their opinions. In business there are calculable numbers—a budget, return on investment, and all the rest. But anybody can have an opinion on a script. The question is whether you respect the person with that opinion." To the smart and fresh graduate of business school, the operation had a distinctly haphazard air. "Two or three films out of every ten had to succeed in order to support the whole studio and nobody really knew which films were going to succeed or fail.''

That was not the most disturbing part. "People were rooting,'' Guber says, "for other people's films to fail.'' Studios saw every film in deadly competition with all others, an unreal analysis. "You were competing for the product,'' Guber says. "It was as if each film was a separate business and each studio was a separate kingdom. There wasn't a great deal of openness.'' Egos ran raw like jarring metal. "There was a great deal of negative talk—backbiting and gossip mongering. Everybody was interested more in whom they were seen with, what the impression was of them, and whether they were at the right parties. You had to use that world to enhance your reputation, to make sure of your exposure and your contacts. But it was a despicable experience.'' There was simple jealousy and envy. There was a sense of danger even in a screening: "There's such an ego identification with the film it's like you were standing there naked in the screening room when the lights go out.''

Like an easterner, Guber arrived with jeans and without a car, Hollywood solecisms. He lacked image and friends at first. Unlike New York where he had known dozens of people, Hollywood demanded bargaining counters before admitting others to be friends. "I had to find something with which to befriend people—a star, a picture, a deal. Everything was business. As I moved up in the business, the economic ladder, so the social ladder expanded, too. You were invited only to the parties of those below you on the pecking order, or of your exact peer group across the agencies and studios. And when I finally did get invited to parties, they were extended meetings. It was like the old high school days—the boys in one corner, the girls congregating in the other, and the boys would always be talking business. There's an old Hollywood story about a man leaving some splendid party and thanking his hostess, very graciously, for inviting him to such a lovely meeting. . . .''

HOLLYWOOD WAS COLUMBIA'S SIBERIA. All the machinery of corporate power lived in a leased building on Fifth Avenue in New

York. Only the plant was on the West Coast. "We were there on sufferance. The three-hour time difference became a joke. You would see executives get up at 6:30 in the morning just to call New York from home, vying for the attention of the East Coast executives. When the men from the East came visiting, you were judged by how much of their time you got. The management was actually undercutting the West Coast. It only took a few producers who realized that you had to go to New York for final decisions, and they began submitting their material direct, bypassing Hollywood altogether. Not only were we all in Siberia, we were low men on the totem pole in Siberia."

There was a brief, phony atmosphere of buoyancy. Columbia had *Easy Rider,* the Barbra Streisand musical *Funny Girl,* and the Broadway comedy *Cactus Flower* translated to the screen. At once, it was making money out of the supposed new generation of youthful, protesting film-makers; and the last of the vast and glossy musicals, this one distinguished by its physical exuberance; and the oldest of formula movies, the adaptation of an undemanding Broadway success. You might think that nothing had changed in the fundamentals of Hollywood; yet around Columbia, other studios were suffering. They paid high interest rates to borrow money to gamble on a handful of huge-budget films. If the films failed, they lost money, lost the interest payments, and had nothing to keep their expensive distribution machinery working. They even lost the chance of the profitable television sale which could usually balance the books for a minor movie. Indeed, as the financial squeeze became worse, television cut its payments for movies. That diminished the assets of the studios, since it reduced the money they could hope to make from films that were past their first release; reduced earnings year by year; and ended the seemingly golden age by revealing the problems that lay beneath. The management was bad, but, ironically, the problems Guber saw were not the simple ones of poor attention to the implacable truth of the balance sheet. "They had business people," he says, "and you need a creative entrepreneur at the top. Business people generally forget that you don't shoot the deal and you don't shoot the budget. You find them shooting some $5 million picture and squeezing the director for the last $2,000 and the director turns round and hates them—yet he's the man they put in charge of their $5 million investment.''

Around him, he says, were empty desks. ''Columbia released more executives than pictures.'' Trouble started slowly. The studio was like Ambrosia salad—''You make it of soft fruit and cottage cheese and if you leave it a little too long or you mix things a little too hard, it becomes a mush.'' Such was the softening and then the exodus that left Guber, six months after he joined the company, the sole survivor of the creative affairs department. He promptly caught a plane for New York and went to see Stanley Schneider and asked to have control of the department which, at the time, he was. Schneider laughed: ''He told me, 'You've come a long way just to get a no.' '' Four months later, Schneider had still not found a head of creative affairs: ''I sort of got the job ex officio,'' Guber says. ''Later, I got the title.''

It was ten months since Peter Guber left business school.

''I was the house youth,'' he says. ''They had their house woman and they had their house black. It was good because it gave me a role to play, but it wasn't a reality. I was just getting position for being young.'' He was resented. ''I sat in my first group management meeting with about thirty executives and I guess I was the youngest in the company. I was thirty-five years younger than the average age of the men who sat at that table.'' It was hard for any executive to hold authority as Columbia began to crack. ''The little man who changed the names on the doors was the busiest one of us all. No longer were the names engraved, they came on Velcro tape. That way, they took only twenty seconds to change.'' It was worse for a young Columbia executive. ''It was very difficult to deal with producers who had been in the business for ten, fifteen, thirty years. I looked like a show-business outsider. I spoke quickly, I was full of piss and vinegar, I said what I meant, and perhaps I wasn't diplomatic enough. That set a whole bunch of people off wrong.'' Anyone with certainties was unpopular. At the heart of the movie operation, after all, was Stanley Schneider, whose father was head of the firm, whose brother had made *Easy Rider* possible, who now proved reluctant to cut overhead or shift executives or fire people. He was oppressed, Guber thinks, by the power of his family all around him.

The young Guber, meanwhile, was finding himself an ally. Ray Stark was in post-production with *Funny Girl* when the two first met. He was a power, both as producer and as financial contacts man. His movies made money, and his banking friends salvaged Columbia. When the corporation needed to be rebuilt, it was Stark who introduced Herbert Allen, of the large and tactful Wall Street house Allen & Company. Stark and Allen had been involved with Seven Arts and its wedding with Warners in the 1960s; they had a way of appearing with the necessary capital when a studio was foundering, and they usually managed a rescue operation. "He traveled in a circle that was just not available to me," Guber says. "He gave me power by association. I became one of the fair-haired boys of the business through him. He taught me, too—about the impermanence of executives, and the fact that although they are impermanent, they make permanent decisions. He understood that because he had been one of the founders of the Seven Arts business, and he had been one of the giants of the agency business with Charles Feldman.

"He was the best single producer and showman I met—old-fashioned Hollywood panache. And he was Machiavelli. He understood the workings and machinations of management, of creative talent, of directors, producers, and stars. He told me when to stay, when to get out." To Guber, Stark bequeathed one of his few enemies within Columbia, the old czar of production, Mike Frankovich, who left behind him, when he quit his job as head of production for Columbia, a trail of losing projects which Guber himself was to inherit. For Guber he was on his way up.

It was sixteen months since Guber left business school. Now, he became head of business affairs.

"As people left," he says, "I accumulated titles—vice-president for janitorial services, that sort of thing. I was the cheapest executive they had, so they kept me." Columbia's troubles were becoming more acute. Like all the industry, its decisions take years to reach the screen and be judged. A wave of response to some imagined shift in public taste may break long after the imagined shift has gone. The old guard's decisions stayed to haunt their successors. "They left behind a string of movies like *Hello Dolly!*, *Goodbye Money!* They were still in the mix long after they had been fashionable. The production line took so long there was no way to stop them."

The disaster struck. It was now twenty-nine months after Guber left business school. He became head of American production for the studio.

"IT WAS LIKE KISSING your sister," he says. "There was no way I could profit." Columbia was struggling with a $180 million line of credit from its bankers; their reluctance was an open secret. The alternative to providing huge funds was to see all their previous investments flicker and die. In the midst of the disasters, Guber had arrived, all bright and vulnerable. Hollywood scoffed. Guber himself was puzzled. "What I found most difficult was to get a handle on what I actually did. I had a kind of invisible respectability as head of American production, except that if a film failed, you were thrown out—like some baseball team's manager."

He installed devices to help him. He had a computer and colorboard which listed every director and showed whether his pictures had come in on time or not, what sort of pictures they were, and whether or not they had made money. It also showed what plans the director had announced for the future. The board dominated Guber's office, stood behind curtains, and had a staff of its own. It was, however, more than the young man's eccentricity, which was what a patronizing Hollywood assumed. After a while, some shy executives began to call Guber asking for the help of the board. They did so with reluctance. "That's the trouble with this business. People would always rather not know someone has made three comedy turkeys in a row before they hire him to make a fourth. They're actually more likely to hire him—on the grounds that he has made comedies before. People hired a director or a writer just on the basis of who they had dinner with last, or who they could recollect at the vital moment.''

The banks had moved in on Columbia. "It made life miserable. Funds shrank. There were no raises, no additional staff. Management was torn down. The accountants were ordered to make pictures profitable and that is something no accountant can do. The advertising department went out to spend more money than was practical to support a picture that was a disaster so that the executives could continue to look good. Ultimately, it made them look bad, when all the chickens came home to roost.

''I went through the whole roller-coaster ride. When I went to Columbia the company appeared to be reasonably solvent, although it had an overlarge inventory that had not been effectively amortized. It went through a tremendously difficult time writing off close to $100 million. It was on the verge of bankruptcy when I became head of worldwide production.''

It was thirty-eight months since Guber left business school. He was running a studio of his own.

"YOU TAKE ALL THE PRAISE or the blame for the executive before you,'' Guber says. In his time, Columbia made *Taxi Driver*, set up *Close Encounters of the Third Kind*, and released *Shampoo*. It also made *1776*, remade *Lost Horizon* as a musical, and released *The Fortune*. It was desperately short of product and reluctant to invest; its resources were now stretched so tight that any large loss would break them. The banks knew what they wanted out of Columbia's shows. "They said they wanted pictures with an 'upside potential,' which meant, roughly, Robert Redford and Paul Newman together, with Barbra Streisand singing, Steve McQueen punching, Clint Eastwood jumping, music by Marvin Hamlisch, all in stereo, on the wide screen, going out as a hard-ticketed road show where you have to book your seats, based on a #1 best-seller which was #1 for sixty weeks and a television show which was #1 for at least a season.''

It was not a helpful formula. Instead, it was the pictures that Columbia bought into, along with some small-budget movies like the police story *The New Centurions,* which saved the studio. Guber's contribution was to help ease the company into tax-shelter deals. Movies could at last be made on money from people who did not necessarily want a profit. They were small-town dentists or Cincinnati accountants who wanted to put off paying the Internal Revenue Service all that they owed. By putting $10,000 into a movie, they could take a tax credit and make a profit. That $10,000 might be matched by money from banks to the tune of $40,000 more; the investor can be thought responsible by the tax man for all $50,000 and defer taxes on that amount. Should the movie make money, he has only delayed paying taxes. Should it lose, he pays even less tax. If the movie's promoter can raise money on the strength of the first round of checks, the movie will get made. It may well be a remarkable movie. Because the creative decisions lay with producers who had the muscle to raise the initial money, and who could then sell their finished product to a studio, independent producers could now take a wider range of risks on subjects. Since studios like Columbia were desperately short of movies to send out through their distribution machinery, most projects would find a home somewhere. It no longer mattered that nine out of ten movies lose money, because the investors and the studios were all backing the tax-shelter movies for reasons other than the direct and certain hope of profit. The movies that were good were also profitable. "We took on Warren Beatty in *Shampoo,*" Guber says, "but only because we wanted to get *The Fortune.*" *Shampoo* had Warren Beatty motorcycling lustfully around Hollywood as an itinerant hairdresser with sexual tastes far removed from the stereotype of that profession. "Everyone was so sure of success on that deal, they were slapping themselves on the back. *Shampoo* was a hit and a tax shelter, so most of the profit went back to the shelterers. So the management got cocky and bought back the tax shelter on *The Fortune*—and that went down the tubes." You may remember *The Fortune,* if you have an unluckily persistent memory: Jack Nicholson and Warren Beatty vied wanly for the fortune of Stockard Channing. It was a caper film.

Tax-shelter products suited the banks who felt trapped and anxious. They also liked the films that Guber bought. There was *The Lords of Flatbush,* brought in for a $150,000 advance, which grossed $17 million; *Aloha, Bobby and Rose!,* bought for even less, which took in $15 million; and *White Line Fever,* bought for $1.2 million, which took in $18 million. Unfortunately, even while Guber was anxiously watching the last days' work on *Taxi Driver,* and trying to persuade Julia Phillips to hire Richard Dreyfuss for *Close Encounters of the Third Kind,* the studio still had its deals with its old and valued friends, the distinguished but ancient film-makers who had always dealt with Columbia. And the studio was counting the cost of this older sort of logic.

The cost was very high, almost the death of a studio. Yet Columbia trusted its old guard. "There were all kinds of pictures one knew were going to be disasters, right from the start," Guber says. "When I was a junior executive at the company I had a deal with Ross Hunter, who had produced *Airport* and *Imitation of Life* and *Magnificent Obsession.* One of the pictures he wanted to make was *Lost Horizon.* Now remakes are always fraught with hazard, especially when the original is as fragile as the Capra version of *Lost Horizon.* With some trepidation, the deal went forward." Like most Columbia deals, it had been done in New York by Stanley Schneider, and by the time it reached the studio in Hollywood there was little left to do but minimize the damage. Besides, by then the project had acquired its own Hollywood logic. There was music by Hal David and Burt Bacharach, who were worth money; a script by Larry Kramer who had written *Women in Love;* and there was Charles Jarrott from British television but, more pertinently, from *Anne of a Thousand Days.* "Ross Hunter had the ability to make the picture. The cast he assembled was first-rate, which is a testimony to Hunter's ability to assemble elements around almost anything. The trouble was the script. It was dreadful and it was the case of the emperor's new clothes—nobody would say anything. Even before the first dailies, we knew it was going to be attacked and castigated and it was unlikely to be special." The result was, indeed, appalling. In the first moments, an embarrassed John Gielgud, bereft of knightly dignity in a woolly hat, shuffles through a studio snowstorm and says: "I am from a nearby lamasery." After that high point, all is decline among heavy green sets and leaden performances. Peter Finch and Liv Ullmann and others spent years trying to undo the damage and shame of the movie.

Nor did *1776* work, although it was a more logical version of the big musical that bankers liked to see. "It was a treat to be involved with," Guber says. "Everybody knew it wasn't going to be a big success, but they knew it was going to be rated PG and there was going to be a television sale, and, besides, it was produced by Jack Warner and he was one of the real moguls of the business." Across a gap of generations, Guber and Warner met and played tennis and Warner, aged 82, won. "Listening to his stories was worth the price of whatever the picture cost. He was alive again. It was splendid to see him parade around the sound stages that he had built. He commanded the kind of respect that nobody I've seen before or since commands." It was a meeting with an old tradition, one that stumbled to an end in 1967 when Jack Warner sold out of Warner Brothers and became an independent producer. It was the meeting of creator and inheritor.

There were movies made more on respect than faith—like Ray Stark's production of *The Way We Were,* in which Barbra Streisand as a mildly Pinko student pursued a screenwriting Robert Redford decade by decade. "As a studio executive you either supported Ray or he got out of business with you," Guber says. "I was a friend of his, so I supported him." Stanley Kramer made *Oklahoma Crude* because Kramer and the studio had a long association, and his *Guess Who's Coming to Dinner* had been a great success—"about one hundred and twenty-six years before *Oklahoma Crude.* Columbia had lost touch with the realities of film-making. They made movies with old cronies, people they felt comfortable with. I was really a figurehead and everybody knew it. The small films were left to me." Some of those were great successes: *The Last Detail,* for example, survived another change of management at Columbia and succeeded. Guber still remembers the first screening. Seventeen times the lights failed and the projector stopped. "I was almost in tears," Guber says. "At the end there must have been only one hundred fifty people left in the whole of that theater. The only thing that preview proved was that my stomach could survive such an experience.''

Still, despite his position, to be on the West Coast was to be ''on the outer limits of an asteroid shower.'' Around him, Guber found ''people who made their careers by killing other executives.'' His position had one staunch support: ''When somebody does not give a fuck about their job,'' he says, ''there is little or nothing that can be done against you. I was young, educated, a member of the bar in two states. I taught at UCLA and I wrote and I had offers. I really was not obsessive about keeping my job.''

IN THE BLACKEST DAYS of 1973, the Columbia management was fired. Guber had already decided the motion picture business was not to be the entire sum and substance of his life, but it was still a painful time. Into the company came the Wall Street house of Allen & Company, represented by Herbert Allen, and their nominee for head of the studio: Alan J. Hirschfield. Within weeks, sixty executives were packing bags to leave. The palace revolution was complete.

''Hirschfield and Herbert Allen came to my office,'' Guber remembers. ''I had already bumped into Allen socially because he was a friend of Ray Stark. They asked me to review all the projects Columbia had. They were going to make all the moves, hiring the new management. I was very candid with them. I went through every project and I told them that ninety-eight percent of them were dogs. There was one that Ray Stark had, and there was *The Last Detail,* and those were the only ones I thought were positive.'' All the others, Guber said, should be scrapped. Inevitably, Allen and Hirschfield asked who was to blame. Guber took some collective responsibility for the sins of the management, but he was careful to add: ''I wasn't in charge of that.'' The conversation turned for several hours. Allen and Hirschfield asked what Guber's plans might be, and he told them he had other offers. He wanted to leave them the courtesy of sorting out their own affairs. They seemed surprised.

They had expected Guber to plead for his job. Instead, he laid out his plans. "Frankly, I was bored with Columbia. I had been through seven years of debacle, and I was not about to go through another president."

He stayed. Two months later, David Begelman took over the motion picture division of Columbia; he had been an agent with what was then Creative Management Associates. "He was an optimist, he was enormously likable," Guber says, "and right then he needed me—maybe only for thirty, sixty, ninety days, but he needed me. I knew that when he had to ask me the way home from Burbank."

Guber, survivor of a past regime, became the symbolic clean survivor. Allen & Company would refund the company; Begelman and Guber would bring in the product, the tax-shelter movies and the independent productions that Columbia desperately needed in order simply to stay a functioning distributor of movies. The division worked, but Guber grew malcontent. He had the position he wanted, which was "executive vice-president," but he had nowhere else to go, unless he wanted to devote his entire life to being head of a studio. He had fallen victim to a Californian enthusiasm and had "raised his consciousness"; in doing so, he decided he was only hovering and drifting in his life and he needed to take control. He could now break out of the corporation, although it would be difficult. People knew him. Columbia owed him favors. He could now become an entrepreneur in his own right. If full control of his work were impossible, since he would always need the moneymen, he could still be free of the routine business of the studio. It was, other things aside, his best and only hope for revenge.

"I ESPECIALLY ENJOY THE FEELING of now being co-owner and chairman of a record company that makes their record company look like a candy dime store, and a film company with three enormous hits in a row." Guber left the studio with the grudging ill will of a number of senior executives. Begelman and Allen, however, were his supports. They had less reason to resent a young man who had survived the troubles and been there when there was again profit to show. "What I needed then was credibility," Guber says. "My game wasn't screen credit, it was bank credit. I left Columbia with nearly $19,000 to my name and that was my sole credit base. That was part of the reason I left. There wasn't any real reward for success or any definite bang on the head for failure.

"There was no way my backing was automatic at Columbia. Usually when executives leave a company they get killed by their successors. The new men want the old management out of the way." Guber did have the friendship of Begelman, and armed with that he became Peter Guber's FilmWorks. His first action was to buy a little story about a boy escaping from a Turkish jail, transform it into a book and wait: "It didn't look as if it had a commercial bone in its body," Guber admits. "It had everything going against it." He needed some movie more immediately, obviously more attractive than his Turkish story. He found Peter Benchley's then-unpublished successor to *Jaws,* a diving story called *The Deep.* "I had to get pictures made," he says. "That was the point. Getting Columbia to pay $500,000 for a Peter Benchley book when his last picture was *Jaws,* I knew that picture would be made. I would become a producer. Now, had *The Deep* failed, I would have soon been gone."

For once, Columbia had the money. There was tax-shelter cash, most of it German; there was money from the British conglomerate EMI, which was buying Columbia's music publishing operations in New York for a fixed investment in three movies at a fixed percentage of the profit; and there was money from Time-Life, again making an excursion into movies. With the money, Guber advanced to planning. The movie would be a logistical nightmare. "Probably," Guber says, "one of the most difficult movies Columbia ever undertook, certainly in all the time that I was with them. Maybe *Lawrence of Arabia* was more difficult. I don't know." Movies made on water were bad enough; the mismatching of shots in *Jaws* is good enough evidence of the difficulties. *The Deep* was to be shot underwater. "All films in water had been disasters in the making before," Guber says. "This one had 11,000 dives," the figures flow like a litany, "10,900 man-hours underwater, over one million cubic feet of compressed air, and 151 days of shooting in four oceans. We had stars acting underwater who had never dived before. You see the problems.''

The plot concerns a plastic holiday-making couple who venture into a Caribbean wreck; there they discover double treasure—a stash of heroin above an ancient Spanish galleon. Their discovery allies them with a maritime recluse, again played by Robert Shaw, who was equally fishy and reclusive in *Jaws,* and it sets them against a crew of black villains with a taste for voodoo and gratuitous sadism. There was also a murderous moray eel and a degree of eroticism that had deliberately been excluded from *Jaws.* Where Spielberg's film had been made in uncertain tides around Martha's Vineyard, with an imminent actors' strike as an additional hazard, *The Deep* needed a slew of underwater locations—wrecks, sea gardens, wonders. The wreck was found off the British Virgin Islands, a satisfactory and spectacular wreck near a hotel; sharks, scarce near the main Bermuda locations, were finally tracked to the Great Barrier Reef; a vast underwater set was built to handle scenes of special effects, of tumbling rocks that open a sea chamber where the galleon lies, and it was built in Bermuda. All this had to be managed in open weather and with a studio that had very good reason to resent the slightest overrun on budget.

Guber turned most of the apparent disadvantages into publicity. He converted the making of the film into an adventure story. Eager reporters dived into the underwater set, where all the beauty was real and all the menace made of stainless steel and rubber. Guber himself wrote the story of the movie, with the story of his anxiety at the studio's anxiety, and made it into a paperback. The ballyhoo was remorseless. Having persuaded Columbia to buy the book by a siege, Guber saw it become a gratifying best-seller. With the movie under way, the publicity machine was sleepless. "If it was a disaster," Guber says, "they would have to determine not to see the film, rather than not knowing that it existed.''

It was during the Bermuda filming that Guber talked with an old friend, Neil Bogart, and they considered the merger of their two companies. Bogart had Kiss and a new singer named Donna Summer;

he proposed the link. Guber did not at first want a partner, but as filming went on, he reconsidered. He could organize his life so much more easily and pleasantly if there was a partner to share the running of his corporation. Each partner could concentrate on his music or movies and share the chores. Guber remembered that buzz word of the 1960s business school: there would be "synergy" between the two companies. For the time being, he put the Casablanca name on *The Deep,* had Donna Summer sing the title song, and waited. On the success of the movie hinged the future of Casablanca FilmWorks.

And it succeeded. It cost $8.9 million and earned $126 million at the box office. Until *Close Encounters of the Third Kind,* it was the biggest popular success in Columbia's history. Guber had been involved in the setting up, writing, making, and selling of the movie. The triumph was personal. It did not, however, buy independence. It did bring a new partner in Polygram, the show-business arm of Philips/Siemens, the Dutch and German electronics giant. Polygram had an almost unlimited bankroll and the sophistication to understand the potential risks and rewards in an operation like Casablanca. "They also give the company a totally different kind of financial credibility," Guber says. "When somebody says bring it to Casablanca, they know we can buy projects for ourselves. We can move aggressively to get them filmed."

BILLY HAYES WAS TAKEN to a Turkish jail, convicted of smuggling hashish. He became an example, a political prisoner. His sentence was increased after his trial, as a deterrent to others. Faced with more years in the foul conditions of a criminal prison, he decided to catch the Midnight Express, to break out of prison and cross into Greece and sanctuary. Guber found the story, encouraged the book, and wanted to make the film. Nobody except Guber believed in it.

"Exhibitors didn't take to it," he says. "It had no great media attraction and it had a dour outlook." With *The Deep,* he says, you had to get out of the way because the movie moved with the momentum of a steamroller. With *Midnight Express,* there were doubts if the film would ever roll. "The management of Columbia had begun to change hands again and there was some dissatisfaction at our success. When a former executive is so successful it makes it difficult for the present executives—at least, if they're directly attached to him. Getting films made has all sorts of political and emotional wrinkles." For a start, the production heads of Columbia changed. "There was Stanley Jaffe and then a new head of production came in after him named Dan Melnick, and then he left and David Begelman left and Alan Hirschfield left and Frank Price came in when *Midnight Express* finally came out. It takes a steady hand to steer through all that executive self-interest. I know. I operated on just the same basis when I was an executive."

The movie side of Casablanca FilmWorks kept moving in the meantime with *Thank God It's Friday,* "a kind of visual album," as Guber says, "and not a work of art," which was coproduced with Motown Records. It was a sampler of disco music with adolescent jokes, as inconsequential as a beach party movie but not so stylish. It was a fine, medium success. It was a time-filler before *Midnight Express.*

For the first time Guber was putting himself on the line. "It was," he says, "my total involvement." He had found and nursed the project, and backed it from the start. He hired the director, actors, and musicians without the customary studio interference. He believed in the project. This was not another element in corporate planning, nor an exercise like *The Deep* in establishing his position. This was the whole point of having such a position. And it appeared, at first, unsalable. Guber had to use every resource of his business background. He had, most of all, to market the idea and movie. He devised the scheme of taking the film to the Cannes Film Festival and selling it there, hard, before repeating the operation in Britain, and only then would he take the movie, trailing wisps of European glory, to America. He controlled the book; he could arrange the mass marketing of the paperback three months before the movie reached the United States. He organized promotional tours by the victim-author of the book, Billy Hayes, to establish some degree of "truth" and "authenticity," at least enough to make the movie separate from the directly fictional stories about the horror of doing time. He organized campus screenings. There were special tests for the logo, a

careful choice of disco composer for the score, television advertisements that managed to show no violence and failed to mention drugs,
but "showed the energy and the excitement." It was a model, ingenious campaign that depended on one man's passionate concern
for the movie. It worked. *Midnight Express* walked away with the
major Golden Globe Awards given by the Hollywood press corps.

It seemed that Guber had his life organized. At least, the figures
said so. Three movies earned, between them, $105 million for Co-
lumbia. At the box office, *Midnight Express* in its first release took
in $60 million, *Thank God It's Friday* took in $25 million, and *The
Deep* topped with $125 million. Guber was hot. Casablanca was
hot. Guber could decide what projects did and did not interest him,
work forever in the Sunbelt and the Caribbean if it suited him,
worry no more about paying the rent. It was a sort of independence;
yet more profoundly it was dependence. The goodwill of Philips/
Siemens provided the necessary capital base. The interest of major
studios made the movies. The corporate states determined finally the
work that Guber would be allowed to do, although for the moment
the decisions all lay with him. He had abandoned the politicking inside those corporations for a treaty with them, a life-style where his
role as client and dependent was less oppressive primarily because
he could make the decisions that he wanted. He compromised in
order to be as free as the corporations allow.

IN ALL THAT TIME, he says, there were three moments when he was
really excited. There was the moment when he dived for the first time
and saw beneath ninety feet of water three stars and thirty-seven
people filming a scene from a movie. The second time was "being
scared shitless when the movie was shown for the first time to an
audience that had paid . . . I could feel my fingers tingle. I could
hardly move. And the third time was after the Golden Globes, when
somebody had said to me you've done a good job on *Midnight
Express.*"

He looks around his chrome and glass office, a few hundred yards
from the Columbia block where he was once executive.

"It has," he says, "been interesting."

6

TREVOR NUNN:
NATIONAL TRUST

THE TOWN IS SMALL and neat and low, modeled for a market and not the cult that it contains. The bookshops have an excess of Jacobean drama; the tea shops are more numerous than you would expect in the usual English market town; the property dealers last century offered two different birthplaces for the town's poet. The streets silt up in summer with alien buses, gaudy and loud. Down by the river, past the weir, by the swans quarreling barbarously on the soft waters and the formal gardens fire-red with civic salvias, is the squat form of the theater. It is the remarkable product of the nineteenth-century cult of Shakespeare, the rediscovery of the English lyric tradition and of the big, imperious gesture from the stage, and of the twentieth-century continuation of that enthusiasm, a duty that followed a cult. It could easily be a deadly enthusiasm, a polite recognition of one safe, known name among the English dramatists who can be honored to the continual profit of the burghers of his birthplace, Stratford-upon-Avon. It is something quite different. Stratford is the center of the largest single theatrical organization in the Western world.

The Shakespeare cult had two direct products: a theater designed to present the work of the poet, in the manner of the 1920s, with very exact attention paid to acoustics and less to sight lines, and a proscenium arch behind which the action lay; and at the same time, a cult so strong that it provided an economic base for the work in that theater to be ambitious and strong. With the help of the Flower family, members of the English beerage who have a tradition of putting the profits from ale into assorted cultural activities, and the inspiration of a succession of Shakespearean actor-scholars, Stratford became a center to which the theater itself attracted visitors. It was at first an accident, and then, after years of success, it became an institution. Tourists and schoolchildren kept it alive. Its name and companies toured the world. It acquired glamour as well as respectability.

Under Peter Hall, it became something more. In the early 1960s, Hall put into practice an idea that had galvanized a sagging British theater. It was the idea of an ensemble, a company that would work together often, on different projects continuously over years, in order to create a shared style, approach, and method. The style would be capable of variation, depending on director, text, and company members, but there would be a fundamental unity of purpose. In the argument for the ensemble, there were always two European examples: the Comédie Française, because Paris gave a public subsidy for a company to live and work together over years, to train newcomers in an approach to classic drama that might sometimes appear restrictive and absurd (the Comédie's lead actors are notorious for moving downstage for great speeches, irrespective of dramatic logic, and facing the audience even at moments when their director had them mangled, dying, bloody, and writhing on the floor), but that provides an essential framework of conventions for approaching otherwise impossibly difficult or elusive texts; and the Berliner Ensemble and the Brechtian tradition, the much more obviously fashionable and influential leader of the idea of an ensemble. Between Paris mechanism and Brechtian device, there was born the Royal Shakespeare Company. To make a range of work possible, and to give the company a proper base for recruiting, the idea of ensemble came to involve a London base. Once RSC had two theaters, it would come in time to need two more—small houses in London and Stratford for more intimate studio work, for smaller-scale productions, or for experiment. With four theaters, four parts of a single company roughly divided into the Stratford players and the London players, RSC needed public money, and never got enough. To make ends meet, the company went out to the West End of London and Broadway. There was *London Assurance, Sherlock Holmes, Wild Oats,* and other great recoveries from theatrical history; there was *Travesties* by Tom Stoppard as a modern work, and occasionally Shakespearean productions, like Peter Brook's production of *A Midsummer Night's Dream,* which went touring the world. Between its national and its international tours and its four theaters, the RSC became a huge machine for making theater, which needed the animation of a leader. It also needed public funds, for which that leader had to arrange, and a degree of public success in commercial theaters to supplement those funds. For all that, for being diplomat and impresario, fairground barker and Shakespearean scholar, RSC required a chief executive and an artistic director. His central problem is always to balance cash and conscience, to maintain the excellence that makes the company worth preserving and the cash flow that ensures its immediate survival.

Trevor Nunn took the job when he was twenty-eight. He is a quiet, unpretentious man, loved within the company. He worked fiercely, but tried always to remain accessible, open, and a democrat. Unlike the model of what any mogul should be, he was modest and retiring, and yet he had the double duties of an institution's keeper and a theatrical impresario. He is now an operator within a corporate structure at least as impressive and solid as that of Columbia Pictures once seemed for Peter Guber, or Polygram is for Guber now. The structure has the added dimension of political activity; in effect, it is possible to appeal to the government for the cash to stage a show. Whitehall is the ultimate banker. Meanwhile, like any mogul, Nunn has to concern himself with the audience and keeping it.

It is a treacherous, demanding business. Trevor Nunn came to it through other people's ambition.

"MY EARLIEST MEMORIES ARE THEATRICAL," Nunn says. "There is a family legend that I announced I wanted to be an actor before

I was five.'' He was born in Ipswich, an East Anglian town where his father was a cabinetmaker. He grew up in the war years when everyone seemed to have a role pinned on them like a badge. Nunn decided that he wanted the role of An Actor. It never seemed likely that he would get it.

He lived down a neat, small street, where everyone was working class. In rural Britain that has an exact force. Nobody was expected to escape this street. At the age of eleven, all children took an examination that decided whether they should go to the grammar schools, which taught academic subjects, or the secondary moderns, which taught some technical subjects and let most of their children go at fifteen. Nunn did well. He went to grammar school. The street never forgave him. ''It was unthinkable that one should go across to that middle-class establishment and join the enemy,'' Nunn says. ''For seven or eight years I had to run the gauntlet of stones being thrown at me, being knocked off my bike, the uniform spat at. The class distinction was very noticeably there.'' Going to university was impossibly exotic; becoming an actor was hardly more so. Nunn talked of both. ''It was sort of understood,'' he says, ''that whatever I did, I was going to decide for myself.

''I went to the theater for the first time expecting to be at home there.'' He smelled plush at the Christmas pantomime and made dramatic readings for his Wolf Cub groups. He remembered the sound of a thin theater orchestra scraping in the pit and had a brief, professional glory at the local theater in a small, boy's part. Before going to Cambridge, he was a schoolmaster for a while and formed a local drama society. His love led to ambition.

He produced *Hamlet*. ''A ludicrous piece of work really,'' he says, ''which lasted almost five hours. It was Wagnerian; a great deal of the effects came from a Gramophone playing extracts from *Tannhäuser*. The costumes were all from the Bayeux Tapestry. I wanted dark, winged creatures wielding axes, all viciously and violently brooding around each other. We built a platform out into the audience and that space was only used by Hamlet for the soliloquies. While that was an impossibly overdemonstrative idea, it did mean the actor had to share the soliloquy with the audience. It was impossible for him to think he was just brooding aloud."

By the time he was at university, he had discovered the job of director as well as the role of actor. "I was thinking," he says, "that it would be nice to have a career as an actor-manager. Of course, I would still be the leading actor on occasions. For my generation, the model was always Olivier."

His theatrical passion was tempered by academic ideas. He wanted to be a pupil of F. R. Leavis, to tackle what Leavis saw as the moral dimension of work, writing, and drama. "He made me insist," Nunn says, "that once I started to work in the professional theater I was performing a serious function." Leavis was vigorous and puritanical, an outsider in Cambridge despite his dedicated, even fanatical, following. He was a teacher, a lecturer in isolation, without university recognition. His isolation gave a dramatic quality to his talk of absolutes. "In any case," Nunn says, "I find the idea of absolutes congenial." Out of this deep seriousness came, in time, Nunn's own idea of a political, philosophic, and critical community within the company of RSC. He once called the company, in a letter to the *Times,* "a left-wing organization," a remark that mortally offended a drab selection of Conservative MPs. He tended to attract coworkers who shared his assumptions, if not necessarily his prejudices; RSC took positions that might seem simplistic, but actually required some courage from a subsidized company. They were possible, in large part, because they were so obviously an organic part of the company. "We do share beliefs," Nunn says. "I think I can say to my colleagues—'This is so, isn't it?' and they are all going to say, 'Yes, but. . . .' At the point where they say, 'Absolutely not,' we're in trouble."

George Rylands, grand and exotic in his rooms above a college archway which his private fortune had restored, was a balancing influence. Leavis was caricatured in open-neck shirts, rope sandals, a self-denying ordinance of cord trousers and morality. Rylands was a sensualist in some ways, and a luxurious man. He invented, for John Gielgud, the reading program, *The Seven Ages of Man,* and directed Gielgud's first *Hamlet*. His Cambridge base was the Marlowe Society, anonymous undergraduates who presented, under anonymous direction, classically exact performances of the text of plays that were usually Elizabethan or Jacobean. "I was in the first production I could be in," Nunn remembers, "playing first gentleman in *Cymbeline,* which is a part that blazes up and is over by the end of Scene two." He watched Rylands at rehearsal, back to the cast, a tiny New Temple Shakespeare clutched in his hand like a score. "It was important," Nunn says, "understanding just how vital the text was. But it was shocking also. Rylands's methods never seemed to me the way to achieve the end."

Cambridge had another gift besides the rigorous and clashing influences of Leavis and Rylands. It had the ADC. Unlike other British universities, it had a theater operated by undergraduates, managed by undergraduates, presenting undergraduate productions. Its final authority was a remote and benevolent senior member of the university. The ADC never stopped to think that it might not be in direct competition with the professional stage. Its output was extraordinary, given the academic commitments that its members, in theory, had to honor. Nunn was involved in thirty-two productions in three years, was solely responsible for twenty, and found the theater "a little like being in a weekly rep" with a change of show every seven days. "I wanted to go on being directed and feeling dissatisfied," he says. "That's a wonderful experience—to be a gripey actor not getting the goods." But more and more he became director and entrepreneur. He managed a Marlowe Society tour of 2,000-seaters through provincial England. He was part of the first Cambridge company to go north to the late-summer festival in Edinburgh.

"Since we understood some of the excitement of getting a touring company together," he says, "a group of us decided we should go to Edinburgh. It was the end of the term when we all had to take finals, and we had all written to a number of theater companies to tell them we wanted jobs." They glowed with Cambridge. "It was a bit of a hothouse," Nunn says, "and there was a sense that it had to be watched. It might be a good thing to give jobs to people who had been influential there.'' The partners went to Edinburgh and waited, expectantly.

ONE STILL SUMMER AFTERNOON in Cambridge, Nunn had been at a loose end. It was 1960. He happened to drift past the Senate House, the academic fulcrum of the university, and he heard the trail of a speaker's voice on the lazy air, followed by laughter. He decided to listen.

"I saw a round-faced young man, unexpectedly young for a Cambridge lecturer, and I saw George Rylands on the platform, and I sidled in. It was Peter Hall talking about his Stratford plans.'' Hall had just moved to Stratford as its director. He was bright, persuasive, son of an East Anglian working-class family like Nunn and a brilliant success at Cambridge. He had soared unimaginably in the stolid establishment of British classical theater. He had articulated his dream of a company like the Comédie Française or the Berliner Ensemble. "He was dreaming,'' Nunn remembers, "of being able to harness those organizational ideas with our Shakespearean tradition.''

It was a passionate vision. It seemed impossibly remote. "I had prepared for a life in a theater of high seriousness,'' Nunn reports. But in Edinburgh, during that festival, he had a telephone call from a bleak Midlands car town called Coventry, from Anthony Richardson of the Belgrade Theater there. It was his job offer. Instead of Hall's vision of a grand company, or Rylands's magical attention to text, or the moral hauteur of a Leavis, Nunn had another lesson to learn. "What happened next was two years in a theater concentrating on survival.''

Richardson worried whether Nunn could direct farce, was not sure Nunn was quite the man he needed, took him on for only two productions, and told him to find some way to subsidize his stay. Nunn succeeded, with a television company's scholarship. "Richardson was not a healthy man,'' Nunn says. "After two or three months, I did my first production. I did ten productions in the first year, and at the end of the first year, I was taken on as resident producer and did another ten productions—at the end of which I had a nervous breakdown.

"I'd done rarefied academic work in Cambridge, and now I was in three-weekly rep, having to stay alive. We did new texts mostly—either London successes into their period of repertory release, so every other rep in the country was doing them at the same time, or else formula three-act comedies with a cast of ten. Occasionally I had to take over productions which weren't always planned ahead as much as they should have been. In a way, those years at Coventry were stultifying."

Nunn's luck lay in distance. Stratford and Coventry are barely fifteen miles apart. "I was," Nunn says, "very fortunate. Peter Hall came over to see my work. There can't have been many evenings when he was free and even fewer when he felt like going to a theater that was not his own. But he came, and during one production, *Caucasian Chalk Circle,* he asked if I would be interested in coming across to Stratford as an assistant.

"It was flattering and it was impracticable. I had quite a few months of my traineeship to run. Besides I knew I was going to do a lot of productions at Coventry and that seemed better than working as an assistant in a huge organization. Still, towards the end of my two years, we arranged another meeting. This sounds corny, but I think the important thing that changed was that we became very good friends. There was a sympathy I didn't dare acknowledge. But I certainly felt it."

So it was that Trevor Nunn joined the Royal Shakespeare Company. The apprenticeship, in ambition, scholarship, and survival, was over. The trials began.

"MY WORK," Nunn says, "was very bad indeed. Peter simply had to be my friend." His first year with RSC could hardly have been less auspicious. Around him, productions folded and actors lost confidence. He was a junior collaborator on the company's massive Shakespearean productions. "They were a fine education, but they were not my own work. I began to feel like a message carrier.

"Then I was supposed to do a musical based on the General Strike of 1926. The actors and me parted company after two weeks. I was overawed by their stature and I lacked the confidence to tell them it would all come out all right. Everything was catastrophic. I didn't understand why Peter Hall didn't say: 'Well, we tried. And now you can go away. . . .' At the end of that year, he made his final throw, which was *Baron Bolligrew,* a children's play by Robert Bolt, and at last I did something which was successful—very, very successful. Then I did *Tango,* by Mrożek, which finally extinguished any flame of hope that I was going to be one of England's leading actors. And then came *Revenger's Tragedy.*"

It dazzled. The text is a Jacobean companion to *Hamlet,* a ferocious series of murders and passions. Nunn made them matter with a drive that was impossible to fake. He set them within a world of black and white, silver and silk, glittering and appalling. It was his debut on the Stratford stage and it made his reputation. It was also an economic accident.

"It was another RSC crisis year," Nunn remembers, "and we had absolutely no money. We had to do revivals for the most part. The only new production planned for certain was Clifford Williams's *Twelfth Night,* and that was meant to pay off at the box office. But right from the beginning of the year, Peter said there would be another production 'to be announced.' He made it into a mystery show. He had to. He knew that halfway through the year he might just have to drop the show discreetly. What he could not afford to do was to announce the production and then cancel it.

"Halfway through the year he told me: 'There's a slot. You're going to do it, but you have to do it within one of the existing sets. I can just about afford a set of costumes.' " It was a brave move, since much of the established company was deeply suspicious of a newcomer whose work seemed so often to turn to dust. "I think the bravest thing that Peter did was to insist that I was formally made an assistant director, six months after I joined. Although I did nothing except make wreckage, he kept to that date. And when it came to *Revenger's Tragedy,* I knew the conditions were right. This time, I chose the play. I knew why I wanted to do it. I was able to cast it myself. The junior members of the company were interested in the idea.'' The only point of dissatisfaction in its success, mounted on the set for *Hamlet* in costumes that had literally been built on the actors' backs for lack of time and money, was the length of time the production took to enter the London repertoire at the Aldwych Theatre. It was two years before its London triumph.

While he worked on productions, Nunn was also encouraged to absorb the business of the company. From the middle of 1965, in his role as an associate director, he was attending the planning committee meetings, ''sitting at the back,'' he says, ''and not making any memorable contributions, but picking up the structure of the company and Peter's relationship with the company. I felt like an observer. I was fascinated by the way he operated. We had taken a number of shocks and blows; the Arts Council were not coming up with the government money that was required; there was a feeling that there should be greater democratization; and we had to agree our next phase of work unanimously. So we discussed doing a new play by Harold Pinter, and after three hours of discussion the vote was seventeen against and one for, and the only person voting for the play was Peter. He simply turned and said: 'I register your view. I know exactly what you feel as a committee. You'll just have to bite your tongues, because we're doing it.' And,'' Nunn remembers, ''everybody in that room responded to him.'' The play was Pinter's masterpiece: *The Homecoming*.

Hall was businessman, impresario, diplomat, politician, and director; and it hurt. ''It is a very nervously draining task,'' Nunn says, ''and he took every decision. It was 1967 and we had a very full year, I remember. We were operating two companies in Stratford, one of which was to be peripatetic and eventually go to America. There were big organizational problems.

''Halfway through work on *Macbeth*, Peter's health collapsed again. He got shingles.'' He also had awkward obligations. RSC had contracted to make a movie, and Hall had hoped to make *Macbeth* with Paul Scofield, who did not want to do the film; so Hall swiftly assembled a rather limp version of *A Midsummer Night's Dream*, tricked out in a patronizing scatter of Carnaby Street mannerisms. The film was brisk; the shooting schedule was only six weeks; it proved a long and vital absence for Hall. "He was away just long enough to feel he had got away," Nunn says. "He felt he couldn't come back."

For weeks Nunn and the other members of the company tried painstakingly to persuade Hall to stay at Stratford. Not only was he the creator of the ensemble idea, but he had been the architect of the company's move and expansion to London. It was Hall who had produced the first government check to subsidize the company, and he was the man responsible for making the RSC a highly well-known, visibly successful organization. "I had two meetings with him," Nunn says. "I really thought I had persuaded him to drop notions of a hasty departure." Hall was identified with the company. It was unthinkable that he should go. Without him, nobody knew what the RSC would become.

"He called me to his house on Buckingham Street, down by the Thames. I thought we were there to talk about productions and we weren't. He said he had decided to leave and he wanted to know if I was prepared to take the job. I said no. He said: 'Think about it.' I thought for a while, and he said: 'You're right to say no if you don't want to make it yours. But if you want to change it and fashion it, then say yes.'

"All these things end perversely. In the end I said yes because I didn't want to change it at all. I wanted to continue it."

"I DIDN'T KNOW THE ADDRESS of the Arts Council," Nunn says. Ten days after his London meetings with Hall, he was before a company meeting in Stratford, being announced as the new director. There was surprise and, spontaneously, there was applause. Nunn was, after all, the actors' friend, the democrat. He spoke of "running the company from among the actors, as it should be." Administration was handed over to an administrative director. Nunn would be artistic director, chief executive, ultimate taker of responsibility, but he would at least sidestep Hall's title of managing director.

"It was paralyzing," Nunn says. "I reckoned I had just about learned how to run a rehearsal at the point where I took over the company. I don't think it was in Peter's mind six months before he left, not who was going to take over. The succession was a very well-kept secret.'' Nunn was convinced that he was simply keeping Hall's job open for a couple of years. It was understood that Hall would stay on, quietly, for some six months while the transition was organized.

Hall was wiser. Having anointed his successor, he left on fortnight's holiday and never returned. Nunn was in control of the Royal Shakespeare Company.

Trevor Nunn had stood, boyish, pale, and shy, before the company meeting and resigned himself to the power that he now possessed. The questions were frequent and complicated. The central one was this: what sort of institution was the Royal Shakespeare Company, and how could Nunn engineer the conditions and the cash that would be needed for the institution to survive? The solutions were not at all obvious. Hall had been able to carry off his own bombastic style, and his success in doing so had shielded the company from the need for answers. Now, Nunn had to find them.

He found a national institution that had become, as the largest and most ambitious publicly subsidized theater company in Britain, a de facto national theater before Britain had either company or building to bear that name. That was the scale of Hall's achievement. But it had been expensive. Up until now, Nunn had worked with the idea of company and ensemble and had handled the immediate tensions but not the problems of structure which Hall's ideas posed. He was confronted with a version of the company's history rather different from the ideals he had heard Hall discussing in the Senate House.

Stratford had been a lovely eccentricity, the enthusiasm of the beerage. With charitable support, and box-office success, the theater had established itself, but it had been a knife-edge operation. Between 1945 and 1960, when Peter Hall took over, it had ended each year with a tiny deficit or a tiny surplus. Bill Wilkinson, finance director of RSC, explains: ''Had there not been overseas tours, or profitable forays into the West End of London with stars like Olivier in the lead, it is doubtful whether Stratford in the long run would have kept its head above water.'' Each year, the company's assets—gifts of property, endowments of shares—had to be raided for a little help in the accounts. The theater's independence became more precarious with each raid. Tours that trailed glory through Europe and Australia were also draining the home theater of a company's loyalty. Stratford aspired to a particular excellence, but the cost was high.

In 1960, Peter Hall had arrived and with him the idea of Stratford as a marginal, worthy theater in the Midlands was exploded. The London showcase for Stratford productions had long been a dream; now, the theater's director was saying that it was an artistic necessity. The troubles were as much structural as financial. To build an ensemble meant offering three-year contracts. Such contracts were new in Britain, and viewed with some suspicion. Actors would not take easily to an exile in Stratford. It is seventy miles from the television studios of London, where the new commercial television companies, rivals to the BBC, were spending high on drama. Rustic exile meant invisibility and isolation from work. It denied the actor's need to be seen by the people who might provide his or her next job. If the company members had families, they had probably made their homes in or near London, since that is the center of television, film, and theater work in Britain. The Stratford move meant resettling families or the dour grind of commuting. The ensemble idea was enticing, but RSC could never pay enough to compensate for the troubles of Stratford life.

The only solution was for the company to have a permanent showcase in London. That, at least, would give actors the exposure, the contacts, and the work they would need. It also served a less pragmatic end. At Stratford, there was little choice about repertory. What filled the theater during the summer was a diet of Shakespeare and nothing else. Yet a company working together needed variety, range, and choice which could all be provided in London. "The reasons were very largely artistic," Wilkinson says. "To remain a company of substance, you couldn't just sit on your bottom in Stratford."

Logic led to two theaters, and aspirations led to a crushing need for money. Box-office earnings were limited by the capacity of the houses and the price the market should be asked to bear. Stratford is an almost absurdly successful theater, consistenly playing to audiences that fill on the average 96 percent of the seats; the record is better than most Broadway musicals during their public honeymoons. In London, with more competition and less surefire product, houses average in the mid to upper 70 percent. "We cost more than other dramatic theaters," Wilkinson says, "but we try not to price ourselves into the rich-only market." Public institutions have some duties to students, schoolchildren, and the community, which high seat prices might prevent. Size of house and the politics of price limit what the company can earn. The need to keep theaters clean, warm, and full of actors and scenery determines what the company has to spend, before the budgets for individual productions. The basic balance sheet is virtually immutable.

It works like this. "Given that we run two theaters," says Wilkinson, "and given that we run in repertoire—alternating different shows night by night and week by week rather than allowing one production to run until it runs out of audience—we have the cornerstones of the whole operation. Now, given the cost of having two buildings, one in the West End of London and the other an enormous complex in Stratford, of which we own the freehold and are therefore responsible for the bricks and the mortar, and given the licensing requirements for public safety and the basic union rates which you have to pay, it's not difficult to put on paper what it costs to keep those two theaters sufficiently staffed to let the public in. And the fact is that just the backup staff absorb our capacity to earn money at our own box office.

"You know how many bodies you need to operate backstage, given you're playing repertory and changing sets all the time. There have to be fifteen stagehands and eight electricians at the Aldwych in London. Below that, you simply can't do the job. You have the same number at Stratford. If you're going to manufacture your own sets and costumes to keep costs down, then there are a number of bodies you must employ in order to cut, plane, and saw, and cut and sew cloth. You need a minimum administrative staff. There are seventy people front of house at Stratford when you count all the cleaners and bar staff and so forth. At the Aldwych we don't technically employ them all because we lease the building, but there are about fifty, including dressers to help the actors. Now that is all before we've paid any actor or designer or built a set or made a costume.

"We need a minimum company of between thirty-five and fifty actors at Stratford, because we have a charter which says that we do the plays of William Shakespeare, and we have to have the actors to fill the parts to do the plays. We pay the actors a small fraction of what they could earn on the commercial stage—in the early 1970s, we paid a top salary of £100 a week, though sometimes we would try to go beyond that, while an Alec Guinness or a Michael Redgrave could easily earn £700 in the West End. Actors used to come to us and ask how in hell they were expected to pay last year's tax bill on the money we could offer."

The company had reserves and property in Stratford, but they could not keep the theaters open forever. By 1963, it was obvious that the survival of theater, company, and ideal was at stake. Having reached the limits of what the box office could do, Stratford needed subsidy.

It came first as emergency money for the 1963–64 season, a check for £47,000 written by a Conservative government. The check was a revolution. Museums and art galleries had always been supported by public money, but theaters were different. They were live, awkward, vital, and hard to discipline; British official philistinism was suspicious of them. Not every town had one, and the theaters stayed put; public subsidy offered some communities advantages over others, which means public growling from public figures that one town had to pay for the theatrical pleasures of another. Theater involved ideas of which any form of politician might, for advantage, disapprove. He might attack the Leftist tendency of a production of *Coriolanus*, a flash of bosom in *Antony and Cleopatra*, the racism of *Othello*. Objections, however absurd, became a serious factor when the men who make them vote the funds for a company to continue. Moreover, theater was a minority taste and the British lack a tradition of preserving and developing the arts. To back Stratford meant accept-

213

ing a public duty to the theater that had not been articulated before. To change and make a precedent usually offends the mind of the civil servant. Stratford was lucky to get its check. When it arrived, it was not enough. Never since the first payment has the government subsidy paid for the difference between income and expenditure for providing live theater in the United Kingdom. Stratford has leeched its reserves, year by year.

By 1966, the principle of subsidy to the arts had been won, although the new, bright Arts Council depended on a stringently managed grant from the all-powerful Treasury. The council promised a "platform of support" for the Royal Shakespeare Company. "They rapidly added," says Bill Wilkinson, "that they hadn't a cat in hell's chance of actually giving it to us."

The subsidy started a deadly game: the theater played to survive. Peter Hall, and now his successor, Trevor Nunn, had to balance their tricky negotiations with government, civil servants, and the Treasury against their own commercial instincts and their duty as a national treasury of theater. It was delicate, difficult, sometimes almost fatal. The risk was actually higher than that of the usual mogul. There was nowhere to lay it off. There was no way to go out of production for a while if that seemed sound strategy. If productions failed, actors, staff, and theaters could not simply be released. For a David Merrick, a flop means a loss to investors and a return to his small, tight office. For a Trevor Nunn, it puts the future of the huge apparatus of his company and theaters at risk. "If we get it wrong by five percent," Nunn says, "we are out of business."

In addition, the RSC is paid to do what it has always done— Shakespeare with excellence. It is inflexible. It is at once industry and museum, and neither is its true nature. It needs to be consistently right in its commercial decisions, otherwise the budget will break and the continuity will end. It needs to be consistently excellent because that is the point of the company. It has peculiar duties to the text of Shakespeare and to the English tradition of handling blank verse on stage. David Brierley, general manager of the Royal Shakespeare Theatre, says: "We are in a high-risk industry, and we're no different from anybody else. There's nothing surefire about even a Stratford season, economically. It's true that life at RSC has something in common with collegiate life—spending your whole working day in one place, with people who come from all over Britain to be here. But for Trevor, the duties are different. He has to be the impresario with the cigar. That is his fundamental obligation.''

THE 5 PERCENT OBLIGATION, the margin of error that determines the company's survival, now lay squarely with Nunn. He was known to be lovable, approachable, and modest. He was not known as a promoter or politician. Peter Hall had been a club sort, sharp, suave, a man for dinner tables with senior politicians. He had a film-star wife in Leslie Caron, and a minor mansion near Stratford. Nunn lived, determinedly, over a fish and chip shop and had a shy, sometimes bloodless manner in public. "With Hall, you got to see his secretary," one company member says. "With Trevor, you get to see him." He was a company favorite—"a sprite," Peggy Ashcroft says—but he could not run an institution on love alone. He was twenty-eight and untried when he took over the company. Some senior company members did not expect him to succeed.

He hated crowds, hated addressing thick ranks of people. Mass meetings were for form's sake; individual meetings always followed them. He did not domineer or impose, as Hall had sometimes done. Instead, "he works by a process of injecting his own ideas into a general debate and drawing from other people's most vigorous ideas," David Brierley says. "He finds their strengths and commitments and matches that to everybody else." His shyness worked against his obligation to beat the drum for the company; he still feels that he has not done enough to maintain that peculiarly high definition required from the company if it is to command the resources that its work needs. His wife, the actress Janet Suzman, says that in public Nunn is "a dampened Trevor, a careful Trevor, a sort of umming, erring public Trevor. But when he is in sneakers in the rehearsal room he's got none of those burdens. They fly away from him. He becomes the real Trevor Nunn.''

Directing plays became a kind of refuge from harsher realities. Nunn had to compromise. He could not administer, direct, and at the same time be totally democratic. He would have to tell tired companies to stay out on the road to save the theater. He would have to learn savage little arts and deal with the Treasury mandarins as much as green room revolts. He had to train himself as mogul.

Although Nunn protested that he was not cut out to be an administrator, he still had to take on that responsibility. His idea of being always available corroded. He also grew under the pressure. "Much can be resolved at a local level," David Brierley says. "But anybody who is distraught, terribly upset, or who is worried about his career and wants to talk authoritatively to that influence which is the greatest—well, he or she is going to want to talk to Trevor himself. That's an enormous number of reporting interests. In the early 1970s, even, I think he would have flaked out under all that, but he's acquired an extraordinary resilience."

At its worst, the gap between his ambitions for democracy and his job as autocrat brought furious, frustrated tears. In one season he directed six Shakespearean Roman plays at Stratford. The productions were glossy and not uniformly successful; they tended to be CinemaScope theater. Nor did the idea of the season finally cohere; between the barbarian world of *Titus Andronicus* and the courtly metaphors and complex politics of *Julius Caesar* there was a yawning gap. With six productions to prepare, and the whole fate of the Stratford season dependent on him, Nunn neglected the more general interests of the company. He had no choice. The atmosphere turned sour. His ambitious season, failing to match its ambitious plan, began to seem an egotistic indulgence. The company sympathy drained away. The coldness was brief but ugly. One night Nunn would be at the theater all night; the next day he would try to rehearse; the next night he would again be talking, watching, or negotiating. "I couldn't really stay awake," he says. "I came up to my office and I fell asleep on the sofa and I was woken at one o'clock and I couldn't stand anymore. I could not be got to stand. I got more and more upset because I couldn't. . . . The frustration just became endless tears."

216

Yet the company needs a man who does not show weakness. He is the figurehead, the father. He must not be seen to have flaws. Nunn takes responsibility for the complex chemistry of the company. At the start of each season, the company rehearses for ten to twelve weeks. It is a long time, but not indulgent. It is essential that company members learn, from working together, how the others walk, talk, and react. Judi Dench, long a member of RSC, says: "It's not like a family, because it is not as comfortable as a family."

His popularity had rested on his work as director. In rehearsal he is open, funny. "In *Macbeth*," says Judi Dench, who played Lady Macbeth in Nunn's studio production, "we almost died laughing." He works from simple, elegant acting exercises that encapsulate emotion. In *The Winter's Tale,* Dench complains, "you have to be jealous within two pages. So for three or four days he told us—it's a warm beach. He had the three main players lie down, with me in the middle. Now when you're lying in the middle, your head has to turn one way or the other. The third person always feels a touch left out." Out of that exercise, Nunn simply and precisely established the relationships he needed for the play. In *Macbeth* he insisted the company listen for the noises that a castle night would hold. He arrived with no grand ideas beyond the idea of a circle within which the action would unfold. "It all grew from that," Dench says. "He is very adaptable; he gets you to do something by suggesting and making it seem to come from you. He makes me feel I could go on inventing things out of the air. But he is very businesslike at the same time, businesslike and meticulous. I have been persuaded by other directors but not convinced. Trevor is convincing."

He has had to trade on his power to convince and on the company's affection. Peter Brook's remaking of *A Midsummer Night's Dream* into a glorious circus celebration, a feast of life, was a company triumph and a commercial asset. It went around the world, first to New York under David Merrick's management and then beyond. It stayed on the road for more than a year, trailing a company who had to recover their joy and enthusiasm each night. It was painful but necessary because the company was on the brink of what Bill Wilkinson diagnosed as a "thundering deficit." The more visible RSC is on Broadway and in the West End of London, the more likely it is to be suffering a financial seizure. *Dream* went touring, with all its cruel demands on emotional and physical resources, to keep the company alive.

The company revolted. The show was too hard, too demanding. They saw no way to keep the necessary life in it. Some had been with the show for a year or more, and were exhausted. Nunn, along with other managers of the RSC, had to meet with the company and explain. If they did not go on, the whole operation was at risk. The 5 percent margin was at stake. The company rebuilt their loyalty quickly, largely through Nunn's persuasion. They went on, according to the company manager, "to have every experience known to actors, and I can't think what they were complaining about. God, we even cured their pox in America." The tour paid off. Without it, Bill Wilkinson says, "at this remove of time, I don't know what we would have done."

The transfers make money, but they do direct damage. When a successful production is taken to a commercial theater, that part of the company becomes a separate unit, working by itself. In London or New York, it is easy for the actors and actresses to drift apart from the Royal Shakespeare Company and the ensemble from which they come. The lead players are now the stars with names above the title. They set the tone for the company. If they take the trouble and come early to the theater and stay in touch with the others, the company may keep its feeling of company. "You don't really have much choice about a transfer," Judi Dench says. "It's nice to be in a success, but it is always completely different from being at the Aldwych or at Stratford."

Sometimes the damage is to reputation. In London, RSC revived, wittily, William Gillette's stage version of *Sherlock Holmes*. In New York, the show launched John Wood on an American theatrical career. Then it left Broadway, and the trouble started. "We had control while the original Broadway cast was in it," David Brierley says, "which was twenty weeks, and we had reasonable control while John Wood was still in it. But then we were separated from it by other commitments. It ended up in a road tour around major cities as a travesty of itself. We didn't keep quality control, and we were desperately upset by what happened. It was very beneficial financially, but we believed the revenue was offset in some places by the bad Press . . . immediate cash, but immeasurable damage. It will not happen again.''

Disputes between British and American Equity, the actors' unions, began later to cut into RSC's ability to earn abroad. The figures, however, still showed how important to the company's survival was the ability of Nunn as impresario, as commercial man. In 1975, the bleakest year in recent RSC history, RSC tours produced an income of $1,631,000—more than the grant the British government provided.

"I HAVE ONE OR TWO MEETINGS, not to say confrontations with the Arts Council every year,'' Nunn says. The contact makes the money come; it is like a sympathetic magic. It also involves another layer of complexity in acting as mogul to the State, for the Royal Shakespeare Company, as well as being a living and breathing theatrical company, is also a royal corporation and a charitable body. It has the structure of an ancient charity.

At the top are the governors, self-elected and self-perpetuating, successors to the original enthusiasts who founded the theater, and still including a member of the Flower family who started it all. The governors form a council; the council forms a finance committee. On that committee, the one that meets most regularly with the theater's management, are the chief executive of a university press, the vice-chancellor of a university, and the senior partner of the largest firm of liquidating accountants in London. The chairman is the vital link. It is he who takes the message from the management and, if he approves it, lobbies discreetly among the more active governors before their twice yearly meetings. The governors can intervene; faced with the need for one dramatic cut, they once dismantled a touring theater operation called Theater-Go-Round. They can create occasional incidents; when Nunn declared RSC publicly a "Left-wing organization," a minor Conservative MP scuttled from the board, trailing dust and recriminations. Usually, though, the governors run like boards of directors—through their committees—and the committees deal most directly with, and most reflect, the influence of the management.

Governors approve or veto plans. They do not originate them. That function lies with the planning committee—associate directors, music director, dramaturg ("when we have one with a separate identity"), senior artists, and senior administrators. "They turn artistic initiatives into what we actually do," David Brierley explains. They meet either in the large, open poster-splashed office that Nunn maintains above the theater in London, or else wherever there is a large room; governors have met in the plush dress circle foyer at Stratford, by contrast, or else in the grandeur of the London Mansion House. Meetings have agendas, but the talk is not recorded. Often, discussion is about options rather than specific decisions. "We like to seem collaborative," Brierley says, "but we don't get there without considerable internal pressures—people not understanding why their lives should be affected by something happening a long way away."

The planners make up a forum, where directors may sometimes stick each other with sharp points. The committee is where the company's internal politics are articulated. Talk can be hot and cruel. RSC always appears to outsiders rather certain, rather smug, as though there could be no dissension inside. There is such dissension, and the planning committee is its main home.

The planners have yet another superior in the hierarchy—the Direction. Trevor Nunn is part of it, along with Peter Brook, Terry Hands, John Barton, and Dame Peggy Ashcroft. It meets only when needed and has no formal structure. It acts as conscience to the company, "high caliber reactors." It puts on paper a little network of friendship and professional respect. Only at this senior level of the company are actors represented.

The last flaw in the RSC democracy is the role of its performers. "We have tried to include them," Brierley says, rather defensively, "but it has never worked. Unless there is continuity of attendance, planning committee meetings are useless. Most committee meetings tend to happen in the evening when performers can't be there. Even during the day, it is ten to one the performer is rehearsing." The arguments show a certain strain. "Besides, much of the discussion in planning committee is to do with performers. Performers find it difficult to be there when their peers are being discussed."

Through this structure emerge the company's plans. Planners agree on them, the Direction may influence them, the finance committee considers them. They are ready, at last, for presentation to the Arts Council.

The government usually has an observer at the monthly meetings of the finance committee, where management and governors look at revised forecasts of what the year's end will show—surplus or deficit. The Arts Council is formally represented at all governors' meetings. There is some friendly interchange while plans are being made. But now it runs into difficulties, every year. The Arts Council does not know what money it will have in the next financial year, which begins on April 5 in Britain. Stratford needs to open its doors for the spring and summer season by the end of March. The company has to start work before its patron in government knows precisely the extent of its resources. In 1978, for example, the formal Arts Council offer of a grant had not arrived by September. The company had been working on assumptions since it opened in March—a good six months. It was already planning the next year's season. "Our knowledge of what our finances are going to be is always hopelessly late in coming," Brierley says.

There is little or no support from private industry, perhaps because music, opera, and ballet seem safer bets for commercial sponsorship. RSC may always do some anarchic Leftist work; the Royal Opera, more likely, will do *La Traviata* again. It follows that when the internal bureaucracy is satisfied, the government offices persuaded, the moneys voted in Parliament, the governors calmed, and the company cajoled and recruited, the finances considered, the company can finally see what it will be able to do. In good years, the logic of money determines what RSC can offer, more precisely than any outside observer would guess. In bad years, the forced decisions can break the heart of Trevor Nunn.

EVERY YEAR, according to the charter, there must be Shakespeare at Stratford. The choice of plays and program is not free. It is determined by the company's structure.

There are, to begin with, thirty-seven possible plays. Excursions into other parts of the Jacobean canon are rare; Nunn's own production of *The Revenger's Tragedy* broke rules. "We have to do five or six Shakespeares," says Bill Wilkinson, finance director. "That whittles away pretty quickly because you've done some plays too recently or you can't find the right King Lear." In a normal year, Stratford must run as many weeks as possible. Staff are paid year-round; actors are on contracts which run for sixty weeks. Gaps lose money. The opening night must be in late March or April 1 at the latest, and "nowadays, we've simply got to run it straight through January for the sake of the extra revenue. There's an audience, and we need the money.

"Now that means the least number of plays you can do is five, and the ideal number is six. We know that from experience. Some years we've done only four or five and we've looked at the level of income towards the end of the season, from late October onward when the last production of six would normally start. There is a distinct slipping away—not massive, but definite. If you have the sixth play, it seems to regenerate interest in the whole season. It's not the only production to do well after October. And that 'marginal' show—'marginal' in economic terms—doesn't cost you much when you've already assembled a company and you're going to keep the theater open in any case. Indeed, sometimes it opens casting opportunities that improve the whole season. When there are six shows in the main house, you've a better chance of offering an actor good parts at least in three—or perhaps a bloody good part in play one, then a couple of decent parts, and something better in the last show. After all, actors are on those sixty-week contracts with us and they want to know they will get a fair number of good parts during the season.''

The six plays have now to be chosen, along with their casts. Nunn has to go out as impresario, a professional seducer of egos at work over the lunch table, a persuader. Actors will not earn much in Stratford; they must be offered great opportunities. They have to believe in what Nunn offers. He may have to revive some past production to strengthen the company next season; *Richard II* was once brought back to save money, because it was a revival, and to persuade its leading players to stay with the company for another year.

Between the programs of past seasons, the state of the budget, the availability of actors, the logic of the season itself, Nunn has a relatively small amount of choice in what plays will appear in the main house at Stratford. In bad years, the choice narrows still further. In the worst year, 1975, it was limited by everything from oil prices to central heating. ''We had to change nature,'' Bill Wilkinson says. ''Our desperate fear was that the change of nature might prove to be long term.''

The start of the 1975 crisis, the worst in Nunn's leadership, was in 1973, and it had to do with the price of oil. When travel costs go up, Stratford suffers. Ninety-five percent of its audience arrives, often long-distance, by some form of oil-powered transport. They drive from London, or are brought by coach from hotels or schools, or come by rail. Ultimately, many are tourists who came by air, who are affected indirectly by the cost of jet fuel. The war in the Middle East and the oil embargo that followed were disasters. ''The moment war broke out,'' Wilkinson says, ''the pattern of our bookings changed drastically. There were simply no bookings for the winter season. Air costs went up, travel costs went up, inflation sent hotel and restaurant costs skyrocketing. Even now at Stratford the cost of a theater ticket is much less than the cost of getting there.'' By early 1974, the impact had become more clearly disastrous. Arts Council grants were not likely to match the gallop of general inflation. ''So we had to decide,'' Wilkinson says, ''how to haul back—how to generate audiences without asking much more of them at the box office for fear of further deterring them.''

223

Economics forced Nunn into structural change. His other pressing
and absurd problem was more literally structural. The middle-aged
central heating system in a middle-aged building could no longer
bring air and heat to the number of bodies in the Stratford auditorium.
Town inspectors arrived to check the plant that was tastefully concealed under decent red brick. They issued an ultimatum. "Either
you renew the heating and ventilating plant," they said, "or we
close you. Or else, we limit the number of bodies in the theater."
Given Stratford's knife-edge economics, the 5 percent obligation,
any limit would be almost as bad as closure. The company had no
money for repairing its own theater. The council could not by law
turn a blind eye. There was an awful stalemate.

"We believed," says Wilkinson, "that if you cut off one major
production at Stratford, you're slicing off a piece of revenue as well.
Only one thing can be cut—one of the major theaters."

In London, the company abandoned repertoire and put on plays
one by one for limited seasons. It lost all flexibility. If a play failed,
it could not be nursed, set aside, and brought back later. It had to
run its time to cold houses. Instead of a true company, sharing different parts in different plays, actors were hired for the run of each
show. Neither actors nor shows could support each other. The nature of the London theater was changed.

At Stratford there was even a further complication. Ironically, it
was the theater's one-hundredth year of incorporation under charter.
It was a year for celebration. There had to be something exceptional.
Yet the company was penniless, the London operation had been
reformed from necessity, and the theater might be closed any day.

"We try to make a virtue of necessity," says David Brierley,
"when we get into a corner like that." The answer was a season for
groundlings, the four Falstaff plays—*Henry IV,* Parts I and II,
Henry V, and the warm and russety *Merry Wives of Windsor*. There
was only one master setting for all four plays, devised by the director Terry Hands. The themes, rhetoric, and comedy all pulled an
audience—until October, when audiences fell right away. "We had
actually budgeted for that," Brierley says, "so we didn't get hurt."
It was a brave, flag-waving front to a financial horror.

"You become schizophrenic sometimes," Nunn says, "thinking I want to do this artistically, but I won't allow myself to do it financially." In 1975, the options were dim. He spent the year before trying to talk the company into accepting the difficulties and the solutions of the thin and expedient season that was to follow. It was a time of dismantling what RSC had been for almost fifteen years, cutting the London connection back to a repertory theater run parallel to the company rather than as a true, organic part of it, and limiting the prospects for the Stratford actors. Nobody knew if the company could be repaired.

It was a time, also, of curious devices. A commercial management, headed by Paul Elliot, came to Nunn and told him that Glenda Jackson wanted to do *Hedda Gabler*. Nunn was interested; Jackson had started her career with RSC and made her reputation there, but there had come distance between star and company. Nunn had long wanted to woo her back, but Elliot's offer involved a new principle. In effect, the commercial management was commissioning a production that would appear across the world under the Royal Shakespeare Company banner, but play RSC theaters only briefly. It would not grow out of the company. RSC would provide only a banner, the director, and, for a little while, the London theater. The deal was tied to a movie version that would be made under Jackson's contract with Brut Productions. The stage show would be wholly financed by Elliot. He wanted to buy the name of RSC.

Nunn agreed. The tour went out from Australia to America and returned only then to London, where it played a short commercial season during the Aldwych's bleak months. The notices, while respectful, were mixed; *Hedda* as a black comedy was thought an esoteric idea, especially since London had too recently seen the psychoanalytical fury of Bergman's production. Nunn himself had wanted to do the show in order to escape for a time his constant diet of Jacobean drama. The reasons paled, however, alongside the basic truth: *Hedda Gabler* paid the bills.

It was a bad time for Nunn and for the company, a season when economic constraints became solid, visible barriers, They did have luck; inspired by the Stratford fare and by relentless appeals, the

theater's Centennial Fund swelled enough to pay for the new venti-
lation plant. That problem at least could be set aside. But it was clear
that harm had been done, and would be done. "We lost continuity,"
David Brierley says. "You were down to fractional groups of people
doing little one-offs. There was a loss of artistic and social community
which actually communicated itself to the audiences. Getting out of
it was a slow process." In the future, it was clear that raging inflation
and the 5 percent obligation were not compatible. The problem is
fundamental.

UNLIKE MOST MOGULS, Nunn also creates what it is his job to finance, administer, and sell. That luxury recedes as pressures grow.
He reckons to spend 50 percent of his time dealing with economic
crises of all kinds, 30 percent looking after the company as a whole,
and only 20 percent actually directing plays.

He recognizes that there is a peculiar role that he must play as
chief executive. He also shares—power, responsibility, and titles.
True company democracy may be an unattainable ideal, since Nunn
cannot always be available, but it is now built into the hierarchy.
Where Hall alone was long the artistic and business chief, Nunn
always had a general manager and a finance director to help him and
shoulder some part of the burden of negotiations with the Arts Council. In the mid-1970s, Nunn acknowledged the problem of handling
companies in both London and Stratford and did what would have
been unthinkable under Hall's old regime: he invited Terry Hands
to be joint artistic director.

He is left out in front of the company, its central figure, its fron-
tispiece, and mostly its spokesman. There has to be a mogul, an
impresario, even within an institution with aims scholarly as well as
commercial. True, the mogul chooses to exercise power by a skein
of contacts and helpers. The institution itself shapes and limits his
powers, but someone has to make the seasons make money, ensure
the company's survival. The mogul is no longer guarantor and
profit-maker. He is helper and keeper of a particular trust, the front

man, visible and seen. He is demonstrably not an absolute power, although he has final say before his governors. He is a shadow-figure mogul like the rest, conscious of the role he plays as the other would-be moguls are not.

Tired and wan in a huge office, talking with passion about plays, he knows the limits of his moguldom. And he is glad of them.

7

ROBERT STIGWOOD:
MOGUL

T HE ROLLS-ROYCE purrs through city streets, white and lush, its floor covered in furs. The suite at the Dorchester is full of pale taste and stuffed books, and vast. The apartment overlooking Central Park is the penthouse, and the Chinese motif glitters in its fields of burlap. The house is rented in Los Angeles, but it has a screening room, and the office in London is a Mayfair house, once the Caravan Club, now full of flowers and sporting prints. The home in Bermuda is white, colonial, dignified, and it graces a whole hill and promontory called Wreck Hill. It is an estate above coral sand, a refuge where moguls should retreat, in a rich man's land.

Those are the proper, outer trappings of moguldom. They belong to Robert Stigwood. He has a faded, ruddy face with strong blue eyes that hold and fascinate. He is sandy haired, self-effacing, quiet. He holds a room on authority rather than any particular contrived stage presence. He is supposed to have trained as a hypnotist; it would explain the exactness of his glance.

Stigwood came from Australia to London to seek his fortune. He succeeded and he crashed. After his company's collapse, he made himself a partner in the Beatles, and eventually became an entrepreneur again. But Stigwood, who failed on his own for lack of capital and excess of ambition, was not a simple mogul. He was employed. Behind him stood Polygram, the entertainment arm of the Philips/Siemens electronics combine. At first they acted as his bankers, willing to fund his business because they understood show business as few bankers do. Then, they were creditors, helping to push ahead the public flotation in London of the Robert Stigwood Organization. As RSO took off, they became the main force in buying out public shareholders and taking control, largely because the organization, as a public company, could not easily handle the weight of debt. Now, they are backers to Robert Stigwood, content to take profit from what he does and not to have their names on his product. They allow him almost total freedom to do what he wants, while he is successful. Robert Stigwood is their creature, but they have no reason at present to exercise direct control. He is making money for them, and that is enough.

The story of Robert Stigwood is, apparently, the story of the brave entrepreneur who triumphs over adversity, makes clever deals, goes public, decides to invade America, and does so with style, making a fortune from movies, records, and theater. His is *Jesus Christ Superstar,* on stage, in concert, and on film; the movie version of *Tommy* and *Saturday Night Fever* and *Grease* are also his. He staged *Evita* and nursed the careers of the Bee Gees, Eric Clapton, and those of various stars from Cream and Blind Faith. The achievement is real and remarkable. But the truth about Stigwood is something different from the legend of an entrepreneur, of an old-style mogul. Only the outer show is the same, for Stigwood has worked for ten years within a corporate structure dictated by a clever accountant, himself an outsider in the City of London, and a major electronics group in Europe. That structure makes him, technically, an employee and actually subject to the interest of the electronics firm. Stigwood is how a mogul can appear with fanfare, glitter, and glory in the age of corporations. He is made and supported by corporate bodies because they need his peculiar flair. He is allowed what public spectacle he wants or needs, and he uses it to establish his public credit as the old moguls did. But his credit goes no further than the credit of his owners. He is the new sort of mogul.

"IT WAS THE MOST ILL-EQUIPPED expedition of all time," Stigwood says. He left Adelaide in Australia, a junior account executive in an advertising agency, and he took the overland route to London. "I took an enormous medical kit and no sleeping bag. In Basra, our first stop in Iraq, we were held up at gunpoint. I was traveling as a journalist at the time. I produced my card and told these Arabs I was on some sort of assignment for the Australian Government, and they were watching our every move. That really got us out of it nicely."

He arrived in London three months later with five pounds sterling in his pocket, twenty-eight pounds lighter, suffering from severe dysentery.

He had come from a solid middle-class family. His mother ran a nursing home and had money of her own; his father was an electrical engineer. He went to private schools, the sort that flattened and homogenized his curiously unaccented voice. His memories of childhood and adolescence are sparse and warm. He once played Toad in *Toad of Toad Hall* and says that was typecasting; he remembers exploring the countryside that sent fingers of life into the suburbia around Adelaide. He flirted with the Church and the idea of becoming a priest, but realized he had no vocation the morning after the family had given a party to celebrate his vocation. Reluctantly, he handed back his presents. When he left school, he went to work for an advertising agency, where he wrote copy and became a junior account executive. His trip to England is variously explained either as the hot pursuit of some girl he wanted to marry, a story which seems to have ended in an abrupt change of mind if it were ever true; or the result of a rare row with his beloved mother; or else the usual Australian rite de passage of the European tour.

In Britain, he survived. He sold vacuum cleaners door to door in Notting Hill Gate, an unsmart area of West London, spent some time working with delinquent boys in a hostel near Cambridge, then went to work in the theater. His first job was on the South Coast at Southampton with the Hector Ross Players, a small-time provincial company. From there, he moved north to Norwich and the Hippodrome, a plush and gilt house that had been built and gilded for better times. Robert Stigwood's career began there.

STEPHEN KOMLOSY was still at boarding school in North London, a bright and handsome boy. He took a vacation job at the Hippodrome, as a scenic painter. His parents were away in the Far East—his mother handled public relations there for the film side of the Rank Organization—and he had some time before he was due to go to university. At the Hippodrome he met Stigwood, and his plans and his life changed.

He abandoned university. "Since my parents were abroad," he says, "they couldn't do very much about it." He decided to stay in Norwich with Stigwood. "The idea was that I was going to be a pop star, but there were a few problems. I'm too nervous and I can't sing. But we got on very well and I left school and we ran that theater together. It went on for about a year—weekly rep, and both of us doing everything from management to scene painting to a bit of acting.

"Then we decided, quite deliberately, that we wanted to be the Grade Organization, and we left." At the time, the Grades were the most powerful force in British show business; the three brothers had television in the Midlands, a string of London theaters, and a vast agency business. The Stigwood ambition was substantial; the reality was less grand. The partners opened for business as a model agency at 41 Charing Cross Road. "In a cupboard," Stigwood remembers. "I could only see one visitor at a time because there wasn't space for two people to sit." Komlosy, reluctantly, was shuttled from customer to customer as the model in residence until the first clients signed on. When they did, Stigwood began to exploit a very sizable gap in the British market. "The big theatrical agencies," he says, "treated the advertising agencies very badly. Even though TV commercials were only thirty seconds long, the agencies wanted those commercials to be like feature films. Vast amounts of money were being spent on time buying, after all." Komlosy says: "We found a niche. There use to be things called advertising magazines on British television in those days, actors discussing products for fifteen minutes. Advertisers who couldn't afford to buy their own commercials would take time on the magazines. It was just starting. It happened that the first two or three people who presented those programs were our clients. In time, there were about eight presenters and we had them all.''

The bulk of the business of Robert Stigwood Associates was with advertising agencies, who were glad to be taken seriously in those relatively early days of television commercials in Britain. (Advertising on television had begun in 1956 with the start of privately financed television companies in a network that competed with the established BBC.) But they had sidelines as well. ''We started handling a few actors in series on television,'' Stigwood says, ''like 'Emergency Ward Ten.' From that, I first got involved in music—through John Leyton.'' Leyton was a personable actor in minor rep who became what Komlosy could not: he was the actor who would become a singer and then a star. ''He looked exactly right,'' Komlosy remembers. ''He was an actor and he could sing well enough. It was the formula we'd often talked about. So we started to peddle around the main record companies—Decca, EMI—and we got turned down everywhere. Eventually Robert paid Jo Meek to make the record— we did it in the bathroom with the bath as an echo chamber. It was a cover, an imitation of an American hit called 'Tell Laura I Love Her.' '' At that time, independent record producers were unknown in Britain. If a singer failed to excite the heads of A&R—artists and repertoire—at either Decca or EMI, he might as well leave the business. Even the Beatles, brushed aside by Decca, were collected by EMI and Capitol quite late in their performing careers. But there was an accident that saved Stigwood's investment in John Leyton. ''Rank were trying to break into the record business at the time, and they took the record,'' Komlosy remembers. Rank at that time were owners of cinemas, a movie studio, and, more important, rights to sell Xerox machines throughout the world. ''The record was released, it began to happen, and we were in clover for a while. Then the week after it was released the Rank record operation collapsed and EMI took it over. Since EMI had released the original version of 'Tell Laura I Love Her,' and they'd already refused our version, we were in trouble.

''That was when there started the most curious and most important stage in the story of Robert Stigwood Associates. We went berserk.

We called them all the names under the sun. We called in the Press. The result was that we had a private meeting with the chairman of EMI, Sir Joseph Lockwood.'' Lockwood remembers later meetings, first with Komlosy and then with Stigwood, and liking the pair. ''Robert and Sir Joseph had a rapport from the start,'' Komlosy says. ''Sir Jo tried to say that EMI would break John Leyton for us after all''—''break,'' in music, means to launch—''but we said we wanted to maintain our independence. Besides, EMI had already turned him down. So Lockwood said he would do what the Americans did and take us on as independent producers.''

It was the start of a curious association that ended in acrimony as Stigwood's firm folded. Sir Joseph was an electronics man, slightly adrift in show business, but quite fascinated. He ran a conglomerate built equally on defense equipment and records. Komlosy and Stigwood were a sort of gift, men to whom he could talk frankly and who had some feeling for the elusive, curious music business. There were walks on Sunday mornings in Regents Park, drinks before lunch, and Stigwood and Komlosy exploited the social links. If their records were not pushed hard enough, Sir Joseph would know. Sir Joseph, in turn, had the sounding board he needed, outside his company but inside the business, to discuss stars and product. It was informal, imprecise, and generous and both sides needed it. Until the final row, it was also a friendship.

It did not, at first, launch Stigwood's records as he wanted. The first John Leyton record died because it appeared too late. The second had more luck. It was the first pale harbinger of Stigwood's later techniques in crossing from medium to medium, promoting as he goes. ''By that time,'' Komlosy remembers, ''we had a number of actors who were working on quite serious shows.'' John Leyton was signed to play a lead part in a prime-time show called ''Harpers West One,'' a saga set in a London department store with a remarkable resemblance to Harrods. ''The first episode was about a pop singer opening the record department,'' Stigwood remembers. ''I had lunch with the director, played him the song we had just recorded, which was 'Johnny Remember Me.' He loved it and it became the theme music. We rather changed the show around—built John a more lavish staircase to walk down and sing.'' The song was already recorded, and it was written by a composer Stigwood and Komlosy had been nursing. Leyton appeared, playing Johnny St. Cyr (in British English, ''Sincere''), and the next morning the record shops were under siege. More than 100,000 record orders poured in. ''EMI were forced to release the record properly, because there was so much demand,'' Stigwood says. The song went to number one on the British charts. Sir Joseph took a benevolent view of his protégés. Stigwood was launched in the music business.

At the heart of his operation was the agency. ''We conceived the idea,'' Komlosy says, ''that in show business you can monopolize all areas of income by controlling and managing the artist. If you start with the star, you control when and where he appears; so if you promote him yourself, you get the promoter's share. If you record him yourself, you become the record company. If you publish his music, you get the publisher's cut. And we always had the 'B' side of records. In terms of mechanical royalties, they make just as much money as the 'A' sides. The idea was not to let anyone in from the outside.''

The master company, Robert Stigwood Associates, took agency commissions. They managed John Leyton, who became immensely successful by the standards of British pop music before Merseyside, and went to Hollywood to play thin blond heroes for the Mirisch Brothers. There was Mike Sarne, whose ''Come Outside'' was the first record Stigwood produced himself, and who went on to a private Valhalla as director of the movie *Myra Breckenridge*. There were other, less durable performers like Billie Davis, a sixteen-year-old whom Stigwood discovered, gave elocution lessons, and set to answering John Leyton's fan mail to the point of bursting tedium. He found for her a song called ''Tell Him'' and it went to number one. The Stigwood roster was impressive in British terms. He was already inventing sounds—the long, mournful bathtub resonance of Leyton— and promoting tours—''one nighters,'' Komlosy remembers. ''They went on for about six weeks, cinema by cinema round the country. Grueling stuff.

''By then we really had the embryo Robert Stigwood Organization—everything under one roof.'' There was RS International, formed in 1962 to act as British representatives for Tamla Motown—''they were just a little Detroit black label then, and we represented them to the point where they became very big. All those people became huge stars—Stevie Wonder, Diana Ross and the Supremes—and we brought them over to Britain and it was great fun.'' There was RSA Music Publishing—''really just a collection bucket for money. We had a deal with Southern Music which handled actual publication. They did all the work except that we did our own promotion of records.'' There was Robert Stigwood Commercials. ''We bought a television studio in the Fulham Road,'' Komlosy says, ''and the idea was that we would make TV commercials on tape, which was not being done at that time. We were extremely successful in selling them—so successful in fact that the film technicians' union, ACTT, called a strike on independent television.'' The studio was to become a millstone, but not yet.

There were also the bizarre, flighty little enterprises that never quite made it. ''We used to run a magazine called *Pop Weekly,* and we were going to do a spin-off from that called *Give-a-Disc Monthly*. We did about three and it didn't work. The idea was that we should do a pop magazine with discs in it—you'd just take the pages out and play them. Somebody came along in the early 1960s with this bit of plastic which looked like paper, but you could play it like a record. The trouble was that people didn't want discs unless they were by stars and the stars were already recording through the record companies. It was a bit early to come up with a daft idea like that.''

''ROBERT IS A GENIUS,'' Komlosy says, ''but he is not controllable in a financial sense. You can't make sense of him on any financial level. As for me, I was just a kid. I'd come straight out of school into the Rolls-Royces and it was too much.''

The partners had drifted apart. Komlosy married early; Stigwood moved into his own luxurious world. At work, Komlosy's patience was sometimes tried; but when trouble came, it was more fundamental. "Robert can recognize what's commercial," Komlosy says, "and he can put it on, but he is not capable of considering what it costs. He shouldn't have to think about it because that is not his talent." Without financial controls of any substance, Robert Stigwood Associates was running into problems. Activity was frantic, but its base was a company without real capital. Besides a few overdrafts at the bank, there was Komlosy's legacy of £5,000 which he had persuaded his mother to put into the company before he reached legal majority at twenty-one; that money was the company's capital at the start. "Beyond that, it was all internally financed," Komlosy says. "Anything we wanted to do, we did with the money generated by the tours, the publishing, the recording, the management side of the agency. And we had no real knowledge of accountancy, either of us." If anything broke the flow of cash, the company would fall apart.

It did just that. The first blow was union reaction to the television studio on Fulham Road. Film technicians were furious that tape was being used. Their jobs were at risk, the studios for film were empty, and the tape business seemed likely to boom. The result was strike action and boycott. ACTT, which had power as the technicians' union in television as well, refused to allow the screening of thirty-second taped commercials. "They killed that studio stone-dead, the unions," Komlosy says. "In fact, they killed Robert Stigwood Associates, because it was that company which really drained us of resources."

Then Stigwood made a rare and major error of musical instinct. He missed Merseyside, the boom in Northern groups led by the Beatles. He admits the mistake and regrets it. Around RSA the whole British music business was changing. It was, for a start, becoming international and innovative. "Suddenly," Komlosy says, "we weren't successful anymore. It took us a while to understand what had happened in the music business—that it had really changed. The single hip-swiveling artist was no longer what was wanted. It was all groups—and they really flooded in. Our cash flow from that area had gone because we were a year behind." An expensive tour with P. J. Proby folded because the star did not appear. The studio costs mounted. The lack of capital told at last.

"When you think what our turnover and our profits had been," Komlosy says, "to go under for a measly £50,000 was unbelievable."

The way to actual collapse was inexorable. Komlosy's mother, Eileen, was on the board, a relic of the days when she had organized her son's inheritance a few years early. On February 6, 1965, she resigned. There was no sense in involving her in the collapse; she had played no active part in the business. On February 19, Komlosy himself replaced the company secretary. Stigwood still seemed confident, living high among his mogul props, the huge marble tables, the silk wallpaper, the real tiger's skin thrown on the floor as a rug. "He would not accept," Komlosy remembers, "that we were in trouble." Sir Joseph Lockwood and the EMI conglomerate offered to buy the company; Komlosy was keen even if it was just a matter of making a deal and quitting within a year. One Sunday morning, Komlosy took matters into his own hands. He drove Lockwood of EMI to Stigwood's flat. Stigwood refused to admit that anything was wrong. He even refused to get out of bed to talk. Lockwood was furious. He would be alienated finally when he discovered some awkward dealings between Stigwood and an EMI associate in America.

Within a week, the liquidator was called in. For £5 15s 6d, the company hired a small room in the Kingsley Hotel, Bloomsbury, and held an extraordinary general meeting. It passed a motion that read, in part, that "it has been proved to the satisfaction of this Meeting that the Company cannot by reason of its liabilities continue its business and accordingly that the Company be wound up voluntarily." Robert Stigwood's empire was bust.

"I LOST MY HOUSE," Komlosy says. "I was married with three children and everything went. It was a very difficult time. Even though the company itself had gone down for £50,000, most of that was personally guaranteed to the banks and lawyers and accountants." Stigwood himself was short on assets, but he met a bank overdraft of £8,500, contributed £5,000 during the decade it took to complete the liquidation, and paid off artists who were owed money. When the final sums were drawn, Stephen Anton Komlosy, owed £2,000 by the company, was paid £27, and his mother, owed £3,500, was paid £47 5s. The dividend, paid on January 17, 1965, was precisely 1.35p on the pound. Komlosy calculates that he had to pay back about £25,000 in all.

Nobody thought Stigwood any less of a genius because of the crash. He has the air of convincing those he meets, a shrewd manner of exactly assessing and exploiting the mood of any group. He had also been successful, shown his flair. Very soon after the liquidator started work, Stigwood was back in business with Komlosy, working from the offices of a firm called Starlight Artists. The partners were to develop and promote stars that Starlight could manage. "It looked as though we were starting to get back on our feet again," Komlosy says. They discovered the Graham Bond Organization, and with it, the drummer Ginger Baker. The flair had evidently not left Stigwood, but Komlosy did, one Friday afternoon. "That Thursday night Robert had been with Graham Bond and he was supposed to have collected our commission, which was about £400 that week. I needed the money to pay the wages. He didn't come in on Friday morning because he wasn't good at mornings in those days. He came in at two in the afternoon. He said he was terribly sorry but he'd lost the money at the Twenty-one Room." Komlosy had taken enough. "I left."

His final view of Stigwood is admiring, not resentful. "He has an uncanny political judgment, this ability to judge very quickly how people will react in any given situation. It is a vital ability. He's a genius, and he is immensely charming and funny and nice. And I like him, immensely."

DAVID SHAW WAS ONE of the bright operators in the City of London, a moneyman of ingenuity. If the City did not always approve what he did, it was for reasons of propriety. He had been a bond-washer, that is, one who avoids income tax on dividends from government stock by selling them with dividend rights attached and buying them back in a few weeks at a lower price when the dividend has been paid out. Shaw and his associates paid lower capital gains tax on the difference between buying and selling prices of the bonds, and that difference would be only slightly less than the dividend paid out.

It was a clever idea but the City, in an overscrupulous mood, did not approve; nor did they much like Constellation Investments. It was the first British attempt to follow an American idea—to allow the public to buy shares in superstars, so that the superstars' income is converted into the capital worth of their shares in themselves. A Susannah York has shares in return for her income, and may trade them as she wishes; the profits she makes will be subject to less tax than her earnings. For practical purposes, the public can buy shares in the success of careers like that of Susannah York. It was again clever, and again the City had communal doubts. It was new, unproven, and curious. Stars were not assets.

Shaw needed stars for his scheme, and he looked hard. He approached Stigwood to ask if Mike Sarne or John Leyton would like to join the scheme. He phoned three or four times, was brushed off, and set the matter aside. But he remembered Stigwood, his client list, and his reputation. When the crash became public knowledge, he talked with a friend, Andrew Gordon. They decided that Stigwood might be worth staking to start up again. There was Sarne still, Leyton having left, and there was the Graham Bond Organization; there was a basic business that could be rebuilt with capital. Shaw and friends wrote checks for £25,000. Stigwood took offices in de Walden Court just off Oxford Street, and the bandwagon rolled again.

The first year was not encouraging. Shaw put in another £15,000 and told himself that all would end well. Then, things began to happen. The Bee Gees arrived, fresh from Australia, on the introduction of Ronald Renny, a friend from EMI who had moved to be head of Polydor. The Graham Bond Organization spawned Cream, and Stigwood added to them Eric Clapton. The Robert Stigwood Organization began to expand.

It was time for a coup.

David Shaw knew Brian Epstein socially, from the round of parties both played, from the faintly raffish edges of musical, financial, and theatrical life. Brian Epstein was manager of the Beatles. He was also bewildered, the heir to a Liverpool department store who had been overtaken and swamped by his glittering music business. He had hard, acute commercial taste, but he did not have his heart in pursuing it. He wanted to browse around pictures and spend his life with bullfighters in Spain. He did not want the responsibility and the sheer scale of his business anymore.

"Brian became a good friend," Stigwood says. "We met when he moved down to London. He was thinking of retiring because he wanted to live in Spain." Together, Shaw, Stigwood, and Epstein set off for Paris—for, Shaw says, "a dirty weekend." Shaw and Stigwood tried to persuade Epstein that he, and his company, NEMS, needed representation in Europe, and that the Robert Stigwood Organization should provide it. What emerged was far more significant. Epstein broke, and his fears and troubles poured out. He was not simply discontent; he was fed up with NEMS. The pressure of being the man who made decisions for the Beatles was becoming intolerable. His personal life simply would not work—it had a romantic, idealized, unattainable core—and pressure would not stop. "And he was responding to pressures the wrong way," Stigwood says. "He was taking uppers to keep himself going, to sustain himself through all the travel and pressures, and he was taking sleeping pills to counterbalance that at night. It had become a vicious circle."

Out of the indulgence in Paris came a deal. Shaw and his City friends looked at NEMS. What they found made it impossible to ask any bank for the money to buy. There were too many unresolved lawsuits lying around, classic double deals on merchandising the Beatles which had them selling two sorts of chewing gum at once. NEMS was a mess. Even if the lawsuits pending were American, and therefore began with exaggerated demands for damages, the bankers were still uneasy. Shaw did not want to push his luck. He proposed a compromise in which NEMS would buy RSO, but Epstein would then give Stigwood and Shaw an option to buy 51 percent of NEMS one year later—if the company could be cleaned up. In effect, Stigwood and Shaw would take over NEMS if they could make it capable of being taken over. "The trouble was," as Stigwood says, "he hadn't told the Beatles. He said that he wanted to do that at the right time."

So, in the fall of 1966, Stigwood went to work on the artistic side of NEMS. Shaw massaged the business back to life and looked for bankers to finance the takeover which might happen in a year. Real bankers were nervous about the idea. Show-business companies were excited. It was a chance to buy half the Beatles for a fixed sum. Polygram, the master company in show business of Philips/Siemens, was more than sympathetic. Stigwood and Shaw were promised half a million pounds when the option fell due, on September 30, 1967. They told Brian Epstein that they would buy.

After vodka and sleeping pills on a night in August, Brian Epstein died. "It wasn't suicide," Stigwood says. "He'd been drinking and he didn't usually drink more than a vodka or two." The situation was chaotic. The Epstein family descended from Liverpool full of natural caution about how their brother's curious enterprise should be handled. Stigwood had the promise of Polygram money and plans for rainbow expansion. Epstein had always kept the Beatles to himself—he told Stigwood: "You've got everything else to look after, but until the option is taken up, the Beatles are mine." When Epstein was suddenly gone, the Beatles turned to the people in NEMS that they knew, and the list did not include Shaw or Stigwood. Since the Beatles were the main muscle of NEMS, they had to agree to any deal. If they did not, the value of NEMS would crumble.

"I met with the Beatles," Stigwood remembers, "and they were very pleasant. They were dreaming up their own company, Apple Corps, at the time, and they wanted NEMS and Apple and Stigwood as one big company. They said: 'You can run it, Robert.' But they started to scare me a bit after that. John Lennon had just discovered his Magic Alex friend, who was going to do everything by computer. It seemed all I had to do was to sit behind the computer and run the business. Now I was starting to have some success with Cream, and just launching the Bee Gees, and I was frightened. I wanted fifty-one percent and they wanted fifty-one percent." The Beatles's dissent reinforced the Epstein family's troubles over death duty and the option itself: there was legal opinion that the option was personal and therefore lapsed with the death of Brian Epstein who had granted it. Inside NEMS, the Beatles listened most intently to those of Epstein's assistants who had most reason to resent the intrusion of Stigwood and Shaw. "After two weeks of discussion," Stigwood says, "I said I'd give up my option for control of the company, take my own things out, and set up RSO separately again." Stigwood and the Beatles agreed to part; Stigwood and Shaw were again on their own.

This time, there was sizable backing. Polygram, prepared to lend half a million for NEMS, were not now likely to stint their protégés. In February 1968, Henring Rintelen of Philips/Siemens said: "We are interested in all forms of show business and are backing Mr. Stigwood because we feel he has the necessary ability to deliver to us business we never got before." The finance would be, for practical purposes, without limit.

There began the razzle-dazzle, the shouting. Stigwood put money into the London production of *Oh, Calcutta!* and he bought the British rights to *Hair*. With both, he fell foul of a crusty court official called the Lord Chamberlain who had the various duties of awarding plaques to the Queen's more regular grocers and censoring the British stage. "It was a very trying time with *Hair*," Stigwood remembers. "The whole script was totally rejected by the Lord Chamberlain's office. I was devastated. But then I had a stroke of luck. Six months later, the Government abolished his office and revised the laws on censorship. I got a six-year run out of *Hair* where before I had no hope of opening it at all." The prurient British were much excited by the thought of a half-dozen kids singing, in half-light, naked. Stigwood, having heard the rumors of the Lord Chamberlain's impending end, had made a shrewd buy.

There came Cream. They were very much Stigwood's creation. He had represented the Graham Bond Organization, and in it were Ginger Baker and Jack Bruce; he took Eric Clapton from the John Mayall Band and created Cream. In the early days of 1967 they were regarded as underground. "It was," Stigwood says, "very difficult to persuade the musical press to print anything about them.'' Their success lay in the small string of central London clubs that have always been vital to any progressive element in rock in Britain. ''There were queues numbering thousands every time they played the Marquee.'' The group became classic, fine. In time, they dismantled their identity as Cream and took another as Blind Faith, adding Stevie Winwood from Traffic. This new group, short-lived, was derided as artificial and greedy, a device to launch a massive American tour before vanishing. It drew 100,000 people to its first free concert in a London park, though, and it was also respected.

There were also the Bee Gees, the Gibb brothers from Australia. In Stigwood's life they come between sons and clients, an extension of family. His ties to them, and especially to Barry Gibb, have always been close. In 1968, he gave them most of his time. Their first hit, the ''New York Mining Disaster,'' came out of a fortunate moment, ragging in a studio corridor when the lights failed. It turned their long but insubstantial career in Australia into recognition in both Britain and America. As Stigwood grew closer to the brothers, Barry would stay sometimes at his mansion in North London, with butler and entourage, and the others would feel excluded. Robin Gibb had moments of jealousy because Barry was also lead singer; he tried to make a career on his own and tumbled. Barry and Stigwood grew apart when Barry found his second wife. The group had massive advances against future royalties, and loans from the company, which became an embarrassment. Their internal dissension hit uncontrolled headlines. ''It was three brothers fighting,'' Stigwood says, ''and when brothers fight that is really terrible. They had American hits for a while, but I think the British public was simply cheesed off. I think the public's attitude was that they were very lucky to be so successful.'' The relationships were strong, and they mended in time, but they left scars. Stigwood's stars were seen to dim, and their estrangement left a void in his own emotions. It was difficult.

It would also prove oddly significant to Stigwood, the mogul. In the future, it would change the structure of his company. For the moment, it is the mid-1960s. Robert Stigwood trails the glory of his links with NEMS. He is thinking of becoming a movie-maker.

BERYL VERTUE LIKES to act innocent. She was secretary then to an agency called Associated London Scripts, which both represented and was owned by a group of top British scriptwriters. She worried about the plumbing and the business and whether there would be a temporary secretary if she went away. In time she worried her way to the board of directors, and as the standing of her writers grew, so did her own stature. She had the gift of shrewd and sideways observation. She might still be overawed by the grand people of the business, and she never liked to admit that she might not know something, but she was good at seeing through people. She noticed that producers came into her office asking for her top clients, and if the top clients might have any ideas that week, saying they had books which they did not, in fact, own. Beryl Vertue saw a way to add a little to her power as an agent.

She saw agency and clients moving into movies, and she cunningly put a salable script—by Ray Galton and Alan Simpson, called *The Spy with a Cold Nose*—into a new company called Associated London Films. "If they want the screenplay," she reasoned, "they have to have the company." She rang the showman Joe Levine to tell him so. "I never doubted he would take the call," she says. "I always assumed anybody would take a call transatlantic.

"I told him I was sending the script and I asked if he really did do it, could we please have our name on it so we could begin to get a bit established. I asked if I could be something on the picture so I had to go in every day—maybe associate producer, not that I knew what it meant. Levine agreed." It began to seem that Beryl Vertue's clients could become a movie company as well as an agency if only there were time enough and capital enough. "I thought, if only we could be with someone else. Not another agency, because that would mean we just had a bigger agency, but someone who was bigger and had things. Somebody with more money, if you like. You can't finance a film company out of a ten percent agency commission."

She talked, in imprecise terms, to Oscar Beuselinck, the London lawyer with show-business connections. She explained her dream. At the same time, on another part of Beuselinck's network, Robert Stigwood was talking about his trials at NEMS and how he wanted to take that company into movies. The marriage was mooted. "For several months we used to meet periodically," Vertue says. "We would have a drink and talk about philosophies and what we liked and didn't like. I was very impressed by that whole NEMS thing." But just as Stigwood and Shaw were going to make an offer, Brian Epstein died. The deal fell through. After a few months, David Shaw called again and explained that Stigwood was now out on his own and Vertue, rather primly, told him that was not at all the same thing as NEMS. It took her time to change her mind and concentrate on the people rather than the corporate names.

"He just seemed to feel that everything was possible," she remembers. Vertue had already sold a British comedy series called "Steptoe and Son" to American television, where it had been remade as "Sanford and Son." Later, she did the same with "Til Death Us Do Part," which turned into "All in the Family." It was the first of the transatlantic "format deals." Her agency had prestige and distinguished clients, even if it was rather short on cash. It had begun to make movies as only a small British company can, a kind of giggling comedy. Stigwood and Shaw bid again; Vertue and ALS joined the Stigwood Organization. "All of a sudden, I didn't even know if the plumbing had gone wrong, let alone have to deal with it," she says. "Robert backed me up with a company and he made me strong. He told the others that I must be called managing director because that was what I was doing. 'She must have the strength of that,' he said. 'It makes a difference to the rest of the world and it makes a difference to me.' " He made friends through his loyalty.

He also excited suspicion. Vertue remembers awkward moments when the crash of Robert Stigwood Associates haunted discussions. She reassured her board members. "He always surrounded himself with the best help he felt he needed at the time," she says, "just because of his financial difficulties in the past."

Stigwood bought himself trouble as well. He bought out the Gunnell brothers, an agency that managed Georgie Fame, Alan Price, and John Mayall. Stigwood was the providential buyer who saved the business. Rik Gunnell was also trusted, supported, and backed by Stigwood. He went to New York to try various American artists, who were not successful, as it happened, and to establish RSO in America. He went, in time, to California, where he collected some $250,000 of John Mayall's tour money and did not trouble to tell the organization of his plans. He was removed as a director of RSO. He was last reported in Spain, working the beaches.

For now, Stigwood was riding high. In London, there was *Hair*. *Oh, Calcutta!*, that long-winded excuse for titillation, was about to open. Bankers and brokers advised the time was right to float the organization and sell shares on the stock exchange. Beryl Vertue had always been impressed by Stigwood's talk of going public and selling shares. She hardly knew what it meant, but she liked the idea. She did know it was an aim almost never achieved after a history of less than half a decade. Now, in 1970, flotation was imminent. It seemed a wild and splendid achievement.

It was actually a necessity. In crude terms, the organization could either float or founder. Its trouble was the brilliance of David Shaw. He created for the company a tax structure in which no dividends were paid, but by a twist of the law, the company was still taxed as an "open" company, one that might distribute dividends to a number of shareholders if it chose. Instead of paying dividends, the company gave its officers, stars, and stockholders generous loans. If a Bee Gee earned £100, he might lose as much as 96 percent of that to the British taxman. If RSO received the cash instead, it would be liable to only 50 percent company taxation. That would leave £50, tax paid, within the company. It was then a simple matter for RSO to lend the Bee Gee—or the director, or the member of Cream—the £50. The system was elegant, legal, and successful for as long as everybody concerned was monitoring the balance between loans, profits, and spending. By the end of 1969, it was clear that something was wrong. On December 31, when the balance sheet was drawn up, it showed that 40 percent of the current assets of the company were represented by loans and advances to directors and artists. Nor was RSO a company rich in fixed assets. Its strength was in the residual value of publishing copyrights, the fees that would keep coming. Offices, cars, and furniture all accounted for only £82,352, and that was the total of fixed assets. If the company was worth anything, the worth lay in the £1,227,915 of current assets, and almost half of those were debt. The profits looked spectacular—£419,612 in 1969—but they were more than matched by the loans—£499,171 in December 1969. Something had to be done.

For a start, the artists were about to find their position difficult. One way out, resolving their debt in one go, was to sell shares to the public. There was no established market in RSO shares that would allow the artists to turn their debt into equity. In fact, what happened was this: loans and advances to artists, as distinct from others, amounted to £318,000. That was cash "lent" by RSO to Polydor who in turn "lent" it to the artists. In this way individual artists no longer owed RSO money. The massive and eminently credit-worthy Polydor did. The artists could work off their debt by making money for Polydor; their real obligation was to provide product and earn the royalties they had already been paid. There was also some £115,000 repaid, according to the papers, when RSO did go public, from the sale of shares owned by artists, including the Bee Gees. The personal bitterness that flared up among artists who were not quite sure of the finer points of a sophisticated system was calmed down. RSO had money again; its cash flow, briefly in jeopardy, was healthy; and by September 1974, some £225,998 of that £318,000 loan had been discharged by the actual earnings of the artists.

Meanwhile, Robert Stigwood had gone public. The shares were offered to a cold and doubtful reception. City of London operators had gone to their traditional August retreats, blasting at grouse in the North. Those left behind did not take kindly to RSO. They saw a machine through which passed appetizing amounts of money, but they did not see its value. They giggled in pubs about *Oh, Calcutta!* and they did not buy the shares. Three-quarters were left with the firm who underwrote the offer. Share prices slumped.

The City was doubly wrong. It neither spotted the real reasons for the flotation, nor did it understand the real strengths of the organization. It could be forgiven one other mistake. Nobody could have anticipated then what would happen to a rock opera called *Jesus Christ Superstar*.

IN THE BEGINNING was the idea, and the idea was a London Museum of Pop Music. Andrew Lloyd Webber was a slight man from the Guildhall School of Music, and the plan was his. He wanted to show the relics he valued. There would be a case for the letter from Decca Records rejecting the services of an obscure northern group called the Beatles and another for a pair of jeans that Elvis once wore. There would also have to be money and property, and Lloyd Webber was not quite sure where to find them. He called on his friend and collaborator Tim Rice, and together they made themselves known on Wardour Street. They went to a small office above a wigshop, with brass plates outside for the Dagenham Girl Pipers. They saw an agent named David Land.

Land, with his partner, Sefton Myers, had property as well as clients. He had garages in the Isle of Wight and shops in Dumfries High Street. Lloyd Webber and Rice explained the idea of the museum to him, and he listened politely. He took a serious interest only when he heard they already had a rock oratorio to their credit called *Joseph and the Amazing Technicolor Dreamcoat*. The two had another idea.

They wanted to write a full-scale rock opera. Its subject would be the last seven days of Jesus Christ, seen mainly through the eyes of Judas Iscariot. Land was enthusiastic. The authors, beaming, promised him: "It's a terrifically good story." Land and Myers wrote a management contract for them. The authors would have a fixed income of a couple of thousand pounds each while they wrote; Land and Myers would take 25 percent of their future earnings. Everybody was happy.

The first results appeared in October 1969, a single version of the title song. The English charts were slightly stirred; in the United States the song made a transit of the lower part of the record charts. Unaccountably, it became a smash hit in Brazil. It took off in Europe through the enthusiasm of Dutch radiomen who heard it, repeatedly, in an Amsterdam gay bar. It was visible, catchy, but not a massive hit. While it was still fresh, Rice and Lloyd Webber made another social call. They remembered that Stigwood had been the only impresario who would deal with *Hair* when the tricky British rights were on offer. They wanted to meet him.

"Tim and Andrew came to see me," Stigwood remembers, "when they had made the single of 'Superstar.' It had made a very minor impression on the English charts. They told me they were doing the album, and I couldn't quite work out why they wanted to see me. They already had a manager, a record company, and a publisher. We talked for a few hours and they said that they really thought that the show could be staged. So, I said, when it's finished, let me have an acetate. The tapes arrived just before I went to New York and I hopped on the plane with them."

In the United States, the word was out about the album. MCA had taken an option on the complete opera in February 1970. Within three months they had the finished score and lyrics; five months after that, they released the album. It was, to the authors, a sort of prospectus for the stage show. "It cost £14,000 to record," Lloyd Webber says. "It must be the most expensive demo disc ever produced." Assorted deals were floated; at one point Shirley Bassey was the most likely Mary Magdalene and Stanley Baker the prospective Christ. Rice and Lloyd Webber were alarmed. They had great trouble with their first joint work and they were determined to keep control this time. The problem, in law, was whether they had any control at all.

In June 1970, David Land made a deal with Leeds Music, the MCA music publishing subsidiary. It concerned the publication of music from *Jesus Christ Superstar*. Across the top is typed, firmly, "excluding grand rights." On page 10, the contract equally firmly includes "grand rights." Now, these rights are an elusive concept, and the sharpest show-business lawyer would be hard put to define them. They are, however, those rights which you must have if you wish to stage or film a show. Perhaps the authors still had those rights. Perhaps they had been surrendered to MCA. Despite the text of the agreement, David Land thought that he controlled them as the authors' agent. "I told them straight," he says. "You can't have the grand rights. Whatever they are."

Stigwood heard the album in the United States and acted with speed. He called the authors and told them he thought it was wonderful and that he wanted to stage it. When they arrived in New York to talk business, he greeted them with a limousine and grace. Their opinion of the man was confirmed. He called Beryl Vertue and told her to summon a board meeting in London. "I want the board to consider buying something called *Jesus Christ Superstar*," he said. Vertue duly assembled the board. "All we knew was that he had seen this record selling, and he had this vision about turning the record into theater. We were sitting there, the rest of the board, with something we'd never heard, and we all agreed that if he was sounding so keen, we should approve it. Robert was always very democratic so we voted on it."

Stigwood now played a simple and powerful card. Before his Cadillac arrived at JFK to collect the impressionable authors, he called their manager, David Land, in London. For shares and cash he bought their management contract. Fifty-one percent of Superstar Ventures, the company with the contract, now belonged to the Robert Stigwood Organization. The cost was relatively low. David Land kept an interest, and his name still appears on the playbills; but Stigwood now had a cut of 25 percent of the authors' income, the rights to stage or film the show if the legal troubles with MCA could be resolved, and the beginnings of what *Variety* later shrieked was the "biggest multi-media parlay of all time."

It was the first, massive Stigwood crossover, although the idea had been dimly present in other deals. He took a project that began in one medium, transplanted it to others, and allowed each to support and reinforce the others. Later, it was the management idea that made a fortune from *Saturday Night Fever* and *Grease*.

The *Superstar* album took off with more speed than anyone had supposed. From Hawaii to Maine, the United States seemed to echo with illicit versions of the show. Stigwood considers that the "star of that show is the music, not the artists," and the point was evidently not lost on other promoters. MCA was unhappy at the legal costs of fighting the pirates; Stigwood insisted. "We had to have local attor neys in every town working on the cases," he says. MCA and Stigwood footed a legal bill of more than $450,000. It was obvious that Stigwood would have to produce the show very quickly, to pay the lawyers and to dampen the growing ardor of the pirates. "We had," Stigwood remembers, "a bare stage with black drapes and it grossed more than $40 million." The concert tour on rudimentary sets was jointly financed by Stigwood and MCA; joint enterprise resolved the squabble over "grand rights." It had no element of gamble. The concert went only where a promoter would guarantee a $50,000 take. In a year, the gross profit was $1.1 million. The members of the cast were unknown, the production costs low, the returns guaranteed. Stigwood was out with the tour; David Land remembers him helping to fix speakers, getting the show on the road. He was naturally enthusiastic. The show was ingenious, clever, and successful.

Lawsuits still mushroomed. "I'd said if people did it in churches, we'd turn a blind eye," Stigwood says, "but I didn't want any professional performances. Then I discovered a group of nuns in Australia were doing a big professional production at $12 Australian a head and I sued them. They were hauled into court. We won. The judge lectured the nuns and told them they were mischievous and devious and the best advice he could give them was to stay out of show business."

The suit had consequences. "We were rehearsing the Broadway production at the time, and the story got around among the cast. I was sitting in the stalls, watching rehearsals one afternoon and the doorman trotted down and said there's a nun in the foyer to see you. This nun started talking to me in an Irish-Australian brogue. It was all 'We had him first, you know.' I was very embarrassed. She started screaming and carrying on and then, suddenly, I heard a few giggles behind me . . ." The nun unmasked was a chorus member, and the impresario laughed, too.

In October 1971, *Superstar* reached Broadway in a glittering, campy production that cost $700,000 to stage. Christ in glory was swathed in lamé. Glory wore high heels. Stigwood's London investors backed the show; they took, in return, between 1 and 2 percent of the gross of all other stage versions, since, technically, the first production licensed all its successors. The show defied lukewarm praise, but it never had the success of the London version. There, the show was stripped down, done almost like a concert against a simple setting. It cost only $260,000, was in the black after twenty-two weeks, and played for more than seven years to packed houses of foreign language students eager for a London treat and out-of-town school parties, all sharing rock that had been sanctified by ages. The New York show, although it was never a runaway success, paid 20¢ profit on the dollar. It folded when the movie of *Superstar* appeared in 1973; "It was not," according to David Shaw, "a difficult decision."

The show stumbled in some territories—the French detested it—and succeeded unpredictably elsewhere—the Australians loved it. The movie, made in Israel by MCA's subsidiary, Universal, had as mixed a reception. It was an unremarkable piece of work by the unremarkable Norman Jewison, but it did show the wisdom of the Stigwood approach to a deal. As coproducer of the concert tour and the stage show, Stigwood had a hefty slice of the profits; but with the authors' management contract, Stigwood also had a part of the 18 percent of the gross set aside for Rice and Lloyd Webber. Between the two, Stigwood would touch more than 20 percent of the distributors' gross.

Lloyd Webber bought a house in Brompton Square. Rice christened his private company Heartaches, but in tribute to Elvis Presley and not the taxman. Eager, even hysterical, stockbrokers scented profit, and told their clients that the once-despised shares in Stigwood were now a buy. Profits by 1975 were sure to reach £3 million or even £5 million. In fact, the profits reached only £898,000. The year after, they disappeared entirely. Robert Stigwood was on the verge of his greatest success—and some of his worst troubles.

"I DID *JESUS CHRIST SUPERSTAR* because I felt I could promote it," Stigwood says. For his next trick he had to promote a movie that no movie company would buy.

Tommy was a rock opera by The Who, a deeply personal project which the group protected adamantly. It was serious, a story of a human vegetable who grows up to be a pinball wizard and a sort of Christ. It had a little smell of art school attached to it, and its natural director was the art school dean Ken Russell, the man whose singular creations have often been the stories of composers made into circus melodramas. Russell has a single unquestioned talent for the imaginative, even perverse, shooting of music when the director has to understand the score. He seemed the right man. The Who agreed. Stigwood was granted rights to make the movie, and Ken Russell was signed.

There now began a melodrama particular to the making of the movie, a spiked progress full of risk and gamble. Distributors who were approached with the project all seemed suddenly to remember that "so-and-so said they had the rights to that." The project had a history. "When it began," says Freddie Gerschon, now president of the Robert Stigwood Group, "no motion picture company in the United States would touch it or give an advance. They thought the idea of an all-singing rock-opera movie was lunatic, and *Superstar* was just the exception which proved the rule. They thought *Umbrellas of Cherbourg* was more in line with what a singing movie would bring. Nobody in Movieland understood what Elton John and Pete Townsend and Eric Clapton meant or were, let alone Tina Turner. Robert had a director with a reputation for being difficult, and a project which had been hawked around a lot. Remember there had been two albums out already."

Still, Stigwood wrote the checks. The superstars were all signed for their bit parts, since, as he promised everyone, the movie would contain a lot of names. Those names needed firm starting dates. They could not stay committed forever. If the starting date passed, the stars would be lost and the film would be dead. There was a sense of urgency, and still no distributor would pay. "It was getting enormously near the start date," Beryl Vertue remembers, "and still we didn't have the money at all. It's the only time I've ever heard Robert even admit something was difficult. He said to me one night in the office: 'Bit of a nightmare this, really, isn't it?' ''

Vertue was frenetic, the executive producer of a project that appeared doomed. Stigwood and the Robert Stigwood Organization were still at risk for the entire $3.3 million budget. ''The orthodox avenues of finance rejected him,'' Gerschon says, ''and so he went to distributors round the world and got them to provide guarantees and deposits. They were subject only to the delivery of a proper print, and he raised $1.25 million.'' ''It turned out to be the best way to do it,'' Vertue says, ''but at the time it was the only way. We sold it territory by territory. I'd say that we wanted fifty percent of the gross because I thought that sounded safe, and I'd say that out of their share the distributors in each country would have to pay a minimum amount for advertising and publicity. And then people had to come to London to discuss it. I remembered selling 'Steptoe and Son' to American television, where it became 'Sanford and Son,' and selling it to people who really didn't know what to do with it, and I never wanted that to happen again.

''They had just about heard of Elton John, the distributors. They hadn't heard of Eric Clapton at all. So they went off and asked their sons.'' The money arrived. At that point, Stigwood took himself to Columbia Pictures and to Peter Guber, and proposed the *Tommy* project. They were not asked to finance the movie—Columbia was too strapped for cash to do that—but only for an advance on likely earnings to help pay production costs. ''He went to Columbia for the same reason he went to Paramount with *Survive!* and *Saturday Night Fever* later, and *Grease,* and for that matter why he went to Phonodisc for his records in America,'' Freddie Gerschon explains. ''He picked the weakest part of the marketplace. Schneider had just been removed. Hirschfield had just been installed. The banks were maniacal. The debt was enormous. Robert said he'd give them the U.S. and Canada for a $1.25 million advance and a fifty-fifty deal on the gross.

''Now we had $2.5 million, and it was only three weeks before principal photography was due to start and we needed $3.3 million.

Robert had to be willing to have a poker face. All this time, The Who were signed and Ken Russell, and Ann-Margret and Elton John and Oliver Reed and Jack Nicholson and Tina Turner—all of them. We had to keep moving forward. And when the word is out that you are moving forward, then everyone is trying to squeeze you. And Robert was still short of the money. So he went to Polygram and said he would create a coventure with their Polydor label in America; like Columbia, they were very weak." At that time, Stigwood produced records that appeared through Atlantic, the division of Warners controlled by his old friend Ahmet Ertegun. But, as he told Polygram, his deal with Atlantic said nothing about soundtrack albums. "I want," Stigwood told them also, "a $1 million nonreturnable advance, recoupable from the profits."

Polygram's powers were reluctant. In the end they produced $750,000, but with many mentionings of doubt. They reasoned that there were two albums out already, and a third would have a rough time; Stigwood pointed out that none of the earlier ones had Tina Turner as the Acid Queen or Elton John singing "Pinball Wizard." But, said Polygram, MCA only released Elton John for the movie on condition that they retained rights to the singles. Stigwood had the rights to Elton John's services only on the album. Stigwood argued back. "When the album comes out," he said, "the most heavily played track will be 'Pinball Wizard.' MCA won't put out a single; they'll ask why they should help me promote my album. So the only way somebody is going to be able to buy that track is to buy the album." And Stigwood was right.

With days to spare, Stigwood finally had $3.25 million to make the movie. "RSO," as Gerschon says, "that famous risk-oriented company, had through Robert's very clever dealings limited its risk to how much over budget the movie might go. It was as though our risk, which had been one hundred percent at the start, had now been limited to the completion guarantee. All Robert had to do was to ride saddle on Ken Russell, and make sure he kept to the budget."

There was one other practical problem. "I had this recurring nightmare," Vertue says, "where I was in a room with loads of brown paper parcels in which were bits of *Tommy*. I rushed into Robert and said, 'I've just realized I've done all these deals and how do we get it there? I don't know how to get the movie there.' " RSO had briefly to go into the business of distribution.

Stigwood's campaign for *Tommy* was splashy and exuberant. It also had a core of iron logic. Beryl Vertue says that when he had the finished movie, "he looked at it like a battlefield, the strategy of bringing something to the public's attention. He looks at all areas of it." On *Tommy* he made an apparently elementary, actually revolutionary, move. He called a meeting of everyone concerned with selling the idea, the movie, or the record. "We used to say very basic things," Beryl Vertue remembers. "Like, if you're advertising on Tuesday, then you others advertise on Wednesday so you don't all do it at once." To help with the promotion, he hired a rock impresario who had the arcane skills of luring an audience of ten or twenty thousand people to a single place on a single night for the appearance of a star. "He'll go to places you people don't know," Stigwood said, "because he'll be advertising the film as he would a rock concert." Vertue says, "I know it all sounds terribly obvious, but it's astonishing how people hadn't done it before and still don't do it."

There was flaming glory as well as logic, lobsters in a subway buffet in New York, a yacht moored at Cannes. "I said we would go to Cannes," Vertue says, "if we could be on the last night. Now it just so happened that on the jury that year, the one announcing all the prizes was Ann-Margret who played Tommy's mother in the film." Stigwood people in Stigwood planes flooded the narrow little town. The yacht and the flourishes may actually have cost less than hotels, but the point was to seem extravagant, to make the grand gesture. The next day, when the last black-paper evening tie had been thrown away, the circus moved on to Paris. In France, there was no distributor who seemed to understand the picture, so Stigwood hired cinemas and showed the film himself—"four-walled" it. He took $1 million out of France when the best distributors' bid had been $50,000.

Stigwood's moves became a philosophy by the time he made *Saturday Night Fever*. "I don't take any nonsense from the distributors," he says. "We buy the properties, we retain the director. If you ever go to a studio and ask them to buy you a novel to produce, that's the end. The other great ploy, usually at the eleventh hour just before the film starts rolling, is to try to change the terms of the deal. If they try to do that with me, I tell them to shove it. They expect you to be in some flat spin if the dollars can't be there on the due day."

There was only one catch in the grand style that shouted and sang for *Tommy*. The cost stood out in a threadbare profit and loss account. Expenses rose as profits leveled. To keep his reputation, Stigwood needed another *Jesus Christ Superstar*.

HIS BUSINESS HAD BECOME a surrogate family, warm and kind. He gathered around him "Stigwood people" who understood mysteriously and quickly whether or not they fitted in. If they did, life was pleasant and demanding, and Stigwood was kind and loyal. If they did not, the effect was rather like a child rejected in a family. It was so painful that the misfits ran away.

Stigwood infuriates some outsiders by his insistence that he enjoys what he does. He does not have a career; he has a life. For the most part, he is working with personal friends. "The artists are friends," he says. "I'm godfather to their children. We don't have formal business meetings. We sit around socially and debate what they should and shouldn't do. We work on a committee basis, really—Eric Clapton and the Bee Gees and of course their young brother because we want to keep him in the family." "He is father confessor, handholder, baby-sitter, and he has the bedside manner of the greatest medical practitioner in Middle America," Freddie Gerschon says. "He looks after his flock, his boys."

He is kind but not, says Stephen Komlosy, consistently. His personal authority can be cloying. "He is a Svengali," Komlosy says. "He dominates you. He dominates your mind. He imposes his will. He is like a father, and the children are all jealous of the father's attention. That's how RSO works—they all respect and admire him." Since he writes his own rules and chooses his own associates, he can insulate himself from unpleasant realities. After the death of Brian Epstein and a phase "when I thought I was going mad," he now devotes much of his time to work and demands eight hours of sleep every night whenever the party, the promotion, the meetings allow him to get to bed. Work and life become the same thing; "My work," he says, "is my hobby."

There could be a cold side to that exact equation between life and work. One old associate says: "Robert thinks he can buy anything, as a result of which he is ultimately very lonely. Business takes priority. If you're involved with somebody and you say you'll be back at eight and you actually arrive at two in the morning without even a telephone call because some business idea has come up, that person is not going to wait terribly long. But Robert expects them to be sitting there at two in the morning as though nothing had happened. You're not going to find many human beings prepared to do that."

Yet Stigwood was around while Eric Clapton was cleaning himself of his drug addiction, and he stayed with the Bee Gees while their careers slumped so far that he had to paper 2,000-seater houses in New York with free tickets to avoid humiliation. The "family" was not bought, and it remains his strength.

IT IS WORTH RECORDING some failures of Robert Stigwood, to spice up the lists of successes. He had molded and abandoned little stars in the early 1960s. He tried to capitalize on the sudden fashionability of pretty Anglo-Indian boys in the manner of Cliff Richard, and he launched Simon Scott with a plaster bust sent to every music journalist in London. Scott went nowhere. He tried to stage a musical, called *Sing a Rude Song,* about the life and bustling times of the music-hall star Marie Lloyd, and the tepid result quickly folded. At the low point of the Bee Gees' career, their gold records were created by "shipping gold"—that is, sending out more than 500,000 records to the shops, on a sale or return basis.

He backed a musical for New York, campy and absurd, called

Rachel Lily Rosenbloom. "I went to the preview," Stigwood says, "and I thought the show was terrible and I wouldn't let it open. I returned the investors their money."

Even in the heady aftermath of his first major film successes, he had what were only minor triumphs instead of gigantic hits. His own standards were by now absurdly demanding. He looked at the box-office figures, week by week, and he said, ruefully, he was waiting for the turkey. John Travolta and Lily Tomlin in *Moment by Moment* did badly, although Stigwood himself was already in profit when the film was finished, since he sold the movie to Universal for an $8 million advance. The much-loved, much-cherished *Sergeant Pepper* project involved minimal risk, since it was heavily backed by German tax-shelter money, but its dim performance as a movie was a sad contrast to the fast, sharp success of the album. Gaps in the record of success begin to seem as important as other impresarios' actual failures or collapses. Stigwood is expected, as a matter of course, to be exceptional, and if he is merely ordinary or successful, that is not quite enough. His privacy, his own self-responsive world, his occasional forays into Hollywood or New York, which demonstrate how far he can remove himself from the day-to-day politics of show business, all make him a target for slick, grudging criticism. He is an outsider, and as such he can be expected to meet preposterous standards. If he does not, he is an outsider and can therefore be deemed a failure.

In any case, the trouble with Stigwood's organization in the early and mid-1970s was not a string of failures, since there were very few. The trouble was a lack of spectacularly successful projects that would keep the record good and cover an ever-more ambitious, expensive life-style. The first attempts to break into American television were dull. "Doing things for the sake of doing them," Beryl Vertue says, "which is exactly what we had never done before." There was a Los Angeles office, but it was impossibly difficult to find projects that were credible, attractive, and worth the effort. "Meanwhile," Vertue says, "I had sold a couple of things—Osborne's 'The Entertainer' to NBC and 'Beacon Hill' to CBS as an American version of 'Upstairs, Downstairs.' Suddenly we thought—we're doing business without having an office and it was happening and why were we having this great big overhead?'' Stigwood, being an outsider, could simply close the television office. ''It caused a fair amount of stir in Los Angeles,'' Vertue says. ''If you're here all the time you realize that people suck in their breath and go 'Good Heavens,' but Robert is rather unmoved by things like that.''

''Beacon Hill'' was the first major series that Stigwood had put together for American television. It was, Vertue says, ''our successful failure.'' At first, she wanted to find some Norman Lear (producer of ''All in the Family'') who would understand the project and bring him in. ''Now Robert never makes you do anything,'' she says. ''He leads you to what you think is your own conclusion. He said: 'You could produce it yourself,' and I said I didn't know how in America. So he asked if I had thought who would write it, and I had, and about the format and how I would present it, and I had; and if I had thought which network I would offer it to, and I had; in fact, I had already mentioned it. And he said: 'Have you thought that you've already done all the important things a producer does? You might as well do all of it.' And that is how we started to produce for television in America.''

''Beacon Hill'' was shot at the same time as ''The Entertainer''; Vertue commuted between the sets, three thousand miles apart. She bluffed her way through in the studio; ''I remember being asked how all this compared to what I was used to in Britain, and for three days I didn't answer. You see, I'd never worked in any television studio before, and I wasn't about to admit that.'' She had to make the series happen at a sprinting pace. ''In American TV you always have to do things with great speed. We were given the go-ahead for the series by CBS and two and a half months later we were actually on the air. We didn't have any scripts ready because I didn't know they were going to do that.'' The series glimmered for thirteen weeks on network; its audiences, between 16 and 23 million, were simply not enough to hold its 10:00 P.M. time slot. The format deal, like ''Steptoe'' and like ''Til Death Us Do Part,'' had been profitable; the cultural translation from Eaton Place to Boston was at least as successful as the earlier comedy shifts. But the series had no particular Stigwood characteristics—except in the selling.

Vertue remembered the rules of the campaign for *Tommy,* and she decided to apply them in television. "I got everybody who was anything to do with the series together. That was very difficult. The network didn't want to do that at all. They're very departmentalized and they resented it, couldn't see the point of it. I invited the people who were publishing the book of the series, which all the TV people thought was very odd, and some outside publicists I had hired and we all met together. I made everybody write down their names and exactly what they did so we would all know. And we discussed. In the end they saw the common sense of it. The man who ran affiliated stations wanted to know if he could have copies of the book for station managers, and he got one for each station; and the person who did women's magazines went off and got cookery writers interested in all the lovely food we had in the series." It is still a model for promoting a TV series.

That kind of marketing common sense, pursued to the point of inspiration, is the key to the next phase of Stigwood. It is the phase of *Saturday Night Fever* and of *Grease.* The elements essential for its success were slowly assembling.

Some simply arrived, like the billowing, gross, and outrageous figure of Allen Carr, agent to Ann-Margret, who had been involved with the marketing of *Tommy* because his client was the star. Carr discovered in Mexico a brutal and silly film called, later, *Survive!* It was an exploitation version of the Andes air crash in which pillars of Latin society had been reduced to eating their dead in order to survive. Dubbed and trimmed, the movie made a great deal of money for Carr and Stigwood. "After that," Stigwood says, "I told Allen that if he had any ideas for movies and wanted them backed, he should bring them to me. I funded the purchase of *Grease* when it was a stage musical. Then Allen was quite sick— he'd had a bypass and I'd heard that his doctors had told him if he didn't have it reconnected within a couple of months, he would die.

So I had to stand up and do the deal with Paramount to finance and distribute that picture.''

There followed the discovery of John Travolta, a hunch based on a brief article in *Time* magazine and careful observation of Travolta's impact on American television in ''Welcome Back, Kotter.'' ''I could see the momentum building for Travolta,'' Stigwood says. ''And I did something the studios won't do. They love to work on an option basis and hedge their bets. I offered him a firm pay-or-play three-picture deal. Whether or not the movies were made, he got $1 million.''

There also had to be some corporate house cleaning. Stigwood made a curious public company. There were assets—music publishing, artists contracts and their residual value—but their future earning power depended largely on the individual talent of Stigwood himself. His intuition and imagination effectively determined the share price. Moreover, *Superstar* had seriously unbalanced what before had been an agency company. It accounted for some 29 percent of the organization's profits. To keep profits steady, Stigwood was obliged to generate comparable hits, and comparable hits were scarce in the history of show business. With only moderately bad luck, profits would slump as *Superstar*'s earning power waned, and the share rating would tumble.

There was also a sizable financial time bomb buried in the company records, which was automatically made live when the accounts were prepared for the year ending September 30, 1975. Necesse N.V., a Polygram subsidiary, had a 15 percent minority stake in RSO Productions, Ltd., which they could compel RSO itself to buy for roughly £750,000 when those 1975 accounts appeared. The actual payment was £770,754—£38,063 for the shares themselves and £732,691 for ''compensation.'' This huge obligation wiped out all of RSO's profit after taxes for that year—£582,698. It represented a hidden, additional subsidy from Polygram to the group as a whole, a little help to dust away the scale of risks and troubles involved in the business. There were more difficulties. At the organization's peak, the City of London shimmered with fine, iridescent promise. Cleverness made sizable profits. The organization had the cash flow; the City had the minor banks. RSO bought one called Roynton. Slickness went out of fashion, the stock market faded, and the money manipulators found their unreal fortunes had been marked and denounced as unreal. Roynton had to go. In addition to the Necesse obligation, RSO had to write off another £223,044 on its demise. Operating profits of £1,214,808 were tarnished to a real-life loss of £373,037. For a public company, such a disaster, predictable from the deal with Necesse, would be deadly. Because of its business and because of its troubles, RSO could not stay a public company, an independent enterprise, much longer.

The trouble with rot in the finances would be trouble only if RSO were public. As a subsidiary of some vast cartel, RSO could easily and healthily sustain the level of risk and reward it offered. Public shareholders, however, would have to see it differently.

That was not the only reason why RSO went private—that is, bought its own shares back from the public. Freddie Gerschon had in 1973 given up his lucrative show-business law practice and come to work with Stigwood. This, from his New York vantage point, is what he saw.

"There was a public company," he says, "publicly traded in an environment where the share price did not necessarily reflect the true value of the company. That was one motivation for a change—nobody received the true fruits of his labors. Even what you did receive through equity participation was subject to a confiscatory tax rate. And that was coupled with Robert's tremendous desire not to abandon England, but to go for the big stakes in America." Gerschon and the Americans were winning Stigwood's ear. David Shaw, in Britain, was losing ground. He valued weekends in the country in his Norfolk manor, life with a family, relaxation. He disliked America, but knew Stigwood's arguments for moving there were unanswerable. The partnership was foundering because Stigwood equated life and work and Shaw would not. Squabbles over Stigwood's expenses—the $350,000 for the Central Park apartment, the huge bills for the Cannes junketing for *Tommy*—made the parting more bitter. Shaw, with due discretion, left the firm.

RSO also faced some technical problems in Britain. "Bank of England controls were so restrictive that they actually stopped the shareholders reaping rewards that were theirs," Gerschon says. Credit in America was impossible, since the sizable British assets, like rights to publish, could not be pledged. Every time RSO wanted to take money out of Britain to invest, it had to pay, like other investors, the dollar premium—a markup on the cost of foreign money for investment purposes. "Instead of wheeler-dealing, Robert had to slow down and think about the balance of payments and whether the company had enough dollar bills," Gerschon says. "None of that ought to come into your judgment on a deal."

American ambitions and a British base were simply not compatible. Stigwood needed an escape.

He had for years been close friends with Ahmet Ertegun, head of Atlantic Records which distributed Stigwood's product in the United States; and Ertegun had been powerful within Warners, which owned Atlantic. It did not seem likely that the ambitious Stigwood would long allow his product to be simply distributed at Atlantic's will. Ertegun knew the relationship would have to change. He had also watched RSO grow, and he saw it as far more than another record production outfit. He began the lunchtime diplomacy that precedes the change from vague responses to solid deals. At the same time, Polygram was unhappy. The public status of RSO was becoming a liability. It made little sense. Instead, the group seemed to need allies—a strong European partner like Polygram and a good American partner that could well be Warners and Atlantic.

Polygram was shocked. Ertegun arranged the first lunch with Stigwood and Steve Ross of Warners. It was the start of a series that wandered between New York and Hamburg and London, but usually settled in Paris, which suited everybody: "Steve Ross was incredibly seductive," Gerschon remembers. "It was a not unattractive deal." What he proposed was this: "I've done my homework and I don't want to buy a third. I want to buy the whole thing. You're the best buy in town."

Stigwood was not at all sure that he wanted to be bought, to compromise the tenuous but ingenious independence he had won with

Polygram's money and public shareholders. But the offer galvanized Polygram into action. "It got them off their ass," Gerschon says. "They never expected someone who was being approached on a one-third basis to come on and try to buy the whole caboodle and re-form the company." Warners did not seem the ideal suitor; Stigwood worried that his movies would be tied to a Warners studio, that his scope for maneuver would be cut. But it was pleasant to be wooed and flattered and cajoled by two show-business powers. He rejected Warners: "No matter how many millions they offered him to sweeten his personal pie," Gerschon says, "he wouldn't do it." Polygram was another matter. They were his first backers, his friends. He knew the dark-suited men from The Hague who arrived to talk group management, but usually allowed him to find and take his own risks. And they were keen, now. "They were crazed," Gerschon says. "They offered him a variety of alternatives, none of which Robert would accept. Finally he said: 'There's only one thing I'll do and I'll do it with you or without you. That is: to find a fair value for my shareholders and my insiders and start afresh.' "

Polygram bought out the public shareholders, the little loyal following, and bought out David Shaw by lending Dutch guilders to Stigwood's own Blanrod company, and made a side contract with Stigwood himself which would have paid him $145,000 a year for his services outside the United Kingdom, plus a generous commission, should the deal by any chance fall through. It did not. RSO went private; Philips/Siemens held all the shares; Stigwood was ready for the great expansion into America.

IN MIAMI TIMES WERE LOW. Robert Stigwood went down to support the Bee Gees while they were recording. Their albums were no great success. Their personal appearances sometimes flopped. The group in which Stigwood had invested so much emotional capital had seen far, far better days.

"I stayed with them while they were recording," he says, "in Miami, before *Main Course*. I didn't like the tracks they were cutting. I told them I'd swallow the cost of the album if they would just start again and listen to what was going on in the business. *Main Course* came from that. It was just that they needed someone to tell them to start listening again.''

The Bee Gees tried again. Stigwood, thick with flu, sat swigging Scotch and Coke in the Criterion Studios, trying to be polite through lackluster sets. Nothing clicked. On "Jive Talkin' " and "Nights on Broadway," the brothers suddenly began to fool around, to imitate a typical rhythm and blues band.

"Do that again," Stigwood demanded.

"We were only kidding."

"You were only kidding the night we did 'Mining Disaster,' " Stigwood said. "When the lights went out in the studio and we sat down in the hallway and improvised. Remember? Let me hear that again."

And from that came the change of style that allowed the Bee Gees to appear as superstars. On the album itself, half was filler material, kept because there was no time to replace it. The rest was classic. "Robert has a golden ear," Gerschon says. "He has this great sense of the hook, of the commercial."

The Bee Gees were on their way back.

"I WAS A KIND of glamorized gofer," Kevin McCormick says. He was in England with his American university; he had arrived at the Institute for Contemporary Arts in London with a program he says was silly and pretentious, called The Body As a Medium of Expression. He knew only one person in Britain of his own age and background and that person was working as Robert Stigwood's personal assistant. In due time, McCormick inherited the job.

"I thought I was going to work for the enemy," he says. "What Robert represented was the commercial. To me the commercial was bad. I guess I thought if I went to work for the enemy, I would do the people's work in a better way later. Instead," McCormick pouts, "my values changed."

By 1976, he had graduated from his three years of assistantship, working eighteen hours a day to handle the phone calls that arrived after Stigwood had retired for his sacred eight hours' sleep, waking early to meet the Stigwood caravan as it moved on. McCormick became head of the RSO film division. Now that the bankroll was Polygram's, along with the risk, Stigwood wanted to expand. He had long ago left behind British comedy *(Up the Chastity Belt)* and become an international producer *(Jesus Christ Superstar)*. Now he was ambitious for massive success, on his own careful terms.

McCormick made the deals that led to *Saturday Night Fever*. "I had come over to America with that *New York* magazine article under my arm and I got on the phone to call about something else and Robert was sitting on the couch in the other room while I was on the telephone. He asked me if I had read the article and I said I'd started it and I thought it was really good. He said: 'Let's buy it.' I had just had lunch with Nik Cohn who wrote the piece a few weeks before, so I got on to his agent and made an offer and within the next three days everyone in the world was trying to buy it." Stigwood now had a magazine story about discos in Brooklyn, their particular culture, their heroes, their ways. He had a star in John Travolta, whose stardom was not yet tested. He had the germs of a production team. He set Norman Wexler to write the script.

He also sat down with the Bee Gees to devise the music. By now, the group had managed their recovery. They were at last allowed some visibility. On *Main Course* there was a logo and nothing else on the album sleeve. On *Children of the World* the group appeared in black leather and white scarves. Atlantic had feared the black audience would realize the group was not black and R&B sales would plummet. Al Coury, new head of RSO Records, disagreed. "I met the Bee Gees," he says, "and I felt we should at least give the audience interested in their music a chance to see what they looked like. I knew that since *Main Course* there was a new audience for their music and it was our intention to exploit that. Robert then agreed that we had to make them more visible." Their change of style brought them airtime on radio stations that specialized in pop music and in rhythm and blues; it doubled their audience. "Atlantic didn't want black people to know the group wasn't black; if they saw three white guys on the cover, that might be a major problem. When I discussed that with Robert, I said we'd have to take the chance.'' It worked. The Bee Gees now had a score that matched the movie Stigwood imagined, and they had a kind of stardom that was in itself a marketable commodity.

The script was sacred to Stigwood; he thinks later improvisation is without value. He liked Wexler's version. He was unhappy when his chosen director, John Avildsen of *Rocky,* started work and changed it. Stigwood was flying into New York and McCormick rushed to the airport to meet him. ''I've got sixteen pages in my hand, I'll meet you at the airport,'' McCormick said, ''but I don't think you are going to like it.'' Stigwood read the material in the back of the car: ominously he asked McCormick to fix a meeting with Avildsen at the Central Park West apartment. ''Robert is almost religious about scripts, and he thought the Wexler version of *Fever* was one of the best film scripts he had ever read. He knew the energy of the picture was going to be in the music. He wasn't interested in having some *auteur* direct the film.'' Avildsen came to the meeting to discuss, as he thought, his changes. ''It was very embarrassing,'' Stigwood says. ''Just as I was having the meeting, the phone rang and it was the news that Avildsen had been nominated for an Academy Award for *Rocky.* I had to shake hands, congratulate him, and fire him.

''My options weren't very many, four weeks before shooting.'' Kevin McCormick remembered John Badham from his impressive films for television like *The Law;* and Badham, having made a timely escape from the top-heavy movie version of *The Wiz,* brought along his choreographer, Lester Wilson. ''I had flown him in to talk about *Pepper* with Robert originally,'' McCormick remembers. ''And now he was out of town when Robert wanted a short list and he had just quit *The Wiz* because he didn't want Diana Ross playing a schoolgirl. I had to spend a whole day trying to reach even his agent.'' Stigwood says: ''I got someone to give him the screenplay, put him on a plane that day, and I met with him the next day. The only problem with the script was that it was slightly too long. I asked him where he thought the cuts should be and they were exactly the ones I had in mind. I said 'O.K., you've got it.' ''

271

Fever went out onto Brooklyn streets. McCormick remembers ten thousand kids trying to kill Travolta. Lester Wilson remembers making dances in a discotheque so small that it was impossible to choreograph even for something as simple as a crane shot, because a crane would have gone through the disco roof. Stigwood watched the dailies, checked the rushes, followed the project closely, but what interested him was a faithful translation onto screen of the script and the score he had already determined. His present project was the selling, harder than any album and movie before, of *Saturday Night Fever*.

Stigwood was in profit when the film was finished, but that was only the start. The movie cost $3.2 million to make; Paramount Pictures paid several millions more for distribution rights. Risk was eliminated. Now Stigwood proposed a scheme to make the movie monstrously profitable. The album of the movie soundtrack would be promoted to the charts; from it, there would be single records that would make radio mention the movie often to the public. Then, and only then, would the movie open, with the audience knowing the music, liking the music, conscious from a steady mentioning on the air of the name and nature of the movie.

The start was the album, and its price. Al Coury at RSO Records remembers the general agreement that there had to be a double album because there was so much music in the movie, and the furious argument over the price tag on the double album. Soundtracks were not supposed to be fashionable. Even Barbra Streisand blockbusters retailed at less than $11.98. Stigwood decided to ask $12.98 for *Fever*. It would after all contain many tracks that had begun on other labels. "We had," says Coury, unblushingly, "to pay a lot of royalties."

Out of the album, RSO picked the first release, a single of "How Deep Is Your Love." Then came the release of the album itself, and the next hit that grew from the tracks that disc jockeys chose to play, the opening number of the movie, "Staying Alive." Then, six weeks later, came the movie. By that time, the free publicity was extraordinary. Each time a single was played, the album was mentioned; each time the album was mentioned there was talk of the movie. For six weeks, the movie's title was on most pop and R&B radio stations in America, with almost monotonous regularity. Moreover, "The Bee Gees' music was," as Stigwood says, "a terrific pre-sell for the movie because everybody knew the songs before they came into the cinema." Record promotion would have been justified as part of the movie's marketing; it also sold 10 million albums. The movie hoopla was justified because, as Al Coury says, "we made that initial investment in the album expecting that the full return would be after the film came out." Together, album and movie established RSO Records, newly brought to full staff as a full-scale record company selling through Phonodisc distributors (a Polygram associate, also) after years as a supplier of custom records for Atlantic release. They also justified the closeness of record and film divisions in Los Angeles, a dialogue that is none too common in the business.

And, it blooded a sales force. For Coury had sent out his new staff to every record station possible on the Monday after "How Deep Is Your Love" went to number one on the American charts of bestselling single records. "The radio men were opening up the trade papers and they could see that the previous record from the soundtrack was on top. That was our timing, and although we had to gauge each market in terms of what records were ahead, we took our chance and our timing was pretty much on target. When our people were walking in, they were coming off a number-one record and handing the radio programmers 'Staying Alive' which everybody was playing off the album anyway. It was a question of one record perpetuating the success of another. There was a snowball reaction."

The mechanically precise selling was a spectacular, notorious success—an album that sold more than 10 million copies within six months, a movie that grossed more than $100 million in the United States alone. Music sold it mostly. "The Bee Gees' score opened it up by thirty-five percent," McCormick says. "It opened it up for people in the suburbs who didn't know disco and who do now." Collegiate audiences swayed to it, Hispanic audiences danced in the aisles, black audiences whistled down Travolta and conceded that the man could dance. In the Caribbean, *travoltear* became a Spanish word for dancing. The product, set so carefully on the market, became a huge and popular success.

THERE FOLLOWED *GREASE,* a movie whose main distinction was the series of spats between Stigwood and Allen Carr. In the end Stigwood pronounced: "I am finding it difficult to deal with Allen Carr now because of the success of the film. I hope he can cope with it. After all, it was Allen's first picture really." There were flare-ups over the casting of Travolta, whose lowering presence animates the gentle spoof of late 1950s rock, and later beach-party movies. "I read that Allen had rung me up to suggest that I sign Travolta," Stigwood says. "I find that particularly irritating as I had to talk him out of using Donny Osmond in the part."

Under the snapping was a marketing operation that differed little in principle from *Fever*. The first release from album and movie was the John Travolta/Olivia Newton-John duet, "You're the One That I Want." It sold even faster than "How Deep Is Your Love." "One of the fastest-selling records I have been associated with in the past five years," Al Coury said. Single sold album; album sold movie. The chances seemed good for the third of Stigwood's American rock films.

Stigwood had put soul and five years' work into the movie based upon the Beatles album *Sergeant Pepper's Lonely Hearts Club Band*. It was a late 1960s classic, nostalgic now, a mess of references to acid, rebellion, time past. When he had the deal on the music, Stigwood retreated and boarded the scriptwriter for more than two years in Bermuda while he finished a script. There would be a Red Pig Records in the movie, like Stigwood's more amiable red cow, and there would be little, skittish references to Stigwood himself. It would be jolly, a $12 million home movie, an indulgence. The Bee Gees would appear. It would be family. At one time Stigwood seemed to edge toward some greater nostalgia, bringing in Jack Nicholson to direct, as though the star of *Easy Rider* would mystically find the spirit of Pepper. Nicholson refused. The movie that was made was more dull, more ordinary than all the promise.

It was expensive, but much of the risk was laid off on German tax-shelter money. It was delayed; "That year," says Stigwood, "it rained in Los Angeles as it never does." Gimmick and effect, however, did not work, and the old devices were obscured by a breakdown in Stigwood's marketing machine.

"The problem was that originally the movie was set to be released as a Christmas feature," Al Coury says, "at the end of November or the beginning of December. Universal asked Stigwood to move it up to the summer, so that consequently put the squeeze on every facet of the production schedule which included the music." George Martin, producer of the album, now had five fewer months to produce the record. He went into studios and, six days later, at nine in the evening, handed Coury a cassette of the final mix of the album at a screening of the final cut of the movie. "Anybody who's been in production can realize what that means," Coury says. "Let me give you an example. If Barry Gibb and the Bee Gees had to remix that many tracks, it would take them about eight months."

Other record companies held rights to performances by the other stars of the movie, Peter Frampton, Aerosmith. Their releases helped the film, but not enough. The main album was in the stores only three days before the movie opened. Manufacturing plants, frantic with the million or so copies of *Grease* that were selling each week, and the residual 200,000 or so of *Fever,* were strapped for capacity to make the new album. With those logistics added to the promotion problems, the Stigwood machine simply could not fall into gear.

There is a caveat. While *Sergeant Pepper* was not what Stigwood had hoped, there were still advance orders for 3 million copies of the album—the disc "shipped triple platinum." The moderate successes need to be seen in some perspective less phantasmagoric than the Stigwood saga.

"THE REAL THINKING gets done in Bermuda," Gerschon says. "That is where the real money is made in the conception of an original thought." It is an enticing prospect, the mogul seated before his promontory surveying a pink sand beach and translating inspiration into dollars.

"He'll look at all the record companies in America, all the motion picture companies in America," Gerschon says, "he'll look at who's running them, all their figures, who's performing how and where the weak points are. Then he'll go off, looking as though he's casually having a lunch or a dinner with some studio head. But he's done his homework and not just on the value of the property that he's selling. It's who needs him, and who's looking to score some points with their own boss by saying 'I just saw Stiggie.' It's who needs product. It's how to extract the best deal. That is Robert the businessman."

That skill protects him when a project misfires, like the quietly absurd *Moment by Moment,* a story of lust across the generations. "There was," Stigwood recalls, "a big outcry over my Travolta/ Tomlin deal, but the studio had nothing to do with the risks in the Travolta deal, or the Tomlin deal for that matter, since she was on a firm pay or play. I said that when I deliver the picture, you, the studio, will pay me $10 million. That's what it would cost you to do it for yourselves. It just so happens that I took all the risks in commissioning, and that's my price. Then, when you break even, we'll split the gross. There was much moaning and groaning at Universal. They couldn't see why I thought I was entitled to make $3 million to $4 million profit on delivery of the picture." The risk is cut, the profit assured, the prospects good if the movie is successful. It is an impeccably logical form of deal.

It looks like power. Stigwood's associates insist that it is. Freddie Gerschon says that Stigwood risks his own bucks, although in reality Stigwood risks not so much actually losing his own money as failing to add to it. "If you look around the world at the men he's dealing with, most of them are custodians of other men's assets," Gerschon says. "Robert is a throwback to an old-fashioned entrepreneur. The man he's dealing with on the other side is usually very bright and an employee. He's the second or third generation removed from the people who had the vision and started the company in the first place—the Roberts, if you like. It colors a man's thinking to know he has two alimony checks to write that week, and the mortgage payments, and if he has two bad years he'll be for the axe. Robert has none of that.''

He has the adventure and the excitement and he revels in it. He has the flamboyant trappings of his mogul status. ''Philips get the money,'' as one old associate says. ''And why should those nice men from Holland in the dark suits want their name on the product, as long as they get the money?'' The corporations are distanced from the risks that Stigwood takes for them; he, in return, is protected by them. He can deal where he wants, do as he pleases, while he has their trust; they need take no more than financial responsibility for what he does. It is a simple, elegant accommodation. It is the new form of moguldom in an age of corporations.

YOU WILL NEED AN INVITATION, and you will find the party something like a circus. There are dragons, still, and stars and fools, new-rich and victims all performing for our delight. Stigwood is seen to be moneyed and powerful, sipping his Louis Roederer champagne, sailing his yacht. He takes brilliant risks. He makes himself a substantial fortune. But he does not fit the oldest myth, the story of Jules Stein for example, the poor boy who makes good through genius, struggling from a shabby home to a monstrous fortune by his own efforts. That is not possible now. In place of the kind uncles that were needed in the old stories of American entrepreneurs, the Horatio Alger stories of rags to riches, the new moguls need corporate protection, kindness from the company satrapies.

If the scale of Stigwood's operation is smaller than Stein's or Paley's—in effect as well as turnover, importance as well as numbers—it remains a glittering performance that is only partly illusion. We might ask why Stigwood is presented so carefully as independent power when he is not, why the megacorporations want us to see apparent entrepreneurs who actually dance to a colder tune. We might speculate. The circus, the party serves some purpose. We might wonder why the vast corporate states decide to conceal themselves behind the individual brilliance of a Stigwood.

Whatever the answer, even if it has to do with a device to mask corporate power while it grows, we can appreciate the party. It is a fine and dazzling affair. It celebrates as once the Astors, Carnegies, or Du Ponts would celebrate. It shows a certain self-confidence, self-esteem. Moguls have changed in fifty years, changed from the architects to the servants of huge corporations, but they remain the dragons of business, the grotesques, and the monsters.

It is an alien land, the land of moguls. We need to be careful of their power, even as we join the party.

BIBLIOGRAPHY

T HE MAIN THESIS OF THIS BOOK rests on Paul A. Baran and
Paul M. Sweezy, *Monopoly Capital* (London, 1977). Material
on the social and economic background to the moguls' careers
is listed, in part, in the bibliography to Michael Pye and Lynda
Myles's *The Movie Brats* (New York, London, 1979). What follows
is a listing of materials useful to the telling of the moguls' stories.
It does not include the vast amount of valuable material to be culled
from *The Wall Street Journal,* since that newspaper is admirably in-
dexed, or *Variety,* since acknowledging that source properly would
require another book. In addition, *Newsweek, Time,* The *Sunday
Times* (London), the *Financial Times* (London), the *Los Angeles
Times,* and *The New York Times* all included valuable information.
Magazine or newspaper articles are listed here only if they are in
sources no longer published and were especially useful. Material on
all the moguls came from the Securities and Exchange Commission,
and Companies House in London; since files are accessible in both
places by company name, I list only those documents of particular
value that might be available elsewhere. Material from the Department of Justice is also available by company name. Where a court
docket number will lead to a valuable source, I have listed it, under
the name of the main witness or plaintiff whose deeds or motives it
illuminates. Documents whose contribution was only marginal are

not listed. What follows is a selective bibliography, containing not the best but the most productive of the sources consulted for *Moguls*.

Balio, Tino, ed. *The American Film Industry*. Madison, Wisconsin, 1976.

Barnouw, Eric. *A Tower in Babel*. New York, 1966.

———. *The Golden Web*. New York, 1968.

———. *The Image Empire*. New York, 1970.

———. *Tube of Plenty*. New York, 1977.

———. *The Sponsor*. New York, 1978.

Bosworth, Patricia. *Montgomery Clift*. New York, 1978.

Braun, Eric. *Deborah Kerr*. New York, 1978.

Brooks, John. *Once in Golconda*. London, 1972.

Brown, Les. *Television: The Business Behind the Box*. New York, 1971.

Brown, Les, ed. *The New York Times Encyclopedia of Television*, New York, 1977.

Cable, Michael. *The Pop Industry Inside Out*. London, 1977.

Davidson, Bill. "MCA: The Octopus Devours the World." *Show*, February 1962.

———. "MCA: A Case Study of Power." *Show*, March 1962.

Davis, Clive. *Clive*. New York, 1976.

Denison, Edward F. *Accounting for United States Economic Growth 1929–1969*. Washington, 1974.

Diamond, Edwin. *The Tin Kazoo*. Cambridge, Mass., 1977.

Elder, Glen M., Jr. *Children of the Great Depression*. Chicago, 1974.

Eysenck, H. J., and Nias, D. K. B. *Sex, Violence and the Media*. London, 1978.

Frank, Gerold. *Judy*. New York, 1975.

French, Philip. *The Movie Moguls*. London, 1969.

BIBLIOGRAPHY

Frith, Simon. *The Sociology of Rock*. London, 1978.

Gelatt, Roland. *The Fabulous Phonograph*. London, 1977.
Grady, Billy. *The Irish Peacock*. New Rochelle, 1972.
Guber, Peter. *Inside* The Deep. New York, 1977.

Hayward, Brooke. *Haywire*. New York, 1978.
Hayward, Leland: mss. in the collection of the New York Public Library.
Hentoff, Nat. "The Octopus of Show Business." *The Reporter*, November 23, 1961.
Hodgson, Godfrey. *In Our Time*. London, 1977.

LeRoy, Mervyn. *Take One*. New York, 1974.
Logan, Joshua. *Josh*. New York, 1977.

Martin, Mary. *My Heart Belongs*. New York, 1977.
MCA: prospectuses dated May 18, 1962; April 17, 1962; October 8, 1959.
Metz, Robert. *Reflections in a Bloodshot Eye*. New York, 1975.

Paley, William S. *As It Happened*. New York, 1979.
Preminger, Otto. *Preminger*. New York, 1977.

Rhode, Eric. *A History of the Cinema*. London, 1978.

Simon, George T. *The Big Bands*. New York, 1976.
Smith, Anthony. *The Shadow in the Cave*. London, 1976.
Stein, Jules: deposition in Los Angeles District Court case 4238, August 8, 1945. File also contains material by Finley, Larry; Bishop, Harold (H.E.); Barnett, Lawrence; Daillard, Wayne; etc.
Stine, Whitney. *Mother Goddam*. New York, 1974.

Taylor, John Russell. *Hitch*. London, 1978.
Thomas, Bob. *King Cohn*. New York, 1967.
———. *Marlon*. New York, 1973.

Thurber, James. "Soapland" in *The Beast in Me and Other Animals*. London, 1977.

Trumbo, Dalton. *Additional Dialogue: Letters 1942–1962*. New York, 1970.

Walsh, Raoul. *Each Man in His Time*. New York, 1974.

Wittels, David G. "Star Spangled Octopus." *Saturday Evening Post*, August 10, 17, 24, 31, 1946.

Zierold, Norman. *The Moguls*. New York, 1969.

INDEX